Teachers' guide 2

Nuffield 11 TO 13 SCIENCE

HOW SCIENCE IS USED

Published for the
Nuffield–Chelsea Curriculum Trust
by Longman Group UK Limited

General Editor,   **Mike Lyth**
Nuffield Science 11 to 13

Consultant General Editor **John Head**

Associate Editors   **Bob Fitzpatrick**
                         Don Foster
                         Jeremy Tafler

Authors of this book   **Jerry Goddard**
                         Ralph Hancock
                         John Head
                         Mike Lyth

Co-ordinator of   **John May**
dissemination

Longman Group UK Limited
*Longman House, Burnt Mill, Harlow, Essex CM20 2JE, England
and Associated Companies throughout the World*

First published 1987
Copyright © 1987 The Nuffield–Chelsea Curriculum Trust

Design and art direction by Ivan Dodd Designers

Filmset in Monotype Plantin and Gill
Printed in Great Britain
by Richard Clay (The Chaucer Press)
Bungay, Suffolk

ISBN 0 582 03009 9

Nuffield 11 TO 13 SCIENCE

CONTENTS

FOREWORD

Nuffield Combined Science was first published sixteen years ago in response to a new awareness of the need for a common course embracing all the sciences for the first two years of secondary school. It has had a remarkable influence on the teaching of science to eleven- to thirteen-year-olds and has been one of the most successful projects Nuffield has ever produced. Indeed, by 1979 (as the survey by Her Majesty's Science Inspectorate showed) over half the schools in England were using the course wholly or in part.

The great changes in education, in science, and in society since then, particularly the growth in number of comprehensive schools and the wider acceptance of mixed ability teaching in the 11 to 13 age group, have indicated the need for a new scheme rather than a revision. Educational research reinforces this view. The new scheme, Nuffield Science 11 to 13, has been produced in response to those changes. The materials have been designed to provide a sound platform for science teaching for the subsequent examination courses.

Nuffield Science 11 to 13 has been prepared under the general editorship of Mike Lyth and with the help of a Consultative Committee under the chairmanship of Professor P. J. Black, academic adviser to the Trust. We are grateful to him and to the other members of the committee. They were G. Brown, Miss K. Chester, M. Coyle, Dr J. Head, R. Lewin, Dr A. P. Matthews, J. May, M. Michell, Miss B. J. Myers, Miss J. Phillips, Mrs B. Schofield, and Dr M. Shayer.

Our thanks also go to M. J. Elwell and C. D. Bingham, organizers of Nuffield Combined Science, and to the team members Ken Wild and J. R. Lance.

I particularly wish to record our gratitude to Mike Lyth, the General Editor of the project. The contributions of John Head, the Consultant General Editor, and John May, the co-ordinator of dissemination, have also been invaluable. Their hard work and their understanding of the needs of pupils of this age group and their teachers have been central to this project. Our thanks are also due to Bob Fitzpatrick, Don Foster, Keith Holmes, and Jeremy Tafler who chaired the teacher groups responsible for writing the first draft of the pupils' material, and to Tony Turner and T. P. Borrows for reading and commenting on the year 2 material.

I would also like, once again, to acknowledge the work of William Anderson, publications manager to the Trust, of the editors Sarah Codrington, Sheila Corr, and Frank Kitson, and of our publishers, the Longman Group, for their assistance in the publication of this book. Their editorial and publishing skills are essential to effective curriculum development.

K. W. Keohane
Chairman, Nuffield–Chelsea Curriculum Trust

Introduction

This Teachers' guide covers the second year of the Nuffield Science 11 to 13 course. The twelve chapters correspond to the paired reader and activities chapters in the pupils' book. In each of these chapters a table is given summarizing its content, followed by notes supplementing the pupils' reader by supplying background information, and notes on the practical activities. At the end of the book there is an apparatus list, which should be useful and convenient for technical staff.

Aims and objectives of the course

These have been spelled out in detail in *Teachers' guide 1,* and only brief comment will be made here.

There is an accumulation of evidence that pupils often have a negative image of science. They only perceive the product, a body of depersonalized knowledge, which has to be mastered by feats of memorization. They dislike the apparent impersonal quality. They fail to perceive the relevance of science to everyday life and people.

In the Nuffield Science 11 to 13 materials, emphasis has been placed on processes, processes by which scientists advance our knowledge of science, and the process by which science is utilized in our society. Stories are told about discovery in science reminding us that science is a construct of human minds. Examples of science in action – the technological applications – are given to demonstrate its relevance. This emphasis on process, rather than products, will help develop a more positive appreciation of science.

The specific objectives to achieve these aims can be summarized as follows.

1 To develop the children's images of scientists as ordinary people doing a special job with a long and interesting history; their images of scientists' limitations, motivations, and range of interests; and their images of scientists' special techniques and skills.

2 To develop the children's images of technologists as multiple-solution problem-solvers, whose main aim is to produce saleable things; and their images of technologists as employers of scientists.

3 To develop the children's understanding of the interaction of science and technology.

4 To develop the children's skill in the use of some fundamental scientific techniques.

5 To develop the children's knowledge of simple scientific vocabulary and observed facts.

6 To develop the children's understanding of scientific ideas and patterns.

The course is intended to make as smooth a transition as possible between the science experienced in primary school and that likely to be met after the age of thirteen. The first year of this course was entitled *How scientists work*, which reflects the emphasis on process. The second year, *How science is used*, represents a slight shift, from people to science in action. This is in order to prepare for the science education which will be met later on at school. The twelve pairs of chapters in *Pupils' book 2* are organized around content, in contrast with *Pupils' book 1*, where the material was organized entirely around processes. Nevertheless, it is intended that the ideas developed in the first year should be constantly employed in the second year. The second year reader materials frequently refer to such processes as observation, measurement, pattern-making, and so forth. Even when such references are not explicit it is hoped that teachers will keep the list of processes in mind and help pupils identify them in the year's work.

The teaching package

The pupils' book has two sections, reader pages and activities.

We cannot envisage a worthwhile science course which did not involve extensive practical experience for the pupils. Such experience is central to the Nuffield Science 11 to 13 project. In selecting practical exercises we were fortunate in that many familiar, well-tried activities, such as those originally developed for Nuffield Combined Science, were at hand and suitable for our purposes. We were aware that schools were unlikely to have funds available to re-equip laboratories and the selection of activities has been made with this in mind. A science department used to offering Nuffield Combined Science should be able to mount the Nuffield Science 11 to 13 project without any major new costs.

The reader pages in the pupils' books are an innovation. It must be stressed that the reader section is not intended to be a conventional textbook and is meant to be used in a different fashion from one. Textbooks tend to be heavily laden with factual information, which may be useful for reference but scarcely makes them enjoyable reading. Such textbooks can discourage the pupils and act as a constraint on the teachers.

The reader section in these materials does not provide every detail of information which the class might need. It is intended to be a resource available to pupils to contribute to their understanding. The hope is that the material can be read with enjoyment. The reader pages have been richly illustrated, and in addition each chapter has a two-page picture spread, usually of a cartoon format. The cartoon form has been employed both because it appeals to the children and is readily understood by them and because it is an efficient mode of conveying complex ideas. We therefore see these cartoons and illustrations as making a serious contribution to the overall utility of the reader sections.

The activities and the reader only provide two-thirds of the total experience the pupil should receive. Discussion between the teacher and pupils, either in the whole class or smaller groups, is needed too. The practical results should be discussed, not least so that the members of a small group can see how their findings compare with others. The reader pages are meant to stimulate and raise questions as well as to provide answers.

Flexibility
One of our concerns in designing these materials has been with flexibility, so that individual teachers have scope to be creative and to develop lessons in the light of serendipity.

The reader chapters can be used in a variety of ways. Sometimes you may ask the class to read them as an introduction to a topic and then, once the scene has been set, use the practical work to explore an issue which arose from the reading. In other instances you might prefer to use the reader after the practicals in order that the class can see how their newly learned ideas are applied in the outside world.

We can describe a number of specific ways of employing the reader.
1 Ask the class to précis part of the content, possibly by drawing a flow-diagram to show how the ideas connect together.
2 Ask the children to come to the next lesson with two or three questions for you based on their reading. Such questions may be of two kinds: those where they fail to understand the text and need assistance, and those where their interest has been aroused and they want to learn more about the topic. These questions should be put down in writing. You can collect them and from the list gain valuable feedback about how the class is progressing with that topic, and plan the next lesson accordingly.
3 Ask the children to undertake some imaginative writing based on what they have read. A letter to a friend or a newspaper report describing an event or discovery outlined in the reader are examples of such exercises.
4 Ask the children to relate events described in the reader to their historical context (what were the major world events then? who was on the British throne then?), thus making connections with other lessons.

We resisted the idea of intertwining the reader and activities passages on the same page as they tended to stifle such flexibility.

For similar reasons we resisted the labelling of sections as 'core' or 'extension'. Discussions with trial teachers revealed an immense variation in the time allowed for science lessons in the eleven to thirteen age range. What might have to be treated as an extension in one school could well be a core activity in another. We have provided enough material in each chapter to keep everyone busy for about three weeks, giving 36 weeks' work in all. Some pupils will have completed all the work suggested in that time. For others, some selection may be needed.

Teachers can also introduce additional material where appropriate. For example, the study of geology in Chapter 6 naturally leads on to the study of the local environment and industries. Such local studies are welcomed, but clearly we cannot outline the exact form such a study might take in each school.

The Nuffield Science 11 to 13 project materials, both the reader and activities sections, provide a bank of resources. They are to be used flexibly, with additions, alterations, and omissions, as deemed desirable by individual teachers and school departments.

Treatment of difficult concepts

In selecting the topics to be included in this scheme we were not only guided by the judgment of the experienced teachers who wrote the material, but also took note of the findings from the immense amount of research which has been conducted in recent years into children's learning of science. (See, for example, Driver, R. '*The pupil as scientist?*', Open University Press, 1983; Head, J. '*The personal response to science*', Cambridge University Press, 1985; Shayer, M. and Adey, P. '*Towards a science of science teaching*', Heinemann, 1981.)

From such research it is abundantly clear that some topics, because of their abstract and complex nature, present undue difficulties to children in the eleven to thirteen age range at the beginning of their science studies. Very few members of the class will understand these topics. Many will come away with confused ideas which might inhibit future learning. Others will conclude that science is too difficult and give up trying to master the subject.

Two topics particularly concerned us: current electricity and the nature of energy. The dilemma is that these topics are too central to science to be ignored. Our tactic has been to introduce a variety of experiences in which these topics are encountered and explored without attempting to provide a detailed explanation. These introductory experiences should provide a sound basis for more formal teaching of these topics when the children are further advanced in their studies.

For example, many instances of energy transformation are met, and a brief introduction to the measurement of energy is provided, but energy is never set as the focus of any chapter. No attempt has been made to take pupils through the traditional circus of energy practicals. This is explained further in Chapter 11. Similarly, the effects of electricity are fully discussed but the nature of electricity has not been laboured.

Use of computers

Suggestions on the use of computers have not been given because both the hardware, and particularly now the software, are changing so rapidly that any suggestions would soon be rendered out-of-date. However, here are some notes on the principles of computer use.

The benefits are obvious. Pupils tend to be positively motivated. More important, computers can simulate practicals which, for reasons of safety, cost, or time, cannot be carried out as actual practical exercises. In that way the range of science which can be studied practically is extended and such simulation can replace the chalk-and-talk mode of teaching in these instances.

Although computers can be valuable in extending the range of things which can be done in science lessons, we do not see computer simulation as being a replacement for conventional practical work. Pupils learn by assembling apparatus, seeing colour changes, smelling gases, and feeling forces or temperature changes. These direct hands-on experiences should not be replaced. Pupils also learn in the actual physical process of drawing bar-charts and graphs and, although it may be quicker to employ computer graphics, that factor may not justify the use of computers with pupils in this age range. The immense advantage that science has over many other disciplines is that is involves all three learning modes – symbolic (words and mathematics), iconic (diagrams), and enactive (learning through the body by manipulating, feeling, etc.) Practical exercises in science involve all three. Computer work involves the first two. Classroom talk only involves the first.

The summary tables

For each of the chapters we provide a brief introduction which highlights the main aims and pedagogic issues relating to the topic being studied in the chapter. We then provide a summary table which allows you to see at a glance what we hope the children will be asked to do. These tables are organized under the following headings.

Target: the pages in the reader to be covered.

Images: the images of scientists and the application of science which are being developed in these reader pages.

Skills: references to those skills which should be developed by pupils undertaking the listed activities.

Ideas: the vocabulary, facts, and ideas which are introduced in the reader pages and might be further developed by class discussions with you.

Activities: the list of activities which we have provided for the children.

Worksheets: the list of worksheets which we have provided.

In the summary tables we provided for the Year 1 work we were able to indicate the key processes being studied in each unit. We cannot pinpoint the processes for the chapters in the Year 2 book, because it is anticipated that the whole range of processes encountered in the Year 1 work will be met again in each chapter of the Year 2 book. Sometimes we provide the children with cues by referring to *patterns, observations,* and so forth. You may like to ask at intervals 'what are the scientists doing?' 'is that an example of . . .?' and so recall the range of processes which they have met.

If you are not clear what the words 'process' and 'skill' mean in the context of the Nuffield Science 11 to 13 project, refer to *Teachers' guide 1* where these terms have been explained in detail.

CHAPTER 1

Life goes on

Introduction

Three main aims have been paramount in planning this topic.

The first is to provide a simple and clear account of sexual reproduction. Without such an account the course would lack credibility in the eyes of the pupils. Furthermore, despite the greater awareness of the 'facts of life' shown by contemporary children, there still remain anxieties and uncertainties which need to be addressed by the provision of a clear lucid account of what is involved.

The next aim, which is a reflection of the overall aims for the course, is to set the physical aspects into a human and social context. Too often teenagers see sexual activity as being something self-contained and removed from any wider context. We have tried to describe the totality of the life cycle, introducing the wider role of the family, in showing the physical elements as integral to life. This social context may help class discussion on issues of parental authority and control and help the children to recognize the difficulties in being a parent and why parents sometimes behave in ways which they find irksome. The social aspects of sex education cannot all be profitably dealt with on one occasion with one age group. It is anticipated that at some later stages other issues, such as that of contraception, will be discussed. On this particular occasion the pattern of the life cycle and child development provides the main theme.

Finally, we want to set the story into a scientific context. The reader chapter starts and ends with material on cells. The activities centre on the use of the microscope to look at cells. From these topics children learn that the familiar scientific processes, from observation to pattern-making, are as relevant to this subject as any other.

Summary

Target Read and discuss pages 1 'Why are people so different?'; 2 to 4 'Patterns of fertilization'; 5 to 6 'The pattern for humans'; 7 to 8 'Being in love and making love'; 9 'Patterns within the family'; 10 'Learning to be a parent'; 10 to 11 'The pattern of development'; 12 to 13 'The idea of cells' (picture story); 14 'Finding out about cells'.

Images Scientists puzzled by inheritance of traits. Development of microscope and recognition of cells suggested that gametes carried the genetic plans.

Skills Using the microscope. Preparing and staining specimens.

Ideas Sexual reproduction allows traits from both parents to be represented in the new generation. The social context; the need for the child to receive care. Patterns of development.

Activities	Use of microscope to look at cells.
Worksheets	16 'Measuring with a microscope' 33 'Make a microbe poster' 34 'How to use a microscope'

Reader pages

PAGES
I to I4

The chapter consists of four interwoven themes:
the variety of life;
the cell as the unit of life, and the history of the development of this concept;
fertilization (in various organisms including ourselves), the adaptations which increase its probability, and those which increase the likelihood that the zygote will survive;
and human sexual relationships.
All four are important themes and it would not have been difficult to put together a chapter for twelve-year-olds on any one of them. A major reason for combining them was to place the work on human reproduction and sexual relationships in a good scientific and human context – neither to bury the work nor to understate its personal importance to the children.

Activities pages

PAGES
110 to 113

The children begin by exercising the skill of using a microscope which they learned in year 1. The subject is a representative of a plant cell such as they have read about. The skills of using a coverslip and staining the specimens are developed.

Prepared slides are studied at the stations of a circus and carefully described; and a set of 'puzzle photographs' introduces an important function of prepared slides and photomicrographs – that is, as a scientific record and a resource for identifying an unknown tissue. A worksheet gives instructions for making a poster to show different kinds of microbes to scale.

Background to the reader pages

WHY ARE PEOPLE SO DIFFERENT?

PAGE
I

The diversity of people and animals stems from the diversity of the genes that programme their development. Each characteristic of a person is determined by at least one, usually several, genes. An individual's complement of genes is inherited from both parents, each of whom supplies half the total. The genes inherited from one parent are not simply half of the genes that determined the characteristics of that parent, because everyone has far more genes than those which were dominant in determining his or her own characteristics, and every time a sex cell (a sperm or an egg) is formed, it is given a different assortment of genes. Thus there are billions of possible combinations of genes, and which of them a child will inherit is a complete lottery. However, the child will get some of the genes that went towards both parents' characteristics, and may thus look rather (but never exactly) like one or both parents. Even when a child has been conceived there is still room for change in its development, as can be seen from identical twins, which have exactly the same genetic makeup but are still slightly different from each other. (Picture 2.) Identical twins come from a single fertilized egg that has divided after fertilization, and are always of the same sex. Fraternal twins come from separate, separately fertilized, eggs and resemble each other no more than do any brothers or sisters. Identical twins' fingerprints have the same general pattern but differ in detail.

An adult person has upwards of 20 thousand billion cells, which vary greatly in size. Red blood cells and the cortical cells of the brain are among the smallest, while the connections of a motor nerve cell may extend for a metre (though the actual central part of the cell is a millimetre across). (Birds' eggs are single cells, though enormously distended by the yolk, a food supply; so the largest single cell is an ostrich egg.) Each kind of tissue – muscle, bone, fat, skin, connective tissue, blood, nerve, brain, and all the different internal organs, consists of many different kinds of cell, making hundreds of types in all. This diversity was achieved from the genetic instructions in just two cells, a sperm and an egg.

PATTERNS OF FERTILIZATION

PAGES
2 to 4

The sperm (or to give it its full name, spermatozoon, plural -zoa) that fertilizes the egg is one of several hundred million delivered at a time (in humans), each one of which is genetically different. Our picture of fertilization was taken in a laboratory dish. Of course, it normally takes place in one of the mother's Fallopian tubes. In order to reach the Fallopian tube, a sperm must swim through the cervix into the uterus, along to the other end of the uterus and out at one of the far corners. Millions of them fail to complete the journey. After the one successful sperm has fertilized the egg, it travels down into the uterus and, with luck, implants itself in the spongy lining which has been prepared to receive it. (The alternatives are [1] that it fails to implant, in which case it will be lost in the course of an apparently normal period and the woman will never realize that fertilization has taken place, or [2] that the fertilized egg will get stuck in the Fallopian tube and begin to develop there. This rare event is an ectopic pregnancy, a potentially life-threatening condition that announces itself by severe pain and must be dealt with by an operation before things go too far.)

Most of the cells in the body have a full set of genetic instructions. (They have a full set for making a complete person, not just a copy of that particular cell, so that in theory it should be possible, by genetic engineering techniques, to make a whole human being from one of his or her cells. This has already been done with plants, and animals up to the level of amphibians.) The only cells that do not have a full set are red blood cells, which lose their nucleus during the course of formation; and gametes. Both male and female gametes (the ovum and sperm cells) have exactly half a set. This halving is made possible by the two-sided nature of the DNA molecule which is carried by the chromosomes (a gene is a short length of a chromosome, enough to carry one instruction). When a cell divides, the DNA splits in half down the middle, like a zip fastener. In normal cell division (*mitosis*) the original 'left' half of the 'zip' makes itself a new 'right' half, and the original 'right' half makes itself a new 'left' half. (Although a DNA molecule is schematically very like a twisted zip, it should be realized that there is no significance in the terms 'left' and 'right'. Both sides carry genetic information coded in the 'teeth of the zip', which are of four different kinds.) Thus in mitosis one set of DNA is made into two identical sets, one of which goes into each new cell. In the formation of gametes of either sex (*meiosis*), the DNA splits but is not copied, so that each new cell gets only half a set of DNA. (Meiosis is actually more complicated than this, and occurs over two cell divisions, but that is the result.) When fertilization takes place, the two half sets from each gamete join up. In fact, since each half set is from a different person, they do not fit exactly; but because both parents are of the same species they fit well enough to work. (In interspecies hybrids such as mules the fit is much worse, which is why most hybrids are sterile.)

Of all fertilization methods, wind pollination is the most wasteful. Billions and billions of male pollen cells have to be produced to give even one a chance of drifting into a female flower. The chances of fertilization are higher in plants that grow close together, such as grasses; but many trees are wind pollinated and the nearest tree of the same species may be many kilometres distant. Nevertheless, such trees do manage to fertilize each other. In general, you can tell whether a flowering plant is wind pollinated or insect pollinated by looking at the flowers. If they are large or coloured, this is to attract insects. If they are small and green, the plant is likely to be wind pollinated.

Many fishes, including sticklebacks, build simple 'nests' for their eggs. After the eggs have been laid and fertilized, the fish may cover them, for example by sweeping gravel over them. Even so, the mortality rate is enormous at all stages of the process. Most of the sperm are wasted; often predators find and eat the eggs; and as soon as the fish larvae hatch they become prey to innumerable carnivorous creatures. Few fishes look after their young, but there are exceptions: for example, the mouthbreeder (a cichlid fish) carries its young in its mouth to protect them.

Frogspawn, a mass of eggs, is transparent and the development of the tadpole can be watched with a hand lens. If you are lucky enough to find some frogspawn in a rural pond, take only a little for study, and when the tadpoles have hatched, put them back where you found them. Many amphibians are in danger of extinction..

Birds' eggs are not always fertilized. Female birds develop eggs whether they are fertilized or not, though the frequency with which they lay eggs varies very much from species to species. Domestic hens are bred to produce eggs every couple of days, and in the conditions of an industrial henhouse, which of course contains only females, these are invariably unfertilized. From an egg eater's point of view, a fertilized egg is edible only if it is absolutely fresh. If the embryo chick has started to develop, the egg contains a nasty surprise.

A woman begins producing eggs in her early teens and continues to produce one (occasionally more) about once every four weeks until she is in her late forties; she will only produce a few hundred in her lifetime. Many female mammals come into season as little as once a year, and their total is even smaller. Therefore elaborate protection is needed for the egg. In comparison, males have plenty of sperm, which in the case of most mammals is produced continuously. (In a few, such as elephants, the male as well as the female has a fertile season.) One male can impregnate many females. So there is no need for special arrangements to protect sperm.

The eggs of mammals have a small amount of yolk which nourishes the growing embryo for the short time needed for the uterus to set up its arrangements. Then the embryo is enclosed in a sac of amniotic fluid and fed through the placenta, which grows along with it and absorbs nutrients from the mother's blood. In contrast, the eggs of egg-laying creatures such as birds and most reptiles must contain all the nourishment for the embryo until it is hatched, so there must be far more yolk.

SEX EDUCATION

PAGES
5 to 11

As was mentioned in the summary at the beginning of the chapter, our aim has been to present human sexual activity in its emotional, social, and scientific context. We are well aware that every local authority and perhaps every school has its own attitude to, and policy about, the teaching of this subject.

Some schools rely heavily on excursions to exhibitions and outside talks; others rely on talks given by visiting specialists; and for others the subject is a matter of course, taught entirely internally by the usual teachers. You may be co-operating with other members of staff, particularly those concerned with English and drama, social studies, and religious education.

Whatever procedure is used, we believe that it is important that the children should be able to ask and have answered any questions which they need to ask about sex. A good way to arrange this is to set up a 'suggestion box' into which the children can anonymously post their questions written on slips of paper. The questions can be read in advance and answers prepared, by the science teachers as a group, with or without outside help.

THE PATTERN FOR HUMANS

PAGES
5 to **8**

No details are given of birth control methods at this stage. Pupils already have quite enough to cope with.

Of the numerous children of a Victorian family, probably only a minority would survive infancy. More would die if the parents were poor, but some even if they were rich. It is only in the twentieth century that infant mortality has declined to a low level, thanks largely to the control of common infectious diseases (see the notes on Chapter 3).

LEARNING TO BE A PARENT

PAGE
10

Obviously, this section is designed to jolt children out of lazy and sentimental ideas about having a baby. Not only is it hard work bringing up a child, it's also expensive. Pupils could be asked to work out the cost of food, clothes, and so on for one child from birth to adulthood. This was estimated in 1984 at as much as £100 000 – though that was for a well-off professional family and included private education.

The mutual love of a mother and child seldom fails to develop, though there are sad cases where it does fail. It happens at an instinctive level through contact between the two, especially during the first few days of life; and several senses are involved, including hearing and smell. A baby learns the sound of its mother's voice even before it is born, a fact which has been proved by experiment. However, if a baby is removed from its mother immediately after birth, the bond which has already started to form does not develop further. The mother will grieve at being deprived of the baby, but not nearly as much as if she had got to know it; while the baby can become fully attached to a foster mother. Many paediatricians and social workers talk (often at wearisome length) about the importance of 'bonding': this is what they mean. The relationship between a child and its father is also influenced by the father being there during the first few weeks, holding and looking after the baby.

THE PATTERN OF DEVELOPMENT

PAGES
10 to **11**

It is important to stress that children acquire their abilities over a very wide age range, and that failure to develop quickly is not a disaster. Many children who were thought to be mentally handicapped have gone on to great things: two examples are James Watt and Thomas Edison. And even if a child really is handicapped or slow, that does not reduce his or her worth as a person.

THE IDEA OF CELLS (picture story)

The microscope was probably invented in about 1600 by Hans and Zacharias Janssen of Middelburg in Holland. It was a compound instrument with two lenses. Like the telescope, the instrument was probably copied by Galileo. A notable early Italian microscopist was Marcello Malpighi (1628–1694), who was the first to see blood capillaries and the stomata on the underside of leaves. Robert Hooke (1635–1703) also used a compound microscope. But these were very imperfect instruments. Two simple convex lenses give a distorted image, focused only at the exact centre and with distracting rainbow fringes. You can get an idea of the effect by looking at a small object through a telescope or a pair of binoculars the 'wrong' way, looking through the objective lens and with the object close to the eyepiece. Nevertheless Hooke's instrument was an improvement on Janssen's, being firmly supported so that it could be positioned accurately and would not shake, and with a stage that allowed both transparent and solid objects to be viewed. Hooke was the first person to see cells, in cork, and he introduced the word cell for them. The rectangular, empty cells of cork, the dead bark of a tree, do look like little rooms. In 1665 Hooke published his famous *Micrographia,* with many beautiful engravings of microscope views – some said to be drawn by Sir Christopher Wren. Another microscope pioneer was the Dutchman Jan Swammerdam (1637–1680), who discovered red blood corpuscles.

Anton van Leeuwenhoek (1632–1723) was a prosperous draper of Delft and an optician in his spare time. He was irritated by the defects of early compound microscopes and his inability to do anything about them – for the multiple achromatic lens which got rid of the rainbows was not invented till 1758, by John Dollond. So he abandoned that design and used a single lens instead. It should not be thought that his instrument was much like an ordinary hand lens. The lens itself was tiny: some of the 419 lenses he made from glass or rock crystal were as small as pinheads. They had a very short focal length and gave a magnification of as much as 200 times. They had to be looked at from extremely close. It seems that Leeuwenhoek was short-sighted, which helped him to look through these awkward little instruments. He was the first to see spermatozoa and bacteria.

Nicolas Hartsoeker (1656–1725) was far from the only person to claim that sperm contained a small human being. For example Gauthier d'Agoty, an anatomist and colour printer, claimed to have seen the embryos of several kinds of animal in the appropriate sperm, and asserted that sperm dropped into a glass of water would develop into an embryo by itself. He claimed to have seen this occur, and in 1750 printed a rather peculiar picture of it. Earlier, in 1684, Zypaeus had claimed to have seen tiny embryos in unfertilized eggs. All this was part of the general confusion of the time about how a fully formed creature could emerge from a featureless blob, and whether the father or the mother was responsible for forming it. Not surprisingly, contemporary opinion favoured the father.

The theory of spontaneous generation was a hard one to disprove, because if any container was not deliberately sterilized it would inevitably contain bacteria or other micro-organisms which would grow if given a chance, even if the container was securely sealed. The first person to challenge it seriously was the Italian biologist Lazzaro Spallanzani (1729–1799), who managed to stop bacteria breeding inside a flask of water by boiling it after sealing. Although bacteria had been seen their true nature was not known, and so those who held the theory of spontaneous generation were not convinced of its wrongness. They said that the boiling had destroyed some vital principle in the air in the flask. Therefore the theory dragged on until Pasteur's work on bacteria (see Chapter 3). However, before this – around 1800 – Nicholas Appert (1752–1841) used boiling to sterilize food in sealed glass jars, and thus invented bottling and canning.

The Royal Society did not take Leeuwenhoek's work very seriously, partly because he wrote in Dutch, whereas respectable scientists used Latin. Hooke quarrelled with almost everyone. His argument with Sir Isaac Newton was about the orbits of planets. Hooke had realized that their path was caused by the competing forces of inertia and the attraction of the Sun, and had suggested this to Newton; but he was not a good enough mathematician to prove it and Newton was. Newton did not acknowledge Hooke's contribution.

Matthias Schleiden (1804–1881) not only elaborated the cell theory of plants, but realized that the controlling force of the cell was its nucleus – a feature which had first been seen by Robert Brown (1773–1858), better known as the discoverer of Brownian motion, the movement brought about by the molecules of fluids.

Theodor Schwann (1810–1882) discovered the first known digestive enzyme, and realized that yeast was a living creature (see notes on Chapter 3). He extended the cell theory to include animals, and was the first to state firmly that fertilized eggs grew by repeated cell division, and that this process continued until it resulted in a full sized organism.

Karl Nägeli (1817–1891) corrected an error that Schleiden had made about the nucleus. Schleiden had supposed that the nucleus produced new cells in the form of buds which split off. Nägeli realized that the nucleus split in half, though the full significance of this was not grasped until Kölliker explained it (see below).

Karl Siebold (1804–1885) was a comparative anatomist, studying the similarities and differences of creatures. He observed protozoa, single-celled creatures, and was the first to understand their true nature. He observed them propelling themselves by waving their cilia, movable hairlike structures.

Rudolf Kölliker (1817–1905) was ahead of his time when in 1861 he published his views on hereditary material. It was not until the 1870s that Walther Flemming (1843–1905) observed this material in chromosomes, and not until 1953 that Francis Crick (1916–) and James Watson (1928–) elucidated the structure of DNA and produced a model for the transmission of hereditary information.

Karl Gegenbaur (1826–1903) was also a comparative anatomist, and studied the development of the organs of embryos, noting, for example, how fish and mammal embryos have similar structures which later turn respectively into gills and ears.

Rudolph Virchow (1821–1902), who despite his Polish name lived and worked in Germany, was a surgeon who made a study of diseased tissue. He realized that disease involved a battle between different cells, but he thought that all the cells involved came from inside the organism (as is the case in cancer), and did not accept Pasteur's theory of 'germs' (bacteria) invading from outside.

The light microscope has a limit of magnification which is due to the wavelength of light. As shown by the German physicist Ernst Abbe (1840–1905) in 1873, in order to distinguish between two particles close together, the light source must have a wavelength no more than twice the distance between the particles. Since the wavelength of visible light is on average about 0.00005 cm, the smallest detail visible in light is 0.000025 cm. Electrons have a much shorter wavelength, allowing details less than one thousandth of this size to be revealed – and this is only the practical limit of today's machines. Already individual large molecules, such as those of DNA, can be seen. Smaller details should be detectable in the future. There are two main kinds of electron microscope: the transmission type, which sends a beam of electrons through a very thin slice of material (cut with a device called an ultramicrotome), and a scanning type which has a greater depth of field and can observe three-dimensional objects, but does not have such good magnification. There is also a hybrid type, the scanning transmission electron microscope (STEM), which combines some advantages of both designs. The picture appears on a video screen. Since it is not in the first place viewed by light, it is of course not coloured. There are certain drawbacks to using an electron microscope. The specimen has to be observed in a vacuum, which means that living tissue cannot be studied. Sometimes it has to be coated with gold to make it show up clearly. It may even not be observed directly, but a plastic moulding made from it and studied to reveal surface detail. As a result of all these operations some observed features may be artefacts of the preparation process, so great care is needed in their interpretation.

FINDING OUT ABOUT CELLS

Flemming (see above) was only one of the pioneers of using dyes to study cells. Another was Ehrlich (see Chapter 3). Chromosomes, the little threads which we now know to contain DNA, are named because they take up a dye and so become visible. The name means coloured bodies, from two Greek words. Between 1857 and the early 1860s,

Gregor Mendel (1822–1884) had worked out the statistical basis of the inheritance of characteristics – quite without understanding the physical mechanism – so he is the true founder of genetics. The importance of his work was not realized until 1900, by the botanist Hugo de Vries. Mendel's work also suggested that hereditary information is carried in the form of units, later called genes. It may be necessary for more than one gene, coding for a particular characteristic, to be present for that characteristic to show itself – for example, two genes may be needed, one from each parent, or more than two – but a gene cannot be diluted: it is either there or not there. Thus it is genes that are inherited, not characteristics. The combination of Mendel's mathematics, the physical observations already mentioned, and Darwin's theory of evolution (which was gradually explained in genetic terms during the early twentieth century) allowed the science of genetics to make rapid progress. William Bateson (1861–1926) discovered that some characteristics are inherited not independently, but in groups. This finding was later explained by the American Thomas Morgan (1866–1945), who showed that it was because the genes for these characteristics were on the same chromosome. Morgan was the first to use that indispensable subject of genetic studies, the fruit fly, which has the great advantage of only four pairs of chromosomes, in contrast to the human 23 pairs.

Notes on the activities

PAGES
110 to 113
The aims of this chapter of activities are to reinforce the children's skill in using microscopes and to add the new techniques of preparing a specimen and staining it. Also to give them direct observation of the cells they have read about on pages 2 and 14; and to make their conception of cells more detailed and elaborate. Problems 1 and 2 are literal statements of these aims – the children are not about to be introduced to cells, nor are they about to 'discover' them. Their existence can be taken for granted, and the emphasis is on the techniques for studying them and the new information which the study provides.

PROBLEM 1: HOW CAN YOU STUDY CELLS?

Getting the microscope ready and making an onion skin slide

PAGES
110 to 111
If the children have used *Pupils' book 1* (page 120) they will have worked through a programme for setting up a microscope. (See also Worksheet 34.) It will be a good idea to revise this with them as a class demonstration before getting them started on step 1. The objective of developing their conception of the size of cells will be easier to achieve if they have measured the size of the field of view of their microscopes. You may like to work through Worksheet 16 from Year 1 again, as a co-operative demonstration.

You will need to prepare in advance some dropping bottles of a solution of iodine in potassium iodide. This will stain the nuclei of the onion cells and make them more visible. Some children will ask how big the two layer 'brick' of onion should be. Of course the answer is that it should fit comfortably on the slide with space all round. Then the interleaved sheet of cells will be the right size. Some children may need help with the change from low power to high power.

Your discussion (step 7 in the pupils' book) should begin with the technique: the drop of water which helps to retain the natural form of the cells; the coverslip which protects and stabilizes the specimen (but often introduces the air bubbles mentioned in step 4); and the stain which colours some parts of the cell but not others (and which the children will have read about on page 14).

You may like to remind the children of the importance of the nucleus – 'the tiny blob which controls all of the complicated things which happen in a cell'.

Alternative specimens for the plant cell preparation are given in 'Additional activities' below.

From an educational point of view, the ideal practical would involve the children preparing their own slides of both plant and animal cells for examination under the microscope. However, concern about the spread of AIDS has led to the collecting of cheek cells from the children's mouths being banned in schools.

PAGES
111 to 112

The best alternative is to show commercially prepared slides of animal cells. (The children can also look at pages 2 and 113 of the pupils' book, which show photographs of animal cells.) After they have examined the slides, it will be advisable to discuss with them the features they observed and the differences between types of cells. Without such a discussion they may not see the purpose of the practical.

The children will probably concentrate on the regular geometric shape of the plant cells compared with the irregular shapes of the animal cells. You may like to remind the children that all cells are surrounded by a very thin bag called the membrane and that, in addition, plant cells are separated by more or less rigid 'boxes' made from the material called cellulose. Advanced textbooks mention the frequent presence of tiny bags of pressurized sap (vacuoles) as a distinguishing feature of plant cells, but the children are unlikely to have seen these.

It is important to compare their drawings with that on page 13, and to point out the impossibility of seeing the complex internal structure at these magnifications. Before the days of electron microscopes, comparatively little was known about this structure. Much of what was known was due to the careful use of a large number of selective stains.

PROBLEM 2:
HOW DO CELLS DIFFER IN THEIR APPEARANCE?

The microscope circus

PAGE 112
Looking at a series of prepared slides is an interesting, even exciting, experience. The colours and shapes of the specimens have a strong aesthetic appeal; and their sectioning, mounting, and staining illustrate one of the great arts of the scientist.

Discussion of the children's answers to the questions will develop their conceptions of cells as being very tiny; shaped like irregular boxes or bags (and not like pancakes!); and varied in shape. Discussion could also introduce the idea of differentiation and specialization of cells: their change in form as they develop to suit a particular job; and the idea of tissues as groups of similar cells working together to do a particular job. The specimens listed and described below under 'Puzzle photomicrographs' have been chosen with such possibilities in mind but there are many alternatives to those we have chosen. In particular, you could provide a set of plant cells or a mixture of both.

The circus format has the advantage that the microscopes and slides can be set up in advance and the children can get straight down to the important job of careful observation and recording. There is also less individual movement and less risk of damage to valuable slides than the alternative, which is to arrange the children in groups around a microscope and have them fetch the slides one by one from the front. However, shortage of microscopes may force you to use this alternative. We hope you will not have to make do with one microprojector – the children still need practice in observing through eyepieces.

It will be a good idea to read through the list of questions with the class before they begin the circus – to answer any questions they have and to transfer the questions to tables of results in their notebooks.

You may like to demonstrate the sectioning of a carrot shown in picture 5; and to make the point that you really need both kinds of section to get a good idea of the three-dimensional shape of the cells. A stack of matchboxes (representing the carrot) can be 'sectioned' in both directions to illustrate this.

The slides will probably be labelled with most of the information the children need, but it will avoid unnecessary handling and movement of the slides if you transfer this information to cards placed beside each microscope.

Puzzle photomicrographs

PAGE 113
Slides are prepared not only for their beauty and interest, but as a record and resource for the identification of unknown tissues. It is worth nothing the importance of identification as a general concern of scientists in all their areas of interest. 'What is it?' is one of their most important questions. As well as being interesting and challenging the puzzle pictures allow these points to be made. The pictures will also illustrate the contrast between thin section photomicrographs and

scanning electronmicrographs; the limitations of black and white photomicrographs; and the difficulty of identifying a new tissue from a sample slide (however good the sample is).

The puzzle pictures show the following:

a *Paramecium* (Magnification on the page × 400.) This subject is included to allow you to make the point that there is a group of animals which are made up of only one cell (the protozoans). The slipper-shaped *Paramecium* is interesting because of the fringe of tiny beaters which surround it, and which are used both for movement and to sweep food into its 'mouth'. The food is stored in numerous vacuoles. The nucleus is well-defined and clearly visible (a feature which distinguishes protozoans from bacteria).

b *S.E.M. of human blood cells* (Magnification on the page × 1000.) The picture shows the disc-shaped red blood cells whose main job is to carry oxygen from the lungs to the tissues; and one of the complex blob-shaped white cells. There are several types of white cells whose job is mainly to deal with invading microbes, viruses, and harmful substances. Red cells in the bloodstream do not have nuclei, but white cells do.

c *Human nerve tissue* (Magnification on the page: × 250.) Nerve cells (neurons) are 'generating stations' or 'relay stations' for the electrical signals which variously represent new thoughts, emotions, and reactions to our surroundings; and which operate our muscles. The cells are clearly specialized for the job, being extended into fine threads (nerves) which connect with other neurons over distances of less than a millimetre or more than a metre.

d *Longitudinal section of striated muscle* (Magnification on the page: × 1000.) The picture shows the highly specialized cells from which most of our muscles are made. The cells are long and made up of numerous fine fibres. The nuclei have been 'squeezed out' to the edges. The dark stripes (striations) which run across the cells are believed to be the sites at which the cells contract to pull on our bones.

e *S.E.M. of human skin* (Magnification on page: × 100.) The slide shows part of the continuous layer of box-shaped cells which, like paving stones, cover the entire surface of the body, internally and externally. Such cells can be specialized for tough renewable protection, production of lubricating mucus, or transfer of useful substances.

Additional activities

ALTERNATIVE SPECIMENS FOR MAKING SLIDES

The children will probably study cells again in later years and you may feel that one preparation will do for now. However, should you want alternatives or additions try thin slices of carrot (use a single-edged razor blade), rhubarb skin (break a stem and peel off), plant hairs (shave off with a single-edged razor blade again), and small leaves such as those of Canadian pondweed and moss.

⚠ Because of the dangers of the spread of AIDS and viral hepatitis, you should not attempt to sample people's blood or cheek cells. See *Topics in safety* published by the Association for Science Education for guidelines.

MAKE A MICROBE POSTER

Worksheet 33 provides the information you will need to make a collage showing a range of types of microbe. With the exception of the 'flu virus, which is non-cellular, the organisms are single-celled, so there is a link with the *Paramecium* on page 113. If you use an A2 size backing sheet (in a dark colour) you can use the scale 1 millimetre = 1 micrometre. The amoeba will be 50 cm long, and you can position it diagonally across the sheet. The result will be most effective if you build up the microbes in relief (like the Queen's head on a coin). Build up the amoeba from layers of polystyrene sheet and sand it to a smooth finish.

Make the yeast by forming modelling clay ovals with sizes ranging from 25 mm to 27 mm, cutting them horizontally in half, and sticking on the halves. The only problem will be that of showing the 'flu virus particles which, to scale, should be less than a tenth of a millimetre across. Grains of sand or tiny seeds stuck to the underside of a piece of matt transparent tape would be one solution – stick down the tape onto a labelled white card attached to the backing sheet. You may like to add a model of a human red blood cell to make an interesting comparison. At our scale it would be 10 mm across.

The worksheet asks the children to find answers to a series of questions for each of the microbes. Here are some of our answers.

Amoeba: a protozoan similar to *Paramecium* (see pupils' book page 113). They have been used for generations as a laboratory subject for scientific research. If some types are swallowed, they can cause the tropical disease amoebic dysentery when they attack the walls of the digestive system.

Yeast: one of a group of single-celled fungi. They are of great technological importance because they produce, as metabolic by-products, enzymes which convert sugars into carbon dioxide gas and alcohol. The gas is employed to raise the dough in breadmaking, the production of alcohol in brewing and wine-making. Yeasts are also valuable as protein-rich foodstuffs.

Colon bacterium: one of the group of bacilli or 'rod-shaped' bacteria. *E. coli* exist in large numbers in our large intestines where they break down waste materials to produce nutrients. They are important laboratory subjects – scientists know more about their genetics than about any other form of life! (Other less benevolent bacilli include those which cause anthrax, tuberculosis, whooping cough, diphtheria, and leprosy.)

Streptococcus: one of the group of cocci or 'seed-shaped' bacteria which include those causing sore throat or scarlet fever (where the 'seeds' are massed in groups rather than linked in strings).

Eberthella typhi: one of the salmonella type bacteria. This one can cause typhoid fever; others can cause paratyphoid or forms of food poisoning.

Clostridium tetani: a bacterium which can cause tetanus. A similar form can cause botulism. They produce toxin which is similar to strychnine but tens of thousands of times more powerful.

Influenza virus: viruses are so simple that many scientists believe that they should not be considered to be life forms at all. Most can reproduce only by entering (and destroying) living cells. This one can cause 'flu; others can cause chicken pox, hepatitis, herpes, measles, meningitis, mumps, pneumonia, polio, rabies, smallpox, and AIDS.

CHAPTER 2 # The body machine

Introduction

The aim in this topic is to see how the normal, healthy body works. In making a comparison to a machine we might be criticized for presenting a too mechanistic model. Our intention is simply to explore in what ways the body can be seen as a machine. We do not wish to imply that humans are simply machines and no more. Teachers may like to discuss with the class the limitations of the analogy. Children at the age of twelve or so tend to be more concerned with how things work than with the more abstract questions of the purpose of life, and for them the mechanistic model is useful.

In addition to dealing with some of the main features of the body – the skeleton, skin, alimentary canal, and so on – two opportunities are provided for opening up the topic. Alongside the study of the alimentary canal we introduce material on foodstuffs and balanced diets. The latter topic needs to be handled carefully, as the prevalence of teenage anorexia in western society demonstrates, but it does make a connection with everyday living.

The final section in the reader deals with the relationship between the mind and body. The treatment has to be brief, but the issue is opened up for discussion. Consideration of the role and function of the mind may lead some children to move beyond the machine analogy in their understanding of human beings.

Summary

Target Read and discuss pages 15 to 17 'The body machine'; 18 to 19 'Finding out about the body' (picture story); 20 to 21 'The food processing machine'; 22 'How is your body controlled?'

Images Scientists learning about the body through observation, such as Harvey's ideas on circulation; serendipity, from war wounds; from recognizing patterns such as the pairing of muscles. This enquiry continues.

Skills Measuring. Setting up fitness tests. Tabulating data. Drawing graphs and bar-charts.

Ideas The body functioning can be compared to a machine. Characteristics of bones, muscles, and skin. Food, digestion, and diet. The role of the brain.

Activities Monitoring personal fitness. Collecting and tabulating class data.

Worksheets 22 'Draw a normal distribution graph'

Reader pages

PAGES
15 to 22

This chapter tries to help children to understand the operation of their bodies by comparing their functions with familiar objects and machines. The chemical substances of which it is composed are described in terms of well known products: whitewash, matches, and so on. The skeleton, which is easy to feel, and the skin, which is easy to examine, are described. Next there is a pictorial history of the discovery of important knowledge about the body. After this, the principal substances in food, their purpose, and the digestive process are described; and finally the control system of the body – the autonomic nervous system – is outlined.

Activity pages

PAGES
114 to 119

The work opens with a discussion of the distinction between 'being healthy' and 'being fit'. This leads to a further study of the scientific meaning of the word 'normal', and of the normal distribution curve. Worksheet 22 on this subject is useful again here. Careful plans are made to collect data on a range of at least eight features of the children's bodies and physical performance. Worksheet 19 'Measuring your strength' will help with the measurements. The notion of a standardized fitness test is introduced and the test tried out. All of the data are carefully processed with the aim of making (statistical) pattern statements, and are presented on charts for the whole year group. A pair of worksheets supports simplified research into the 'energy values' of the children's diet (see important note on energy in the introduction to this teachers' guide). A further worksheet (37) gives instructions for making a collage which shows schematically the various systems of the body and the transfer of substances between them.

Background to the reader pages

PAGES
15 to 22

The list of substances making up the body is highly simplifed. Lime (calcium hydroxide) is mentioned because it is a well-known compound of calcium. Most of the body's calcium and phosphorus are in the form of calcium phosphate, which forms the hard structure of bones. Most of the carbon and sulphur are in protein, and almost all the rest in fats and other lipids (the chemical group to which fat belongs; another lipid is cholesterol which, despite its evil reputation, is a necessary component of cell membranes). Most of the iron is in the red blood cells which carry oxygen around the body; the iron gives blood its red colour. Other elements in the body include large amounts of oxygen and hydrogen which, apart from making up water, are also found in protein and fats; a good deal of nitrogen, most of it in protein; chlorine and sodium, mostly as salt (sodium chloride); potassium which, with sodium, mediates electrical activity in the body; and small amounts of magnesium, zinc, manganese, chromium, copper, fluorine, molybdenum, selenium, cobalt, and iodine. These less abundant elements have roles in some of the complex chemical reactions in the body. For example, the thyroid gland uses iodine in regulating the body's metabolic rate; and cobalt is a constituent of vitamin B_{12}, involved in the creation of new cells, particularly red blood cells.

Bone is not just a lump of calcium phosphate. The hard mineral is formed into a strong, light honeycomb structure whose lattice is aligned in the direction of the load on the bone. A full-size X-ray of, for example, the head of the femur shows that its interior structure is as organized as the girders of a large bridge. The calcium phosphate is intimately combined with living cells (mostly collagen, a protein) which constantly maintain and renew the structure – not only to mend fractures, but responding to stress of all kinds. Astronauts who spend more than a couple of weeks in the weightless conditions of a space station begin to suffer loss of bone because there is not enough stress on it to keep the renewal process going. Bone loss in space can be slowed by frequent, strenuous exercise.

Bone is slightly flexible, more so in children than in adults. The ribs are particularly flexible, bending at each breath, because they have 'hinges' of cartilage ('gristle', largely composed of collagen). In babies a large part of the skeleton is made of cartilage, which gradually changes to bone during childhood.

The discs in the spine (see picture 8) are also made of cartilage. Each disc is enclosed in a little bag of fluid, the whole making a combined flexible joint and shock absorber. Excessive strain on a disc causes it to bulge outwards and backwards, pressing on the spinal nerve and causing pain – a 'slipped disc'. The pain is often felt in the leg because the nerves from the leg run up to the spinal cord and join it in the neighbourhood of the vulnerable lower discs. The discs become compressed during the day and recover at night, but they do not recover fully, so that adults get shorter with increasing age.

Muscles end in tendons, strong cords of collagen fibre which attach them to the bones. Often the tendon is quite long: the muscles which move the fingers up and down are in the forearm, and move the fingers by means of tendons running over the wrist. Muscles consist of fibres.

At a molecular level, each fibre consists of long protein molecules which slide over each other, causing the muscle to become shorter and broader when it contracts.

The outer covering of insects and other arthropods, including crustaceans such as crabs, is made of chitin, which is not a protein but a carbohydrate, and not found in the bodies of vertebrates. In big marine crustaceans it is stiffened with calcium salts in the same way as bone. The shells of molluscs (such as oysters and snails) are made of protein and calcium salts. The fingernails, hair, hooves, horns, and so on of vertebrates are made of keratin, a protein. Some primitive fishes, mostly extinct, have external plates of bone. There are specks of bone in the skin of sharks, which is why it has a sandpapery texture. These fishes have skeletons made entirely of cartilage. Higher fishes have bony skeletons and keratin scales. Tortoise and armadillo shells are of bone covered in keratin. These animals have normal bony skeletons.

Skin consists of two main layers. The inner one, the dermis, is composed of collagen interspersed with blood vessels, nerves, etc. The outer layer, the epidermis, produces cells which turn into keratin and die, forming a tough outer layer which is renewed from inside as it is worn away. Hair follicles, sweat glands, and sense receptors penetrate both layers. Under the dermis there is a layer of fat. (See picture 10.)

FINDING OUT ABOUT THE BODY (picture story)

PAGES
18 to 19

Hippocrates (460 to *c.* 370 BC) was born and worked on the Greek island of Cos. It is likely that he was one of a hereditary line of what we should now call witch doctors, and also that many of the line were called Hippocrates. This makes it hard to tell which of the many (over fifty) books attributed to Hippocrates are actually by him, but the best ones have a strong personal style. They include *On ancient medicine,* in which he discusses the importance of variety, balance, and preparation in the diet as a means of preserving health. (This is 'ancient' because it had already been instinctively arrived at – Hippocrates is trying to give it a rational basis.) In his *On the regimen* he lists the properties of various foods. Most of this is fanciful, but it does show that he understood that dietary fibre is needed to prevent constipation. Most of the explanation is in terms of the 'four humours': four bodily substances (blood, phlegm, black and yellow bile) which must be kept in balance to ensure health. Each food promoted one or more of these humours, which was why they had to be mixed. This was to become the dominant doctrine of medicine until well into the 18th century AD. More usefully, Hippocrates was the first to argue that disease had a physical cause rather than being due to evil spirits; and his emphasis on correct diet is similar to modern views.

Galen was born and had his first medical post in Pergamon in Asia Minor. He was the doctor in charge of the gladiators at the local arena, which gave him useful practical experience! His dissections of animals were thorough and careful, though he did not realize how the heart worked – difficult to guess in a dead animal. There was a belief in classical times that the mind was situated in the heart, and that the brain was a mysterious organ which might have something to do with cooling the blood. Most mammals, but not people, have a network of blood vessels (the *rete mirabilia* or 'wonderful net') between the nasal passages and the brain which does cool the blood (that is why dogs pant), so Galen's work reinforced this wrong theory. However, Galen did realize the role of the spinal cord in carrying messages to the limbs to tell them to move. By cutting it at various places in live animals and observing the paralysis this caused, he was able to roughly map the layout of the motor nerves. He also developed some simple substances which are still in use (and still called 'galenicals'); one of these is cold cream.

Before the time of Vesalius very few people dissected human bodies, and then clandestinely. Plenty of bodies were available from frequent wars and executions, but the church authorities forbade dissection because of the Christian doctrine of the resurrection of the body. If you had been cut up you might have difficulty reassembling yourself on the Day of Judgment. Vesalius was Flemish, and his name is a Latin form of Wesel, his home town. But he taught in Italy, where the enlightened attitudes of the Renaissance permitted dissection. His near contemporary Leonardo da Vinci also dissected and drew human bodies. Much of Vesalius' fame is for the quality of the illustrations in his *De corporis humani fabrica* ('On the structure of the human body'). They were drawn to his meticulous instructions by Jan Stephen van Calcar, a pupil of Titian. Vesalius realized the true function of the brain as the seat of the mind and controller of the body, though it was for others to work this out in detail later – see below.

William Harvey (1578–1657) also studied in Italy. He made his discovery both by dissecting human and animal hearts and by experiments on living beings. It was this combination, and his grasp of experimental method, which led him to his conclusions. He described them in a short book (badly printed in Holland), *De motu cordis et sanguinis* ('On the movement of the heart and blood'). It took some time for his conclusions to be accepted, as they contradicted Galen's belief that blood oscillated back and forth along the vessels. Harvey was not helped by being given the nickname Circulator, which is Latin for quack. Harvey was not the first person to describe the blood as circulating – Hippocrates had done that – but he was the first to understand the path it took. Previous researchers had not understood how blood goes from arteries to veins by seeping through the tiny capillaries, which had led them to propose that it soaked through tiny pores between the right and left sides of the heart. There are no such pores, of course, and the two sides of the heart act as separate pumps.

Opposing pairs of muscles, not only the biceps and triceps but many other pairs in different parts of the body, can be observed to contract by feeling them while pushing against a resistance in the appropriate direction. For the biceps-triceps pair, sit at a table and try to raise it by pressing with the hand from below while feeling the front of the upper arm with the free hand, then press the hand down on the table while feeling the back of the arm. Picture 9 shows these muscles. Not all the muscles in the body are paired; for instance, the sphincter muscles are not.

Albrecht Haller continued the work begun by Galen, charting the nerves carrying sensations from the limbs and motor impulses to them. Unlike Galen, he realized that all nerves lead through the spinal cord to the brain. He experimented on animals by stimulating or damaging parts of the living brain and observing the resulting movement or paralysis. It had been thought that the nerves were tubes through which an invisible 'animal spirit' flowed to carry messages. Haller showed that nerves were solid. But it was not until 1771 that Galvani (see Chapter 5, pages 42–3) suggested that the signals were electrical.

Burke and Hare were only the most notorious of many grave robbers. However, according to Hare, who turned King's evidence at the trial in Edinburgh, Burke increased the supply of corpses by strangling at least 15 people. Burke was hanged. Hare was imprisoned but later released, and is said to have died a beggar in London in the 1860s.

Surgeons dealing with combat injuries have always been leaders in anatomical discovery, from the time of Galen and before. Perhaps the most famous was the French barber surgeon Ambroise Paré (1510–1590). Unlike most surgeons before the nineteenth century, he realized the importance of cleanliness during surgery. He introduced trusses for hernias, invented several new surgical instruments, improved the design of artificial limbs, and wrote several illustrated books on subjects including general surgery and the treatment of gunshot wounds.

The general adoption of anaesthetics in surgery was extraordinarily slow. Homer mentions anaesthesia through the use of 'nepenthe' – we do not know what this drug was. Herodotus (c. 485 to c. 425 BC) describes the use of hemp. In the Middle Ages Theodoric of Bologna (1206–1298) describes a 'soporific sponge' impregnated with drugs and held over the face, apparently invented by the Arabs. Medieval painkilling drugs included hemlock, mandrake, and lettuce sap (similar to opium but less powerful – though primitive lettuces had much more effect than modern ones). Another method, mentioned by Severino in 1646, was to apply ice to the part being operated on to numb it. But none of these was in general use. The anaesthetic effect of nitrous oxide was discovered by Sir Humphry Davy in 1800, and that of ether by Michael Faraday in 1818 (for both people, see Chapter 5, pages 42–3). But neither was used until 1842 when an American doctor, Crawford Long (1815–1878), gave a patient ether before removing a neck tumour. He did not publish an account of the procedure, and credit for the discovery is usually given to an American dentist, William Morton (1819–1868), who used ether during extractions in 1846. Chloroform was used by Sir James Simpson for childbirth in 1847 in Edinburgh. Many doctors refused to give anaesthetics to women in labour because they claimed that the pain was natural and proper. Queen Victoria quickly put a stop to this by insisting on chloroform for the birth of her next child, and her example was copied. Local anaesthetics were first used by a Dr Richardson in Glasgow in 1866 – an ether spray. Cocaine, much more effective, was used in eye surgery by C. Koller in Vienna in 1884. A wide variety of compounds will work as general anaesthetics, and the action is not properly understood.

The germ theory of disease was worked out by Louis Pasteur (1822–1895). This story is told in Chapter 3, but notes on it are given here because they are relevant at this point. In 1856 Pasteur was called in by the French wine industry to discover why a lot of wine was going sour, which led him to work on yeast, a primitive fungus consisting of a group of independent cells. He realized (as Semmelweiss had earlier – see the notes on Chapter 3) that yeast was a living organism, and its action fermented grape juice to wine. Other, undesirable organisms might also get into the wine and turn it sour. The cure was to heat the wine gently to kill all organisms in it, a technique which was called pasteurization. The discovery made him famous, and in 1865 he was asked by the French silk industry to find the cause of a disease that was killing their silkworms. He found that the larvae were infected with a parasite introduced on the leaves they fed on. The only cure seemed to be to destroy all infected silkworms and trees. Pasteur went on to speculate as to whether all disease might be caused by micro-organisms. In the same year Joseph Lister (later Lord Lister; 1827–1912), a surgeon, read of Pasteur's work and began to use carbolic acid to kill germs during surgery, dramatically reducing post-operative infection which until then had killed a large proportion of patients who survived operations. Pasteur went on to discover vaccines against anthrax and rabies made by heating live germs to weaken them, so that they would not cause the disease but would stimulate the body's defence mechanism to produce antibodies to the disease, thus creating immunity to it.

Karl Landsteiner (1868–1943) was an Austrian-born American. Before 1900 blood transfusions had been tried as a way of restoring blood loss after injuries. Sometimes they worked, but more often they quickly killed the patient. Landsteiner discovered that people had blood which was always one of four kinds. If someone was given blood which was of a different group from his or her own, the result might be that when the two bloods mixed the cells clumped together like milk curdling, with fatal results. However, this clumping could be observed by mixing blood samples in a dish, making it possible to test blood before transfusion. The four groups are A, B, O (all discovered in 1900), and AB (1902). Blood of the O group may safely be given to any of the other groups. The discovery began saving countless lives almost at once. Landsteiner later discovered other subgroups which do not affect transfusion but are useful in discovering the paternity of a child (groups are inherited). In 1940 he and others discovered the Rhesus factor in blood. This works rather like an allergy. A mother whose blood is Rhesus negative and who has a Rhesus positive child becomes sensitized, and if she conceives a second Rhesus positive child there may be a reaction which harms it. Trouble can be averted by testing the mother's blood during the first pregnancy and administering a drug. 85 per cent of the population is Rhesus positive.

Transplanted organs are less easily matched than blood. Each person's body tissue is of a completely individual type. If a person is given an organ from another body, his or her own defences will recognize it as foreign and gradually destroy it. Transplant patients must be given anti-rejection drugs which depress their immune systems, and must go on taking the drugs as long as they live – which makes them prone to infections of all kinds. There are main groups of tissue types, and in order to survive for any length of time a transplanted organ must belong to the same main group as the recipient. The closer the match the better. Often a brother, sister, or other close relative can give an almost matching kidney, since a healthy person can live normally with only one kidney. The most highly publicized transplants are heart transplants, the first of which was done by the South African surgeon Christiaan Barnard (born 1922) in 1967. The patient, Louis Washkansky, lived only 18 days; but later heart transplants have prolonged life for several years. Sometimes the donor's lungs are transplanted as well as the heart. Livers and corneas (the transparent covering of the eye) are also transplanted successfully. In the future, genetic engineering techniques may overcome the rejection problem by making the recipient insensitive to the donor tissue.

The pineal body has long puzzled researchers. A New Zealand reptile, the tuatara, resembling a 60-cm long lizard, has a pineal body strongly resembling a third eye set in the top of its head. The tuatara is an extremely primitive reptile, and appears to be a link with past creatures far older than the dinosaurs and which may have had a working third eye. In humans, the pineal body seems to respond to signals from the eyes by releasing a hormone. The well-known sense of depression associated with gloomy weather has been attributed to this pineal activity.

The main problem in finding a cause for cancer is that it is not one disease but many. All kinds of causes are known for various cancers: irritants such as tobacco smoke, asbestos, and strong sunlight; unsuitable diet; and certain viruses. A tendency to cancer is inherited. People are more likely to get most kinds of cancer in middle age or later, as if the body has got tired of reliably producing new cells of the right kind, and slips into making incorrect cells which rapidly multiply into a cancerous growth. However, there are also cancers that principally affect children, and anyone of any age can fall victim. Another theory is that the body makes mistakes in cell copying the whole time, but that the defective cells are normally wiped up by the body's defences. At some time bad health of any kind may weaken the defences and allow a defective cell to survive and multiply. This fits observed facts rather well: for example many men get cancer suddenly after they retire, and this may be precipitated by the depression that often accompanies retirement. Treatment for cancer includes surgery to remove growths, drug treatment (chemotherapy), and radiation treatment at the site of the cancer. In many cases treatment can do no more than prolong life somewhat, and the side effects are often worse than the disease. However, certain types of cancer – for example simple skin cancers caused by sunbathing – can be cured quite reliably. One of the most promising treatments is the use of monoclonal antibodies, genetically engineered substances which on introduction into the body will travel to a particular type of tissue and cling to it. These can be linked to anti-cancer drugs so that they will deliver a powerful, concentrated dose to the growth without poisoning the whole patient.

THE FOOD PROCESSING MACHINE

PAGES
20 to **21**

Further information on nutrition is so readily available that no general remarks are needed here. A recommended source is the Nuffield Home Economics course, published by Hutchinson (1982–5). This is intended for 13- to 16-year-olds, so that more able pupils will be able to cope with the third year book, *The Basic Course*. As usual, pupils' books are backed by teachers' guides which will be useful in any case.

A few particular points on the text.

1 kilocalorie is 4.1861 kJ. Kilocalorie is often written as Calorie, with a capital C, intended to distinguish it from a calorie but actually causing endless confusion. Many larger supermarkets have begun to mark food packages with quite detailed dietary information, including both kCal and kJ value and amounts of protein, fat, and carbohydrates. (This will be useful in the later activities, to rate foods not covered by Worksheet 36.)

Dietary fibre is in fact a carbohydrate. Not all carbohydrates can be digested by humans. Sugars and starch are; cellulose (the cell walls of plants) is not, and this constitutes fibre. Its action in aiding the working of the bowels is mainly mechanical. It absorbs water, swells up and provides bulk, sweeping other waste products away with it. Although fibre is not digested it may contain digestible and useful substances: for example bran is full of B vitamins. That is why wholemeal bread contains more vitamins than white. Brown sugar contains no fibre. The impurities from the sugar cane that turn it brown give it a pleasant taste but little else of value.

The substance in saliva that starts digestion is an enzyme, ptyalin. Other enzymes play an important role in digestion, stripping sugar molecules out of starch, breaking down fats and proteins into their components, and so on. The hydrochloric acid in the stomach, though strong, could not do this by itself.

The end products of digestion are substances used in the maintenance and operation of the body – these include the amino acids which are the components of protein, used to replace body proteins; vitamins; minerals (see the minor items on the list of elements at the beginning of this chapter); and other essential substances that the body cannot make, for example linoleic acid, which is found mainly in vegetable oil. Energy comes from glucose, a simple sugar and the final substance into which the energy giving part of food is transformed. The liver stores some of this sugar in the form of glycogen, and breaks it back down to sugar and releases it into the bloodstream as it is needed. Any excess sugar is turned into body fat, a long term energy store.

The lining of the stomach is not invulnerable. Even taking aspirin can make it bleed. Sometimes the lining breaks down, and this is a stomach ulcer. If the damage goes right through the wall of the stomach – a perforated ulcer – the result is peritonitis which can lead to death unless treated swiftly.

HOW IS YOUR BODY CONTROLLED?

PAGE 22

The control system of the body is known as the autonomic nervous system. It works completely automatically and is not consciously perceived (though its effects are) or consciously controlled (except by people such as Indian fakirs, who have learned to do so). This system is separate from and independent of the motor and sensory nerves. It is co-ordinated by parts of the spinal cord, and the medulla and hypothalamus in the brain. It controls some muscles, for example those that move food down the gut and constrict blood vessels. These muscles have a different structure from the voluntary muscles, and are known as smooth muscles, as opposed to striped. Of all the muscles controlled by this system only the heart muscle is of the striped type. The autonomic nervous system is divided into two parts. The larger is the sympathetic system, which runs to the limbs and skin, controlling functions such as sweating. The smaller parasympathetic system runs to the internal organs. One obvious effect of the autonomic nervous system happens when we are frightened. The system causes the adrenal glands (on top of the kidneys) to send adrenalin into the bloodstream, inducing alertness (not to say unease), stimulating the muscles and temporarily stopping some functions so that essential materials can be rerouted to the muscles. For instance, digestion is halted, causing a sensation of 'butterflies in the stomach'.

In addition to the involuntary control of the autonomic system and the conscious control of the motor system one could also discuss reflex responses. In such instances, as with the leg kicking when the knee is struck, the motor nerves are stimulated by an external happening which has not been mediated by the brain.

A further point which may come up in discussion is that of co-ordination – how we learn to sequence and synchronize movements for effective action. Some co-ordination seems to be innate, as displayed with the young child feeding, but more often, as seen with a child learning to walk, considerable effort is required. Once sets of movements have been learned and repeated then co-ordination does not require conscious thought. It is difficult for us now to explain how we walk – we just do. Similarly, once the skill of riding a bicycle or changing gear when driving a car has been acquired then the coordinated set of movements no longer require thought.

Notes on the activities

PAGES
114 to 119
This chapter of activities aims to reinforce the children's skill in using measuring instruments, reading scales, and drawing bar charts of their data. It provides the opportunity to develop understanding of the scientist's use of the word 'normal', and some simple statistical ideas. It stresses the important idea that every human being is different and explores the dimensions of that uniqueness – the range of features in which we differ. This emphasis on organic difference balances the impression of mechanistic similarity which is inevitable in our treatment of the reader pages.

It is important to note that the chapter concentrates on fitness rather than health, which will be the subject of Chapter 3. Taking the two chapters together it is worth mentioning that the relationship between health and fitness is an increasing concern of new PE curricula. It is likely that the PE department at your school will be interested in knowing in advance about these activities, and co-operation between departments may be possible.

PROBLEM 1: HOW CAN YOU MONITOR YOUR FITNESS?

Health and fitness
PAGE
114
The work is intended to start with a discussion. You could begin by asking the children to say what they understand by the words 'healthy' and 'fit'. Is there a difference? Are the two connected? How can you keep a check on your fitness?

This should lead to the idea of measuring some of your features and keeping a check on changes in the measurements as time goes by. The questions: 'Are there standards of tallness, or heaviness?', and 'How do you know how tall or heavy you should be?', lead the discussion towards the statistical idea of normality as follows.

What does 'normal' mean?
PAGE
115
The answer to the question is not simple. 'Normal' is a slippery word with many colloquial meanings such as: natural, neutral, balanced, moderate, middling, commonplace, everyday, ordinary, usual, rout-ine, socially acceptable, conventional, regular, standard, orderly, and according to rule, custom, or criterion. So you have to be careful how you use the word.

The discussion could continue in this vein, gradually leading up to the point that everyone is different, and the differences have to be taken into account when you talk about normal values. Next you could choose to look at some theoretical distribution graphs, basing your presentation on the following notes; or, alternatively, you could suspend further discussion until you have some graphs of actual measurements to put before the class.

Distribution graphs
If the children have followed the first year of Nuffield Science 11 to 13 they will have drawn bar charts of their 'vital data', and they may have coloured in the boxes on a worksheet to produce a classic normal distribution graph. This worksheet is referred to on page 115 of the activities.

The artificial data used to plot the graph are as follows:

Class	1	2	3	4	5	6	7	8	9	10	11	12
Frequency	1	2	4	9	15	19	19	15	9	4	2	1

Of course, in practice, the class numbers would be replaced by groups of values of a variate such as length (eg. 140–144 cm). The following set of data provides an interesting contrast:

Class	1	2	3	4	5	6	7	8	9	10	11	12
Frequency	1	1	1	3	3	7	11	17	30	20	5	1

The resulting graph is what is known as a 'skewed' distribution (negatively skewed actually – remember it by saying that the 'pointed' end of the graph, 'like a skewer', points in the negative direction). Suppose this was a graph of the weights of 100 children in the second year, against the number with each weight: what would you conclude about the second year as a group? What would be the normal class for the second year?

What is 'normal'?
There are three answers to this question, depending on whether 'normal' means balanced ('average'), or middling, or most frequent (popular). The average is the value you would get if you cut out a piece of cardboard the same shape as the outline of the graph and balanced it on a pencil. It is the 'centre of gravity' of all the values on the graph. Of course you can calculate it using our values by multiplying and adding like this: $(1 \times 1) + (2 \times 1) + (3 \times 1) + (4 \times 3) + (5 \times 3) + (6 \times 7)$ etc., and dividing the result by the total number of values (100 here). You will get a result of 8.25. The average is often taken as the 'normal' value, but it is difficult to explain and interpret.

The middle value, called the 'median' is easier. This is the value which divides the population into two halves (of 50 here). You can see that with 44 below the 9th interval and 26 above, the median is somewhere in the 9th interval. In fact it is $6/30$ above the bottom of the interval. This actually has a value of 8.5 because, for a continuous scale, the 9th interval stretches from 8.5 to 9.4. So the median is $8.5 + 6/30$ or 8.7.

PAGE
115

Finally there is the most popular value which corresponds to the peak of the curve. On our scale it is the middle of the 9th interval or simply 9. This value is called the 'mode' of the distribution.

It goes without saying that whenever a scientist hears the word 'normal', he or she is anxious to know in which of these three senses it is being used.

Organizing the collection of data
In order to establish 'normal' statistics you will need to pool the results for all the children in the year, and for each of the variates the children measure. It would be ideal to end up with a display consisting of the bar graphs for each variate pasted onto a large backing sheet. It would be worth while to take some trouble over the label for this sheet, using rub down lettering on a piece of white card to say: 'Second Year 1988: Vital Statistics' for instance.

A good way to organize the collection of data is to set up a series of postboxes made from shoe boxes: one for height, one for chest size, and so on. The children can write their names (important this) and measurements on slips of paper and post them in the boxes.

Later, for the counting and bar graph construction, you can share out the boxes amongst all of the classes in the year. You may like to add to the list of variates in our table so as to increase the number of postboxes and decrease the size of the group responsible for each. One good addition would be shoe size (See *Pupils' book 1* activities page 148 and *Teachers' guide 1* page 133). You will need to decide whether or not to draw separate graphs for boys and girls, and this may take some discussion. The procedure may seem elaborate and time-consuming, but the children are developing some important new ideas, and the experience of handling large amounts of data is relevant, interesting, and valuable.

TAKING THE MEASUREMENTS

PAGES
116 to 119 The actual measurements are straightforward. It will be worth emphasizing the need to use correct units (particularly in parts B, D, and E) and some children will need help in reading the scales, and in using the calibration graph in part G. Some other points relating to specific parts are as follows.

Part C: Frame size
As we have presented it, you will need to compare the bar graphs for parts A and C to answer the question at the end. Another way would be to ask the children to divide their frame size by their height and to plot the quotient, which is normally 1 (mode) for the whole adult population.

Part D: Strength
Worksheet 19 from Year 1 is used here.

34 Chapter 2 Activities

Part E : Lung pressure

A suitable U-tube would be that from the Nuffield Physics Bristol pressure kit which consists of a 6-metre length of plastic tubing clipped to a 2.5-metre backing board. Plastic mouthpiece tubes (to be kept in a beaker of Milton diluted 1 to 80) are part of the same kit. You should try to prevent the children from being too competitive and over-exerting themselves, which could lead to hyper-ventilation.

The units of pressure – which the children are meeting for the first time – are newtons per square metre or pascals, called to honour Blaise Pascal (1623–1662), the French scientist. The pressure due to a 1 cm column of water is actually 98.06 Pa, which is conveniently close to 100 Pa.

Part G : Reaction time

While the children are working on this you might like to show them a well-known parlour trick. Hold a five pound note vertically in the same position as the metre scale in our diagram and say: 'You can have it if you can catch it when I drop it'. It's a good risk!

We used the equation of motion:
$s = ut + \frac{1}{2} at^2$ ($u = 0$, $a = 9.8 \, m/s^2$)
to draw the calibration graph. Any error caused by ignoring air resistance will be completely swamped by that in reading the catch point on the scale – but this is nit-picking in the present context – the important thing is to give the children another opportunity to use a graph as a computing device.

You will probably have modern electronic stopclocks in the science department, and these will be fitted with two pairs of terminals which can be connected together in various combinations to start and stop the clock. You could demonstrate this to the children and set them as a design challenge to work out a circuit which will start the clock when a light is switched on (or buzzer sounded), and stop it when a reaction button is pressed.

Part H : Step-up performance

PAGE 119

It will be a good idea to treat the Harvard Step Test separately from the other parts. It gives an opportunity for discussion to bring out the need for standardized tests where planned training and selection are necessary (as, for instance, in preparing a national Olympic team, or in the armed forces). You might start by saying: 'Suppose you were getting together a team and you wanted to choose only those who had reached a certain level of fitness – how would you go about it?' You could follow the discussion by giving a personal demonstration of the step test: it does need practice to get the rhythm right, and this is particularly so if you have to use steps or stairs ('up three treads . . . down three treads . . . up three treads . . . .').

There is an extensive bibliography on the subject of tests such as the Harvard Test. Two of the most useful books are as follows.
COOPER, K. H. *The new aerobics.* Bantam Books, 1970. ('The Official

Exercise Program of the United States Air Force, The United States Navy, and the Royal Canadian Air Force'. The chapters 'Indoor exercising', 'I'm glad you asked me', and the appendix are particularly interesting and useful.)

COOPER, M. and COOPER, K. H. *Aerobics for women*. Bantam Books, 1970. ('The world's most popular physical fitness programme – now adapted specifically for women'. Again, the appendices are excellent.)

Additional activities

Probably the most highly motivating subject for any group of children (or adults) is 'Ourselves', and the possibilities for sure-fire additional activities are legion. You need to remind yourself that the children will return to the subject, probably several times, in later years, and resist the temptation to spend too long on it now.

On Worksheet 37 we have provided a starter for making a very general poster to show schematically the various systems of the body and the transfer of materials between them. You might like to follow this by designing another collage to show the major organs of the body – very few twelve-year-olds have a good idea of the locations and relative sizes of these. They will enjoy colouring and cutting out the organs from one worksheet and sticking them on an outline (similar to those used for dress-up doll cut-outs) on another. An excellent reference for such work is Barnett, C. H., Lumby, H. G., and Taverner, D. *The human body*. English Universities Press. You may also like to consider purchasing one of the cut-out skeletons marketed by Fisher & Miller Limited, 27a Old Gloucester Street, London WC1N 3XX.

BINARY DISTRIBUTIONS

It will be valuable to complete your collection of data on individual differences by looking at some features which do not vary continuously through the population. Good examples are the ability to roll your tongue (you can or you can't), attachment of your earlobes (they are or they aren't), and your ability to taste phenylthiourea (you can distinguish between the taste of plain filter paper and PTU-soaked filter paper – ugh! – chewed for about half a minute, or you can't). Possession of freckles is a good subject for discussion!

⚠ Caution. Phenylthiourea is toxic, and only minute quantities must be used for a taste test. The danger comes from those children who do not detect a bitter taste and are tempted to try more of the substance. Never allow children access to the solid reagent. The best procedure is to make a solution of the phenylthiourea in water (0.5 g per litre) and soak a piece of filter paper in this solution. The paper can then be allowed to dry and small pieces (about 1 cm × 8 cm) allocated to the children for testing.

WORKSHEETS 35 AND 36:
'MONITOR THE ENERGY VALUE OF YOUR FOOD'
AND 'ENERGY VALUES OF FOODS'

We would like to highlight the attitude to the concept of energy which is implied by the introductory text to Worksheet 35. As understood by a mature scientist, energy is an entirely abstract idea. Statements which refer to energy amount to no more than convenient forms of words for describing and ordering complex interactions in the world of observations. For example, to say: 'Your food provides you with energy', is a convenient (and useful) way of side-stepping description of the complexities of part of the function of foods. In fact it says no more than: 'Your food provides your body with the raw materials which it needs for movement and the production of heat.'

In so far as it can be simply defined, energy is the ability to cause movement or change in movement. This idea – that we have a word for the ability or capacity to produce particular effects – is far too difficult for most eleven- and twelve-year-olds, so nowhere do we attempt to introduce it. We avoid such statements as 'Your food provides you with energy' because we believe that they teach the children that energy is a thing or a kind of stuff. Instead we use statements such as the longer one above, which do not require it. This argument is developed further in Chapter 11.

When it comes to the energy *values* of foodstuffs the common usage is so strong that we cannot ignore it, but we use the phrase 'energy value' with care, simply as the name of a certain kind of measurement. So the answer to the question: 'what is energy?' can be 'It's just a number'.

The children will enjoy keeping a record of their meals (for our purposes, one boiled sweet is a meal, as is one cup of coffee with or without a biscuit); and will enjoy finding out the total energy value of their diet. Provided, that is, that they do not get bogged down in a lot of unnecessary arithmetic. We have used the idea of picking up counters to make sure that they do not. As a result our values may seem far less precise than those appearing in other lists. However we would argue that such precision is unjustifiable, not least because of the rough and ready way in which 'portions' are commonly estimated; and that our system will give a total which is within 10 per cent of that which would be obtained from more careful measurements. Incidentally, one of our units is approximately one megajoule (MJ).

Finally, it is important to note that we had to say in our table: 'aim for the top end if you want to put on *more* weight' because, of course, at their age the children are putting on weight all the time.

THE NACNE REPORT

In step *4*, the children will almost certainly find that most of their counters came from fat, and what we would now call refined carbohydrate – starchy and sugary foods. Ten years ago this would have been entirely acceptable; increasingly, it is becoming less so.

In recent years a quiet revolution has been raging in our understanding of, and attitudes to, diet, and confusion is only just beginning to give way to a new consensus. The most famous expression of the consensus is to be found in the recommendations of the National Advisory Council on Nutritional Education, a body which was constituted in 1979. Their recommendations are as follows:

1 Fat intakes should be reduced by 25% to provide not more than 30% of the total energy intake. Saturated fatty acid intake should be on average not more than 10% of the total energy intake.

2 Average sucrose intake should be reduced by approximately 50% to 20 kg per head per year. Of this not more than 10 kg should be derived from snack foods.

3 Fibre intake should be increased by 33% to 30 g per head per day. The increase should come mainly from a greater consumption of wholegrain cereal.

4 Salt should be reduced by approximately 25% to 9 g per head per day.

5 No recommendations either to increase or decrease total protein intake have been made. Other recommendations would however ensure a greater proportion being consumed from vegetable sources.

6 The energy content of the diet should be sufficient for individuals to maintain optimum body weight and allow adequate exercise.

Essential reading for anyone interested in the area or responsible for teaching it is: Tudge, C. *The food connection*. BBC Publications, 1985.

CHAPTER 3

Keeping well

Introduction

We move on from the discussion of the healthy body in Chapter 2 to issues of ill-health and medical care in this chapter.

Threatened by high mortality rates, particularly in childhood, and subjected to periodic plague epidemics, people have always been concerned about the causes and prevention of illness. The work of Pasteur, Ehrlich, and Fleming illustrates how the application of scientific methods and ideas can bring immense benefits to mankind. Alongside that account of success we have tried to suggest that much more needs to be understood and undertaken if such contemporary problems as heart disease and cancer are to be overcome.

Summary

Target Read and discuss pages 23 to 25 'Keeping well'; 26 to 27 'The microbe story' (picture story); 28 to 29 'The war of the cells'; 29 to 30 'From herbal remedies to modern medicines'.

Images Early treatments for illness tried out by hit-and-miss methods. Recognition of micro-organisms lead to systematic methods. Further research needed – and is being undertaken.

Skills Handling microbiological materials. Setting up controls.

Ideas Without scientific medical care illness can devastate populations. Recognition of role of micro-organisms led to control of many infections. Antibiotics. Contemporary health problems.

Activities Growing micro-organisms. Identifying presence of micro-organisms.

Worksheets 38 'Health do's and don'ts'
39 'Make a medicine survey'

Reader pages

PAGES
23 to **30**

This chapter is about the prevention and treatment of disease. It opens with pictures of ancient and modern treatments, some of which are to be dealt with in more detail later. The seriousness of infectious diseases in the past is stressed by reference to the Black Death and the Great Plague. Old remedies are discussed, making the point that some of them were useless but others quite effective. Prospects improved with the discovery that many diseases are caused by microbes. Today, if a micro-organism can be identified, the chances are that the disease which it causes can be cured or even prevented. Ways in which infection is transmitted are described, as are the body's defence mechanisms which avert many diseases. The rest of the chapter tells the story of the growth in our knowledge of the causes of diseases and ways of treating and preventing them. The account uses both text and a pictorial sequence.

Activities pages

PAGES
120 to 126
The work introduces a new range of skills and techniques: those of the microbiologist. We begin with a two-part investigation of the growth of microbes in a liquid medium. The first part illuminates good experimental design. It shows how the optimum conditions for the growth of yeast can be demonstrated. The second is a modern version of Louis Pasteur's great swan-necked vessel investigation. We use fermentation locks to do the same job as the S-bends of the original flasks. Problem 2: 'How can you catch a microbe?' (if you can't see it!) introduces the technique of culturing microbes under controlled conditions on agar plates (see special note below) – the effectiveness of varying degrees of washing your hands is assessed. Problem 3: 'How can microbes give themselves away?' illustrates the use of established pattern statements about microbes in the design of a method for evaluating the freshness of milk. Worksheet 38 'Health do's and don'ts' supports mini-project work based on the children's collection of sponsored materials on health care; and Worksheet 39 'Make a medicine survey' supports a survey of the medicines stored in the normal home.

⚠ Two special points should be made regarding the work in the chapter. The first is that the work is covered by a body of safety requirements, which must be followed rigorously (see 'Notes on the activities' below). The second is that the first three activities will take some time to give results, and you will need to plan for the waiting time.

Background to the reader pages

PAGES
23 to 30
Administering medicines by hypodermic injection is a relatively modern technique. Large syringes were used in ancient times, but only for squirting fluids into existing body cavities as one might today put drops into the ear. Hippocrates (see notes on Chapter 2) described such a device: a tube with a pig's bladder attached. The technique of injection was invented in the fifteenth century not for living patients, but to preserve or stain anatomical specimens, using mercury, ink or wax. Before the nineteenth century drugs were sometimes rubbed into the skin, which might be blistered first in an attempt to increase uptake. In 1844 in Dublin Francis Rynd (1801–1861) first used a

hollow needle to introduce narcotic fluid under the skin. No syringe was attached to the needle, so only a little fluid could be inserted, simply by the drop in pressure under the skin caused by withdrawing the needle. The first proper syringe was used by Charles Pravaz of Lyon in 1853, to treat aneurysms (bulges in the wall of a blood vessel). He had previously used a needle with a fluid filled bag attached. In the same year Alexander Wood of Edinburgh used a syringe to inject a painkiller in a case of neuralgia. The introduction of local anaesthesia (see notes on Chapter 2) led to wide use of the new device.

Acupuncture, treatment of disease by pricking with needles, is said to have been invented by the Chinese doctor Huang Ti around 3000 BC. There were 367 points at which needles could be inserted. Since then the technique has been greatly developed, so that a practitioner must study for more than a decade before he or she uses the technique in earnest. Great accuracy – to the millimetre – is needed to hit exactly the right spot. The points are situated along 'meridians', lines through which the life force, ch'i, was said to flow. The meridians mostly do not correspond to any visible bodily structures, and the points are remote from the organs to be treated. However, there are some correspondences: for example, some of the points for heart treatment are on the line running from the chest down the left arm along which the pain of angina pectoris, symptom of a heart condition, is felt.

Acupuncture is used to treat complaints of all kinds. One of its most spectacular uses is to induce local anaesthesia for operations. For an operation on the oesophagus three needles – one in the body, one in the left ear, and one in the left forearm – are said to give complete insensitivity. Many Western doctors have been sceptical about such claims, saying that pain relief is slight and mostly caused by suggestion. Others disagree.

It may be that the slightly painful insertion of the needles stimulates the brain to produce endorphins, natural painkillers. Once the needle has been inserted there is a sensation of tingling numbness at the site. The 'gate control' theory of pain states that pain signals can be blocked by sending a signal that travels up a nerve faster than a pain signal (which is slow moving) so that the nerve is occupied and won't carry any other signal.

Bleeding is a treatment that has been carried out since ancient times. According to legend, shortly after the siege of Troy, Podaliarius, son of the god of medicine Aesculapius, bled the daughter of Dametus king of Caria, after she fell off a house and knocked herself out. She recovered and he married her. The Greek physician Erasistratus (c. 304 – c. 250 BC) believed that many diseases were caused by an excess of blood, and that bleeding would cure them. This theory fitted the earlier doctrine of Hippocrates, later worked out in detail by Galen (for both see Chapter 2) that disease was due to an imbalance of the four humours of the body, one of which was blood. Bleeding was widely practised for centuries. It might be done by cutting a vein (phlebotomy) or by applying leeches to suck blood. The gold knob on a barber's pole represents a bleeding bowl. In 1820 the physiologist Marshall Hall (1790–1857) attacked bleeding as useless, and over the next 25 years the practice greatly diminished.

The picture of a modern operating theatre shows the importance of sterile conditions to prevent infection during operations. The surgeons, anaesthetist, and nurses wear sterile gowns, caps, and masks – even breath can transmit germs. The instruments are sterilized. Smaller ones, such as scalpels, are disposable, and are supplied in sealed packets. The entire room is lined with washable surfaces. The picture also shows the quantity of electronic equipment used to monitor the patient's condition during the procedure.

The idea behind the stethoscope came from Leopold Auenbrugger (1722–1809), a Viennese physician, in the 1750s, who realized that the state of the chest cavity could be diagnosed by tapping the chest and listening to the sound. The technique was extended in about 1816 by René Laënnec (1781–1826), who listened to the heart and other chest sounds through a straight wooden tube. The original motive may have been to preserve the modesty of his female patients, who didn't like having a doctor's ear pressed against their bosoms. But Laënnec found that the tube amplified the sound. The modern stethoscope has two sound pickups, one narrow and one wide with a flexible diaphragm, which can be switched around. They are for listening to sounds of different frequencies.

PAGES
24 to 25
The Black Death was so named in the nineteenth century. At the time it was simply called the plague. The disease is thought to have arisen in China and slowly spread westward. (Picture 8a.) Since it was a new disease, people had no natural resistance and the death toll was enormous. After a while it died down, partly because, although there was no cure, people learned to isolate plague victims and avoid stricken areas. The city states of Italy devised quite effective hygienic precautions such as quarantine: anyone coming from a plague area had to spend 40 (*quaranta*) days in isolation before being allowed out in public. However, plague never quite disappeared and there were less severe recurrences such as that of 1665 in London. (Picture 8b.) There is some disagreement about what disease or diseases these plagues were. The usual theory is that both the Black Death and the 1665 plague were bubonic plague, characterized by large swellings (buboes) in the groin and armpits. Bubonic plague is spread by rat fleas infected with the plague bacillus, and which may leave their host to bite humans. But from descriptions of the symptoms it seems likely that at least some of the cases of Black Death were anthrax, another disease caused by bacillus and whose symptoms include black and red swellings (Greek *anthrax,* a live coal). The 1665 plague may have been typhus, which also causes skin lesions. There is a 1665 plague pit under the triangular site in front of London's Victoria and Albert Museum. Recently the site was excavated to build the Ismaili Centre. If the

disease had been anthrax there might have been an outbreak, as spores of this bacillus can lie dormant in the soil for centuries. All three diseases are still prevalent and there are occasional outbreaks.

Doctors are re-examining many ancient herbal remedies and finding them effective. Salicylic acid is also found in the herb meadowsweet. Meadowsweet tea has for centuries had a folk reputation as a pain reliever. It is superior to aspirin in one way, since the natural gums in the herb prevent the acid from attacking the lining of the stomach. Another forgotten herb that is now being taken seriously again is feverfew, a wild chrysanthemum. This was used to treat fevers and headaches (its name is a corruption of febrifuge, an antidote to fever). In recent controlled trials it has been found to give at least some relief from migraine in 70 per cent of cases. Traditional herbal medicine is still practised in many countries, notably China where the government gives equal favour to herbal and western-type practitioners. The Chinese are also scientifically investigating many plant substances. One of these is gossypol, a possible male contraceptive of the future. It is made from cotton seeds, and the effect came to notice when a high incidence of male sterility was observed in an area where food was cooked in cottonseed oil. Gossypol is certainly effective, but troublesome side effects have to be eliminated. Such work is not confined to China: for example, western drug firms use a hormone-like substance from a tropical yam in the making of the ordinary female contraceptive pill.

Spa, in Liège province, Belgium, has been famous since the 14th century for its mineral springs. But it is by no means the first 'spa'. The Romans were enthusiasts for bathing in hot springs. The first bath house at Bath in Avon was built by them, and parts of the original building are visible today. The great age of spas was the eighteenth century, when fashionable people would go to a spa each year to 'take the waters', bathing or drinking as prescribed by their doctor in an attempt to undo the previous year's over-indulgence. (See picture 9.) The presence of such fashionable people accounts for the grand and beautiful buildings to be found in many spa towns. Spas have declined in importance since modern research has belittled the curative properties of the water. But many are still going strong, for example Aix-les-Bains in France which is thronged with invalids. Russian doctors often prescribe spa treatment. The claims on Italian mineral water bottles have to be read to be believed (*L'acqua la più radioattiva nel mondo*, etc.) (The most radioactive water in the world.)

Legionnaire's disease was first observed at the Philadelphia convention in 1976, but afterwards it was realized that some earlier mysterious outbreaks had been of the same disease. At the time they had been explained as anything from influenza (Legionnaire's disease has symptoms like those of severe 'flu) to mass hysteria (always a favourite when doctors can't explain an epidemic). Since then the disease has become quite common. The bacterium, *Legionella pneumo-*

phila, grows strongly in lukewarm water. The air conditioning system of the Philadelphia hotel included a water spray on the roof from which droplets were carried in the wind down into the street, so that some passers by got the disease too. This greatly confused the researchers. Some later outbreaks have been traced to showers, where there is always a residue of water and the temperature is never high enough to kill the organism. Once the source of an outbreak has been traced it is fairly easy to eradicate the bacterium by chlorination and altering the water system so that stored water is kept cold. But a lapse in precautions can lead to a new outbreak.

THE MICROBE STORY (picture story)

PAGES
26 to 27
The useful effects of micro-organisms include fermentation caused by yeast, which digests sugars and – in the case of bread/beer/wine yeast, which are different strains of *Saccharomyces cerevisiae* and a couple of closely related species – produces alcohol and carbon dioxide. Oriental fermented foods, many of them made from soya beans, are produced by various yeasts and moulds: for example soy sauce is made by *Aspergillus* moulds, several bacteria and a *Saccharomyces* yeast. Milk products are made by bacteria which ferment lactose (milk sugar) to lactic acid, which gives them their characteristic sour taste. The process begins with bacteria that create acid which prevents non-lactic bacteria from working, thus preserving the food from decay. These bacteria cannot tolerate highly acid conditions, so stronger lactic bacteria take over and produce more acid until they too poison themselves and stop growing. Yoghurt is made by *Streptococcus thermophilus*, then *Lactobacillus bulgaricus*. Other organisms may be involved: some local yoghurts are alcoholic through yeast fermentation – a Central Asian one appropriately called *busa* is about as strong as a light white wine. Vinegar is another product made by bacterial fermentation: the organism, *Acetobacter aceti,* turns alcohol to acetic acid. (But the cheap 'non-brewed condiment' in chip shops is made by a straight chemical reaction.) Many cheeses owe their flavour to a *Penicillium* mould on the surface (such as Camembert) or inside (blue cheese). The species that produces penicillin is different; the original type was *P. notatum* but now various other moulds are used to make penicillin and other antibiotics.

Anton van Leeuwenhoek is discussed in the notes on Chapter 1.

Theodor Schwann (1810–1882) was the first to discover a digestive enzyme (see notes on Chapter 2), the stomach enzyme pepsin. He went on to try to disprove the current theory of spontaneous generation – that microbes or even mice could be created by rotting matter – and this led him to study yeast under a microscope, and to observe its cells dividing. He published his results in 1839, to the scorn of all the leading scientists of the day. It was not until 1854 that Pasteur continued his line of enquiry.

Ignaz Semmelweiss (1818–1865) was a Hungarian obstetrician

working in a hospital in Vienna. He noticed that childbed (or puerperal) fever affected women in the hospital, but not usually those who gave birth in much less hygienic conditions at home. In 1847 he forced the doctors he was in charge of to wash their hands in calcium chloride solution, which was known to be effective against infections (Sir John Pringle [1707–1782], a military surgeon, had published the results of experiments with various substances in 1750). The doctors resented this not least because, although Austria and Hungary were nominally united at the time, there was still a lot of nationalistic feeling and Austrian doctors didn't like being told what to do by a Hungarian. In 1849, when there was a revolt in Hungary, Semmelweiss was sacked. The doctors stopped washing their hands and the disease returned. Meanwhile Semmelweiss went back to Hungary, where he eradicated childbed fever at Budapest maternity hospital. He did not know about the germ theory of disease since it had not yet been proposed – that was done by Pasteur between 1856 and 1885; see the Chapter 2 notes on Pasteur and Lister. All he knew was that somehow the doctors were carrying the disease on their hands, and he took highly effective steps to prevent it.

Robert Koch (1843–1910) began work on anthrax in 1876 after an outbreak of this disease struck the cattle near his home in Breslau. He transferred the disease to mice, and later managed to grow the bacteria in blood serum at 37 °C. Thus he observed how the bacilli lived, and in particular how they produced the hardy spores which make anthrax so hard to eradicate (see the Chapter 2 notes on the Black Death). Later he introduced the modern method of growing bacteria on agar jelly. Julius Petri, who invented the dish, was his assistant. In 1882 he made his most important discovery, the tubercle bacillus that causes tuberculosis. He did not manage to produce a cure (though he thought he had in 1890). Nevertheless, now that bacteria could be isolated and studied outside the body, it was only a matter of time before people such as Ehrlich began to find antibacterial agents.

THE WAR OF THE CELLS

PAGES
28 to **29**
Germ and microbe are only general terms. Many diseases are caused by bacteria, for example tuberculosis, typhoid, and leprosy. Bacteria are among the simplest of living creatures, having single cells without nuclei. They are roughly classified by shape: bacilli (rods), cocci (berries), spirochaetes (spirals) etc., each group including many different species. Some diseases are due to larger organisms such as amoebas, which can cause a severe kind of dysentery. Amoebas are still single-celled, but have nuclei like the cells of higher creatures. Larger still, but still microscopic, are parasites such as the flukes which cause schistosomiasis (bilharzia), a tropical disease spread by standing in rivers containing infected water snails. Certain diseases are caused by yeasts and moulds, which are primitive fungi. Common fungus conditions are thrush and athlete's foot. At the bottom end of the size

range are viruses. A virus is a casing of protein containing a strand of DNA, the material which acts as a store of information for the processes of living cells. When it comes into contact with the cell it injects its DNA through the wall. The cell is now programmed with false instructions that cause it to copy the virus over and over again, resulting in a virus disease. Such diseases include colds, influenza, measles, AIDS, and some kinds of cancer.

Blood contains a large range of cells, collectively known as white cells or lymphocytes, which attack invading organisms. A cubic millimetre of blood contains only 7500 white cells of all kinds, in contrast to 5 million red cells. However, white cells are carried by the circulation to any source of infection and congregate there.

According to the theory, we imagine that antibodies recognize foreign substances by their shape. An antibody has a site on its surface whose molecules are arranged so that they fit exactly into a matching site on the foreign body. The fitting reaction also signals to a white cell to come and destroy the invader. Antibodies may be produced against almost anything: not only germs of all kinds but also transplanted organs ('foreign' because they are of a different tissue type to that of the host; see notes on Chapter 2), and many harmless substances that are breathed in or eaten by a person, who subsequently becomes and remains allergic to that substance. The antibody mechanism can even mistakenly be activated against the body's own tissues, as in muscular dystrophy. So this defence mechanism can be excessively and inconveniently active. At other times it can break down, as in AIDS, which is caused by a virus which is thought to evade detection by antibodies and to go on to destroy an essential kind of white cell called the T helper lymphocyte.

Edward Jenner (1749–1843) was a doctor who systematically studied smallpox. It was a particularly virulent disease because it had arrived in Europe from the east only a few centuries before – the first recorded English case was in 1241 – and the population had no natural resistance to it. It was highly infectious and often fatal. Those who recovered were often badly disfigured by pockmarks. Before Jenner's time it was known that if you got smallpox and survived, you wouldn't get it again. We now know that this is because an antibody is developed. There was a dangerous procedure invented in Turkey whereby you deliberately infected yourself from a mild case of smallpox in the hope that you too would have the disease mildly and thereafter be safe. Sometimes people were inoculated with pus from the blisters of a smallpox sufferer. The skin was scratched and the matter rubbed in. This was called variolation (French *variole*, smallpox). Jenner heard of a belief in Gloucestershire that if you got cowpox you would be immune to smallpox, and resolved to try. He inoculated a boy with cowpox, waited for the mild disease to subside and then inoculated him with smallpox – a most risky gamble, but the vaccination (*vaccina*, medical Latin for cowpox) had worked and the boy didn't get the disease. Jenner became famous not only in Britain but all over Europe. In 1807 Bavaria was the first state to vaccinate everybody. The first child to be vaccinated in Russia was named Vaccinov and exempted from school fees for his entire education. So effective was mass vaccination that between 1967 and 1980 the World Health Organization managed to completely eradicate the disease, the first time this has ever been done (though there was one death later as the result of a laboratory accident). Vaccination works because the cowpox virus has a surface of the same shape as the smallpox one, so that the antibody formed to attack one will also attack the other. Antibodies will react to certain bacteria even if these are dead, provided that the matching site is not damaged. Bacteria can also be weakened by heating so that they do not cause a disease, but still create antibodies. This was the basis of Pasteur's vaccines for anthrax and rabies: see the notes on Chapter 2.

FROM HERBAL REMEDIES TO MODERN MEDICINES

PAGES
29 to **30**
Chlorine is so poisonous that even the tiny amounts in swimming pools give people sore throats and inflamed eyes. There are less unpleasant ways of disinfecting the water, such as treatment with ozone, but they are more expensive. Although drinking water is treated with chlorine, nearly all of it is removed (see notes to Chapter 7).

Paul Ehrlich (1854–1915) began studying the staining of bacteria while he was still a medical student, using the new aniline dyes which had recently been invented, and which were made from coal tar. He also created a cure for diphtheria, then a leading killer of children. By 1890 there was a rough understanding of the nature of antibodies, though not how they worked. Ehrlich inoculated animals with diphtheria and extracted antibodies from their blood to make an effective treatment for humans. But he kept up work on stains. After a while he found a red stain that was quite effective against the trypanosome (a single-celled parasite) that causes sleeping sickness. It was called trypan red. Ehrlich continued the search for something better. Number 606, which he reached in 1907, was not effective against trypanosomes, so he put it aside and went on. It was actually one of his assistants who in 1909 found that 606 was effective against the spirochaete that causes syphilis – then a very grave disease. But Ehrlich was quick to make use of the discovery. These two substances mark the beginning of chemotherapy, a word invented by Ehrlich. The modern name of salvarsan is arsphenamine.

The most important subsequent advance in the fight against infectious disease was the discovery of penicillin, a substance produced by a natural mould whose effect was first noticed in 1928 by Alexander Fleming (later Sir Alexander; 1881–1955). A dish of bacterial culture was accidentally infected with the mould, and Fleming saw that the bacteria died in its vicinity. Most of the credit for the isolation and manufacture of penicillin belongs to Howard Florey (also knighted later; 1898–1968) and Ernst Chain (also knighted later; 1906–1979). It was the first of many antibiotics – substances that have an effect against a range of bacteria.

Most diseases caused by bacteria are now curable. Viruses are harder to deal with: antibiotics are generally ineffective against them. Some of these diseases can be avoided by immunization, for example measles. Others, such as the common cold, remain unavoidable and untreatable. But so many diseases can now be cured or alleviated that most people are living longer and dying from different causes. These include illnesses brought about by stress and an unhealthy lifestyle, such as various heart conditions and many cancers (see the notes on Chapter 2). The fact that these illnesses are now more prevalent is not a sign of failure; everyone has to die of something, and if some of the causes are removed others become more significant. If the current campaign for a healthier lifestyle manages to reduce heart disease and lung cancer, other conditions will claim more victims.

Every few years a new disease appears and causes severe problems before it is brought under control. Examples are Lassa fever, a virus disease first seen in 1969, not common but very infectious and usually fatal; Legionnaire's disease (see the notes above); and AIDS, another virus disease which reached the west in the early 1980s.

Scientists have estimated that, if we could remove all diseases, people would die sometime between their 100th and 150th year as a result of irreplaceable loss of cells, particularly of the brain.

Something that has not been mentioned in this chapter is the effect of the mind on disease. Faith healing, in which a practitioner convinces the patient that he or she is going to get better, can alleviate many diseases. It is more effective on unsophisticated patients, for obvious reasons. In many cultures there are witch doctors, shamans etc. who can cure (or kill) their charges more or less at will by the use of impressive rituals. There is a parallel to this in western society: the placebo effect. If a patient is given any drug, whether or not it has any medical value, he or she is likely to feel better and may even recover from a genuine disease as a result of being given a worthless preparation. In tests up to 60 % of patients have shown this effect. New drugs are tested by a double blind test, in which neither the patients nor the doctors know whether the substance administered is active or inert – this prevents the doctors from unwittingly showing signs of confidence or scepticism which might have an effect on the patients.

Notes on the activities

PAGES
120 to 126 In this chapter of activities the children are introduced to a new range of skills and techniques – those of the microbiologist. The topic gives some of the best opportunities which exist for developing the idea of a controlled investigation. The children are able to experience some of

the happenings which they have read about in the reader chapter, including a modern version of one of the most important experiments of all time – that in which Louis Pasteur demonstrated that decay is initiated in a material by the introduction of microscopic solids from its environment, rather than from within its own substance. Finally, there are opportunities to develop understanding of the practical usefulness of scientists' hard-won knowledge about microbes.

The investigations involve the culturing of microbes so will take some time to produce results and this has implications for planning. You could go right through, setting everything up, making notes, and answering questions, and returning to the beginning again when things have had a chance to happen. This could cause problems of storage (and safe storage), and would interfere with the logic of our progression. We suggest that you treat each problem as it comes, using reading and discussion of the reader pages to fill in any 'awkward gaps'.

⚠ *Before beginning the investigations* (and particularly those of problem 1 part B onwards) you must check your LEA requirements and/or CLEAPSE Hazcards on microbiological work to make sure of the techniques you intend to use. Some LEAs require that a member of your department must have attended a course on the subject; and you must be aware of the DES regulations regarding the disposal of microbiological samples. The precautions embodied in these documents exist because some 'safe' microbes in the air and on our skins are only so because they are 'diluted'. When 'concentrated' on an agar plate or in broth they can be very dangerous. We have suggested the children's fingers as a relatively safe source, but you will need to emphasize that the children should not open the sealed dishes after they have been incubated, and that the dishes must be autoclaved before disposal, including incineration.

PROBLEM 1: HOW CAN YOU GROW MICROBES?

PAGES
120 to 123

Problem 1 was a real problem for several generations of scientists. Following Anton van Leeuwenhoek's first sighting of bacteria in 1677, it was almost exactly two centuries before they could grow pure strains for investigation (see notes on Robert Koch's work under problem 2 below). However, the social and commercial importance of brewing made sure that the culturing of yeast was fully investigated if poorly understood. (Even in the 1850s Liebig and Pasteur were arguing bitterly as to whether it was a purely chemical or a microbiological phenomenon.)

Part A : What do yeasts need to grow?

PAGES
120 to 122

Before letting the children read the instructions for this, you may like to discuss their experience of the use of common yeast, see how many of them know that yeast is a micro-organism, and ask them to suggest what it might need to live. Of course we are not able to interact with our readers so our instructions assume that it needs four things: sugar, water, air, and a certain amount of warmth. We have not suggested an investigation of the optimum temperature. You might like to do this as a buffer for faster groups. Each component is excluded in turn from tubes A, B, D, and E, the other three being provided. Tube C provides all four and is the only one which should show fermentation.

The investigations suggest that the children should be organized into groups, each group taking responsibility for one set of conditions and components. You may like to provide a duplicate set of the test-tubes to halve the size of the groups (and as a form of insurance!). Dividing into groups will prevent the children from directly comparing the tubes, but provision is made for doing this as a discussion activity in step 6 of the instructions.

The children may need some help in setting up the fermentation locks properly.

Part B : How can you demonstrate Pasteur's great investigation?

PAGES
122 to 123

Pasteur's work with the swan-necked flasks was in fact much more of a demonstration than an investigation or experiment. Personally he had ample evidence in support of his theory that air-borne dust and spores produce decay. His problem was to demonstrate what was to him a fact in such a way that the results were beyond dispute. He had to use a medium known to produce decay; and he had to make sure that the medium was open to the air. Had it been sealed some of his opponents would have argued that a 'vital principle' in the air over the broth (necessary to start spontaneous generation in it) had been destroyed by heat during the sterilization process. Others would have argued that 'bad smells' in the air, which they believed to be the cause of decay, had been excluded. At the same time Pasteur had to make sure that the dust and spores could not get through to the broth; and did so by adding the S-bend as a dust trap (probably as a result of much trial and error!).

These points are relevant to your discussion of the questions which the children are asked to answer in step 8. Hopefully, their answer to the first question will be that the microbes will have got into the test-tube from the air. Other possibilities are that the glassware or fermentation locks were contaminated or that microbes were in the broth to begin with. The second question deals with this possibility – we hope that boiling the broth has sterilized it. In fact, heating to 100 °C will have killed most of the bacteria themselves but the higher temperatures of an autoclave or pressure cooker would be needed to destroy their spores. (You could say that spores are tiny, inactive, but well-protected packages containing all the chemicals needed to start a new bacterium – including the special chemicals carrying the instructions for doing so – when conditions improve.)

A fermentation lock is designed to allow gases (carbon dioxide usually) to escape from a vessel whilst keeping the air and air-borne microbes out. We use it as a dust and microbe trap.

We have a second, open, test-tube treated in an identical way because we want to demonstrate that there is nothing, other than the exclusion of dust, to stop decay. If neither or both of the tubes showed decay at the end, the dust trap could not have made the difference.

Finally, you may like to ask the children what, in Pasteur's shoes, they would have done next, and it will be one of those high points in your science teaching if someone suggests Pasteur's follow-up! This was to suck air through a pair of sterile filters, and to show that the first filter, but not the second, would initiate decay.

PROBLEM 2: HOW CAN YOU CATCH A MICROBE?

PAGES
123 to 124

This too was a real problem which scientists had to solve in order to get to grips with diseases caused by bacteria. Of course, you can only catch a microbe by making it betray its presence, and the culture does this. Pasteur could be said to be the chief pioneer in the use of nutrient media, though he was more interested in gross effects than in individual microbes.

There is an inherent problem in the use of liquid media: the infestation consists of a number of species of bacteria and separating them is tedious and time-consuming. In the late 1870s Robert Koch at the University of Berlin was using blood serum as a culture medium to investigate the life cycle of the anthrax bacillus. He developed the use of microscope slides coated with 'gels' carrying the medium. Bacteria could not move on the gel so would produce patches of single species. The gel used by Koch is still used. It is agar–agar, a complex carbohydrate made from seaweed. One of Koch's assistants, Julius Richard Petri, suggested in 1887 that the coated slides should be replaced by shallow glass dishes with lids; these bear his name today.

The warnings about microbiological work given above are particularly relevant to this investigation; it is important to follow the procedure exactly and it will be advisable to read through the instructions with the children before they begin.

A control plate is always necessary when you culture a microbe. You have to be sure that any colonies which appear come from the subject microbe and not from others to which plates have been exposed. If, at the end, the control shows the same colonies as the sample plate you have to assume that both were contaminated and dispose of them. If there is a big difference at the end you can assume that it is caused by your subject microbe (see step *13*).

The Bunsen burner provides a sterile space extending at least to the edges of its heatproof mat. Probably its chief effect is to provide an updraught of air which carries spores and bacteria way from the plates. It is obviously important to seal the dishes with tape. Seal them crosswise, not around the circumference, otherwise anaerobic organisms might thrive.

When the dishes have been incubated you should find extensive colonies in quadrant A, fewer in quadrant B, and fewer still in C. Quadrant D is interesting – you may find extensive colonies again.

These will be made up of different types from the others, having started from bacteria dragged up from deep crevices in the skin.

The two questions at the end are intended as a link with problem 3. It will be a good idea to discuss them with the children before you go on.

PROBLEM 3:
HOW CAN MICROBES GIVE THEMSELVES AWAY?

PAGES
125 to 126

The problem illustrates an application of our modern knowledge of decay, as expressed by the two pattern statements: 'the fresher the milk, the fewer the microbes in it' and 'the fewer the microbes, the more oxygen in the milk'; and their conclusion: 'the more oxygen in the milk the fresher it is'.

The method makes use of a dye, resazurin which changes colour from blue to red to colourless in the presence of oxygen, and at a rate which depends on the oxygen concentration. The relevance of the method to anyone involved in the production, marketing, or buying of milk is obvious.

⚠ Resazurin is somewhat toxic. Children should not be given access to more of the reagent than they need for the practical work, and they should wash their hands at the end of the lesson.

We have suggested using different kinds of fresh milk and one-day-old milk, kept open or closed, and in or out of a fridge. This is a convenient and realistic range of conditions, and sufficient if our main interest is the developing of skills and understanding of process.

However, the difference between the results may be relatively slight and you may like to have ready samples of four-day-old milk – some kept in a refrigerator and some at body temperature in an incubator – to produce more dramatic results. You will probably have to set up a rota for periodically checking the state of the incubated sample over several hours. The following information may be useful.

Sterilized milk: heated to over $100\,^{\circ}C$ and held there for 1–5 seconds.
UHT milk: heated to $130\,^{\circ}C$ and cooled again in 4 seconds.
Pasteurized milk: heated to $75\,^{\circ}C$ for 5 seconds or held at $63\,^{\circ}C$ for 30 minutes.

The last method has the least effect on the taste of the milk; but, though it kills most of the harmful bacteria, it allows the acid-forming types which sour the milk to survive.

The children are asked to study the McCartney bottles and discuss them with you. The bottles are a good example of a carefully designed piece of scientific apparatus – designed specially for microbiological use. They have double caps – an inner rubber one which fits tightly in place, and another metal one which screws down to tightly seal the rubber. The metal cap has a cut-out at the top which reveals enough of the rubber to allow a hypodermic needle to be inserted (not needed in this investigation).

As mentioned in step *4*, if pipettes are used more than once they must be rinsed in sterile distilled water each time. It is worth making a big thing of this.

In step *8* the children are asked to work out a way of showing the results on a diagram. A good way would be to draw a large stopclock face and mark on it the times when each sample decolourized the resazurin. Perhaps you might do this by sticking on small milk bottle shaped cutouts with appropriate labels.

Additional activities

NOT ALL DISEASES ARE CAUSED BY GERMS!

If you followed Year 1 of Nuffield Science 11 to 13 with the children you may like to recap the section on vitamins (reader pages 74-5 and *Teachers' guide 1* pages 130–1) and spend a little time discussing the subject. Perhaps the children could draw up their own tables of vitamins. The point of this is to make sure that the children do not get the idea that all disease is caused by microbes. It is worth remembering that the idea of deficiency disease pioneered by Christiaan Eijkman and developed by Frederick Gowland Hopkins (later Sir Frederick) met with some resistance at first because of the obsession of the scientific establishment with the splendid new 'germ theory of disease'.

SIMPLE BIOTECHNOLOGY

There are rich opportunities for extension work, by carrying out mini-projects on some of the following:

Bread production: (as part of their normal metabolism, yeasts produce carbon dioxide which makes the bread rise).

Sour cream, yoghurt, butter, and cheese production: (cultures of various bacteria produce chemicals which change the milk in various ways and produce distinctive flavours).

Blue cheese production: (various moulds, often inocculated into the cheese, produce the blue veining and distinctive taste).

Wine and beer production: (as part of their normal metabolism, yeasts produce enzymes which will convert sugars into alcohol).

Malt vinegar and wine vinegar production: (cultures of bacteria convert ethanol to ethanoic acid).

Linen production: (microbes strip fibres from flax stems).

Leather production: (microbes clean the leather and produce chemicals which partially cure it).

Antibiotics such as penicillin: (produced by moulds).
⚠️ Actual practical work should not be attempted in this instance.

Raw materials such as acetone: (produced by bacteria during fermentation).

The list lends itself to presentation as an exhibition (perhaps as a puzzle: 'What do these things have in common?'). Bread-making investigations such as those described in Revised Nuffield Biology

Text 1, page 156 could follow. As always, the question is when to call a halt, bearing in mind work planned for future years.

WORKSHEET 38 'HEALTH DO'S AND DON'TS'
The worksheet provides a starter for the children's study of printed materials collected from health centres, doctors' surgeries, dentists, opticians, chemists, etc.

You may like to augment their collections with a collection of the free materials listed in the catalogue of the Health Education Council (78 New Oxford Street, London WC1 1AH. Tel: 01–631 0930). There are opportunities here for teaching the children to be selective but balanced in their studies of 'second hand evidence', and to make efficient summaries. It goes without saying that the language skills of the children are crucial.

WORKSHEET 39 'MAKE A MEDICINE SURVEY'
This reflects the frequently expressed concern regarding the overprescription and waste of medicines (at great cost to the taxpayer), and the dangers of keeping old medicines within the reach of children.

⚠ You should emphasize the need to secure the agreement and co-operation of parents and relatives – some may object.

CHAPTER 4

A colourful world

Introduction

The material in this chapter cuts across many subject boundaries. It involves physics, in dealing with the nature of light, chemistry in describing the manufacture of dyestuffs, and biology in the section on chlorophyll and photosynthesis. In addition, links can be made with art and design, for example through the activities of dyeing and making batiks.

Connections are also made with industrial and social issues. The development of dye manufacture was an integral part of the coal-tar industry in the nineteenth century which had the side-effect of removing the demand for natural products. The section on photosynthesis opens up opportunities to discuss the problems of World food supplies and the conservation of tropical rain forests.

Summary

Target   Read and discuss pages 31 'A colourful life'; 32 to 33 'What is colour?'; 34 to 35 'The dye story' (picture story); 36 to 37 'One thing leads to another'; 38 'Green for life'.

Images   Newton identifying colours in white light. Use of natural dyes and discovery of artificial dyes. The development of the coal-tar industry.

Skills   Observing. Testing. Making comparisons.

Ideas   Nature of light and colour. The coal-tar industry and its products, and how they affected everyday living. Role of chlorophyll in photosynthesis. Plants as basis of all food.

Activities   Extracting dyes from plant materials. Dyeing fabrics, including tie dyeing and batiks. Testing for fastness. Techniques to improve dyeing.

Worksheets   40 'Test your own dyes'
41 'Do a food dye survey'

Reader pages

PAGES
31 to 38
Unlike most mammals, we humans can see colours, and this has important effects on our lives. The chapter explores this idea and discusses the nature of colour and our perception of it. The importance of dyestuffs technology is sketched, as is the use of dyes in science (as stains), and in medicine. The picture story tells of the development and use of dyes from ancient times to William Perkin's Prototype Purple, and the beginning of the modern dyestuffs industry. The

importance of coal tar is explained. Finally, the scientific study of chlorophyll, and scientists' ideas about its function are outlined.

Activities pages

PAGES
127 to 133

The activities are more to do with technology than with science. That is, they are more concerned with the development of (at least potentially) marketable products, and less concerned with observation, measurement, and explanation. However, there are good opportunities for developing observing, recording, and communicating skills, and the designing of investigations and objective comparisons. A range of natural dyes is produced and tested on different fabrics. A worksheet introduces the long-term testing of dyed samples. The difficulty of achieving fastness leads to an investigation of the use of mordants. Finally, some methods of decorative dyeing are tried out.

A further worksheet supports a survey of the use of coal tar dyes as food colourants and introduces 'E numbers'.

An important additional activity would be the study of dyes as indicator substances. We hope that this will be possible, and have provided notes on it under 'Additional activities' at the end of this chapter.

Background to the reader pages

PAGE
31

The painting in picture 1 is called 'The visit to the child at nurse' by George Morland (1763–1804).

The Victorians liked deep, rich colours for their furnishings, as well as for women's clothes. Surviving fabrics of the period are much discoloured, blackened by soot from coal fires and faded from exposure to light, and do not give much idea of what they looked like when new. A much better idea comes from contemporary paintings. Natural fabric colours, some of which will be mentioned again later in the chapter, include: for blue the vegetable dyes woad (European) and indigo (Indian); for red and pink another plant dye, madder (European), or a dye made from lichen, archil (European), or from brazil wood (originally from the east; the country was named after a similar tree found there), and also kermes (Spanish) and cochineal (American), both from scale insects; for yellow the plant dyes weld (European, from mignonette), safflower (Indian) or fustic (from an American tree). Green was a mixture of blue and yellow, and brown could be obtained from many common plants, including raspberry leaves. Black was made from iron sulphate and oak galls, which made a chemical dye, iron tannate; or from logwood (an American tree). Pigments for paint included red cinnabar (mercuric chloride), Paris green (copper arsenite and acetate) and other metal salts: for example cobalt blue, which was used from the sixteenth century to replace the

56 Chapter 4 Reader

extremely expensive lapis lazuli, a blue semiprecious stone that was powdered to make paint.

WHAT IS COLOUR?

PAGES
32 to **33**

Humans and other primates, birds, and most insects and fishes can see colours. Colour vision depends on there being three different kinds of cone cell in the retina at the back of the eye, each of which responds most strongly to red, blue, or green light. The eye also has rod cells which cannot distinguish between colours but are more sensitive to low levels of light – that is why you can see shapes but not colours in semi-darkness. The brain assesses the relative stimulation of the three kinds of cone cell in each area of the image, and decides what colour is being seen. It is not a straightforward process, since the colour vision centre of the brain 'knows' that colours look different when brightly lit or in shadow or next to other colours, and it corrects the picture to give what it considers a reasonable interpretation. It is not often misled. (See also *Teachers' guide 1*, page 46.)

Bees need to be highly sensitive to colour because they live by finding flowers. Since they can see a short way into the ultra-violet, flowers look quite different to their eyes as compared with ours. Many flowers that we see as white are a brilliant ultra-violet to them. The radial marks on the petals, which they use to aim at the centre of the flower, also stand out more clearly in ultra-violet light. People who have had the lens of their eye removed because of cataract and replaced with a plastic lens can also see a short way into the ultra-violet, because the natural lens included material that filtered out ultra-violet; but apparently they do not see things very differently. In contrast, owls can see a short way into the infra-red, which helps them to see at night.

Sir Isaac Newton (1642–1727) was never keen to rush in to print, and also was distracted after his experiment with the prism by his work on calculus, so the book in which he describes his work on light, the *Opticks,* was not published until 1704. It was in English not Latin, which was unusual at the time; indeed it had to be quickly translated into Latin so that foreign scientists could read it. Newton's eyesight seems to have been rather odd and possibly defective – though it never failed, even when he was in his eighties. The indigo colour that he saw between blue and violet is not at all obvious, and most people would simply say that blue shaded into violet. Also he does not seem to have noticed any of the dark lines in the spectrum of sunlight, although the stronger lines would have been visible with even his simple equipment. At least he did not mention them. Maybe he thought them due to a flaw in the glass.

The spectrum of visible light is a narrow band of the much broader spectrum of electromagnetic radiation, from gamma rays (wavelength less than 10^{-10} metre) to long radio waves (wavelength several thousand metres) and beyond. Its wavelength ranges from 7.8×10^{-7} metre (red) to 3.8×10^{-7} metre (violet). Beyond this range infra-red rays have a longer wavelength, and ultra-violet shorter. The colour of objects can be explained in terms of the structure of their atoms, and the ways in which their 'charge clouds' interact with the very short waves of light. The theory is complex and will not be explained here. The apparent colour of an opaque object is due to the wavelengths it reflects, and of a translucent object to the wavelengths it allows through. Some translucent objects have different colours when lit from behind or in front. One kind of coloured 'Perspex' sheet looks green when light falls on it but pink when held up to the light. Gold leaf lets through green light. Most coloured objects reflect or transmit a mixture of wavelengths which we perceive as a single colour. An object that reflects yellow light looks yellow, but so does an object that absorbs yellow light and reflects red and green light in certain proportions. Additionally, some objects fluoresce: that is, they absorb ultra-violet light which we cannot see, and this stimulates their atoms to emit visible light. This phenomenon is used in the fabric brighteners that are added to washing powder. The hybrid nature of the colours we perceive sometimes causes two objects which look the same colour in the daylight to appear quite different in the light from a bulb and different again in the light from a fluorescent strip lamp.

Make-up seems to be as old as the human race. No doubt the earliest humans painted themselves with coloured earths such as yellow ochre, and with plant juices, just as the tribesmen of, say, New Guinea or Brazil do today. One of the oldest cosmetics still in widespread use is kohl – antimony trisulphide, a common ore. This is what the ancient Egyptians used to give themselves those long black eyes. It was and is believed to have a protective effect, and at least it does no harm, unlike galena (lead sulphide) which is made into a black eye make-up and ointment in parts of Asia. Deadly nightshade is also known as belladonna, Italian for 'beautiful lady'. It dilates the pupils, making the eyes look dark and lustrous. This reduces the depth of field of the eye, so it is hard to focus and everything looks blurred. If you have ever had atropine (the active principle of the juice) dropped into your eye to dilate the pupil for examination of the interior, you will be familiar with the effect.

Dyes are used to stain cells because these are generally colourless and translucent, so it is hard to see, for example, bacteria against a background of plant cells. Early researchers had realized the problem and had tried colourings such as ink and indigo, which were not very selective. It is no good staining everything blue. The breakthrough came with the introduction of aniline dyes (see below), some of which could be made to stain bacteria and nothing else, and which were used by Robert Koch, whose work stimulated Paul Ehrlich to look for antibacterial agents based on dyes (for both people, see the notes on Chapter 3). Stains can even be used to distinguish between types of bacteria, a fact discovered by Hans Gram (1853–1938), a Danish bacteriologist. He used iodine followed by alcohol to divide bacteria into 'negative' (where the alcohol washed out the brown colour) and 'positive' (where the colour stayed). The distinction was to be important later, as some antibiotics attack mainly Gram positive and others mainly Gram negative bacteria.

THE DYE STORY (picture story)

PAGES
34 to 35

The main pigment used by cave painters such as those who painted Lascaux in France was ochre, a natural hydrated form of ferric oxide, Fe_2O_3. This can be red or yellow, according to the impurities it contains. Black came from soot. These are long lasting colours, but even so Lascaux has been closed to the public because the lights and the humidity were making the paintings come off the walls. Visitors now walk through a full size glass fibre copy of the cave.

The ancient Egyptians knew of many of the Old World plant dyes and pigments mentioned at the beginning of these notes, and their painted artefacts and murals could be most colourful. What we have of these comes from the tombs of kings and noblemen and was decorated regardless of cost. It is a curious feature of the wall paintings that the men are painted reddish brown (with ochre) and the women are almost dead white. The ancient Egyptians were not the same race as modern Egyptians, but were probably about the same light brown colour. A fair skin was considered beautiful for women, and noblewomen would have preserved it by staying indoors as much as possible, while the men went out wearing nothing but kilts and got deeply sunburnt. Paintings of visiting Cretan men show them the same colour as the Egyptians, and Africans from the hinterland as realistically dark.

The purple dye of ancient times is called Tyrian purple, as it was traded through Tyre in what is now Lebanon. The best kind came from *Murex brandaris,* a sea creature similar to a whelk. Each snail yielded only a few drops of a colourless liquid. Exposed to air and light it darkened and finally became a brilliant purple. The dye was so expensive that a kilo of wool dyed with it cost almost £1000 at today's prices. There were laws restricting its use. Even a Roman emperor would have just a purple edging to his toga. He could wear a completely purple one only while taking part in a triumphal procession.

The indigo plant is one of various species of *Indigofera,* a leguminous plant (the pea and bean family). When dyed, the fabric is at first colourless but goes blue on exposure to the air as soon as the dye solution dries up or is washed off. You can mimic this rather dramatic effect by bleaching a piece of authentic blue denim, which is still today dyed with indigo (though cheap imitations aren't) by using 'Dygon'. Take the white fabric out of the solution and splash plain water on it. Each drop will cause a spreading blue stain. Woad comes from a cruciferous plant (the cabbage and wallflower family), *Isatis tinctoria,* which grows mainly around the shores of the Mediterranean but is still sometimes found wild in Britain. The dyestuff is chemically similar to

A colourful world **59**

indigo, and has the reputation of being very durable.

Many metal compounds are strong pigments, and often these are poisonous. The colour that may have affected Isaac Newton would have been cinnabar. In fact his nervous breakdown may equally have been caused by overwork in trying to conduct scientific research and run the Royal Mint simultaneously. He is not the only famous victim of his décor. Napoleon's death on St Helena was probably caused by the Paris green of his bedroom wallpaper. As late as the 1950s Clare Boothe Luce, American ambassador to Italy, nearly died because flakes of white lead paint from the ceiling of her crumbling palazzo kept falling unnoticed into her food.

William Perkin (later Sir William; 1838–1907) would never have managed to synthesize quinine. It was far too complex, and was not achieved until 1944, by Robert Woodward and William von Eggers Doering in the USA. August von Hofmann (1818–1892), who taught Perkin at the Royal College of Chemistry in London, was interested in what could be made from coal tar. He had already prepared aniline by treating benzene, a simple coal tar derivative, with nitric acid to make nitrobenzene, from which it is a short step to aniline. This led to various aniline type compounds one of which, allyl toluidine, seemed to him similar to quinine. He put Perkin on to the task of turning this into quinine. All Perkin could make was a useless reddish brown sludge. Perkin tried again starting with aniline and got a black sludge which, when he mixed it with water, gave a strong mauve colour. He tried dyeing a piece of silk with it, and discovered that the colour was fast. So he sent some of the substance to a Scottish dyeing firm, who were impressed with it and wanted to buy more. Now came the difficulties which are typical of those facing the young entrepreneur. The Patent Office was reluctant to give him a patent as he was only eighteen, under the age of majority which was then twenty-one. In fact he never managed to patent it abroad, so that later foreign firms pirated the substance. No chemical firm would supply him with aniline, so he had to make it himself from benzene – and he couldn't even get nitric acid and had to make that too. Nevertheless he and his father and brother were making his 'aniline purple' at Greenford within six months. Perkin made enough money to let him retire at thirty-five and go back to pure research. One of his later achievements was to synthesize coumarin, the main component of the odour of vanilla. This is used in the perfume industry. Meanwhile foreign competitors were copying his dye, and developing other colours. The name mauve is the French for mallow, a plant which yields a slightly pinker natural dye, alizarin. (Alizarin is also the basis of the natural plant dye madder.) However, this was the first time the name had been used for a colour. It was an obvious choice because Mauve was also the name of a fashionable painter of the Hague school. The new dyes included Hofmann's own violets; rosaniline, also called fuchsine because it was fuchsia pink; rosaniline blue; chrysaniline yellow; and aniline black.

In the same year as the last of these was discovered, 1863, Peter Griess in Germany discovered a new family of colours, the azo dyes, which give oranges and yellows. Adolf von Bayer, founder of the Bayer chemical firm, created red phthalein dyes (the chemical indicator phenolphthalein is related) and also synthetic indigo and Tyrian purple. An assistant of Bayer's, Karl Graebe, synthesized alizarin, and the firm patented the process in 1869 one day before Perkin, who had been working on the same problem, patented it in England. Baeyer's indigo process was expensive, but when in the early 1890s the Badische Anilin und Sodafabrik (now the giant BASF) devised a cheaper way of doing it, the Indian indigo industry was almost wiped out – though some real indigo is still used to this day. Other synthetic colours followed rapidly. Now any fabric could be dyed any colour with a durable synthetic dye. At the same time the Germans had won a lead in the business of producing not only dyes, but also many other synthetic materials such as synthetic rubber. Today most products of all these kinds are made by using oil as a feedstock rather than coal. But if in the future oil becomes uneconomically expensive it will be possible to return to coal as a starting material for any of these products.

ONE THING LEADS TO ANOTHER

PAGES
36 to **37**

There was some talk of using gas for lighting at the end of the seventeenth century. For example, Dean Clayton of Kildare, Ireland, experimented with coal gas in 1688. In 1765 Carlisle Spedding, the manager of a colliery near Whitehaven, piped the dangerous firedamp (methane, natural gas) that collected in the mine to his office and used it for lighting. He wanted to install gas lights in the town, but wasn't allowed to. The first real success came when William Murdock (1754–1839) built a coal gas retort at the back of his house in Redruth and used the gas to light his house. He sold the idea to factory owners who were already using coal for steam engines. It did not need a large plant to make enough gas to light a factory. The coal was heated inside a sealed cast iron cylinder and piped to a small gasholder – much like a modern one, bottomless and floating in water so that it could rise and fall and remain gas-tight, but only 3 metres high and wide. The gas was not cleaned and must have smelt foul. His first commercial plant was built at Boulton and Watt's Soho Foundry at Birmingham, where James Watt's steam engines were made. Later Murdock installed a water spray inside the retort to remove the sticky coal tar which clogged it. The tarry liquid was piped off at the bottom. At first a useless material, it did not become important until later – see above. The first public coal gas lighting was installed in Pall Mall, London, in 1807 by Frederic Winzer (1763–1830), a German entrepreneur who changed his name to Winsor and founded the large Gas Light and Coke Company which was the main British firm until it was nationalized in 1948. Early gas lights had plain burners and gave no more light than a Bunsen burner's 'luminous' flame. In 1885 Baron

Carl Auer von Welsbach (1858–1929) invented the first successful incandescent gas mantle, a dome of woven fabric impregnated with thorium and cerium nitrate. When the flame was lit the fabric burned away and the chemicals turned to thoria and ceria (oxides) which glowed brilliantly. The composition of coal gas is, on average, 50% hydrogen, 30% methane, 8% carbon monoxide, 4% other hydrocarbons, and nitrogen, carbon dioxide, and oxygen together 8%. From 1967 onwards, Britain began to be converted to natural gas. Northern Ireland still uses coal gas.

A list of some of the commoner synthetic food colours is given on Worksheet 41. (See 'Additional activities' below.)

The E160 carotene colours, whether natural or manufactured, are actually good for you, as they break down in the body to yield vitamin A. The commonest, beta carotene, found in oranges and carrots, is simply two vitamin A molecules joined end to end. The carotenes are a group of substances ranging from colourless through yellow and orange to a weak red, lycopene, found in tomatoes and pink grapefruit. Other natural vegetable colours include the anthocyanins, red, purple or blue pigments found in red cabbage, raspberries and other berries and the skins of red apples. (There are also proanthocyanins, such as the colourless substance in quinces which turns pink when they are cooked.) These substances are rather unstable, and most of them will give an attractive red only in acid foods. Red cabbage is normally cooked with vinegar or citrus juice. If it isn't, the slight alkalinity of hard water makes it go an appalling greenish grey. Iron makes anthocyanins turn blue or black, which causes problems when fruit is canned in a tin with a slight scratch on the plating inside.

GREEN FOR LIFE

PAGE
38

The green plant pigment chlorophyll is quite similar chemically to the red blood pigment haemoglobin, but instead of iron it contains magnesium. There are several slightly different forms found in higher plants, blue-green algae, and photosynthetic bacteria. Chlorophyll is actually a bluer green than you would expect from the colour of leaves, since these also contain a yellow carotene colour. It looks green because it absorbs red (and some infra-red) light, and it is these wavelengths that initiate photosynthesis. The reaction is highly complicated, but can be simplified to:

$$CO_2 + 2H_2O \xrightarrow{\text{light}} (CH_2O) + O_2 + H_2O$$

The expression (CH_2O) represents not an actual substance, but a 'building block' of more complex carbohydrates – sugars, starches, cellulose, etc. Thus the plant is supplied with the substances it needs to build itself up, and incidentally recharges the oxygen in the atmosphere that is used up by animals breathing and the burning of fuels. It was the first photosynthetic organisms that released free oxygen into the air and made it fit to breathe. For a long time, plants produced more oxygen than animals could use up. When the plants died, the extracted carbon formed underground coal and oil. Now human beings are burning this at such a rate that the amount of carbon dioxide in the atmosphere is rising steeply, too fast for any amount of plants to correct (and not helped by the rapid destruction of tropical rain forests). Climatologists fear that the extra carbon dioxide will alter the way in which the atmosphere absorbs sunlight, leading to an uncontrollable rise in temperature – the 'greenhouse effect'. Meanwhile, they are also trying to duplicate photosynthesis in the laboratory, since it is far more efficient than any other means of using sunlight, such as solar cells. It could be used to make sugar which could be turned into alcohol and used as a fuel, or in many other ways. The first small-scale laboratory tests have been moderately successful despite the complexity of the reaction, and better things may follow.

Notes on the activities

PAGES
127 to 133
Although this is more a chapter of technological activities than of scientific ones, there are rich opportunities for developing observational, recording, and communication skills; and the investigations can include testing and the making of comparisons which can be structured in an objective scientific way.

It is interesting to note that all of the techniques on show here have been known for centuries and owe little to science for their development. They were developed by trial and error and, by and large, the pattern statements which recorded success were handed down by word of mouth. The first great *scientific* contributions came in the second half of the nineteenth century following the work of William Perkin and August Hofmann in discovering and developing synthetic dyes; and that of Friedrich August Kekulé, who explained their structures.

PROBLEM 1: HOW CAN YOU MAKE NATURAL DYES?
PAGES
127 to 128
If you need help in obtaining the samples of fabric, the Home Economics department should be able to help. They should also be interested in what you are doing and there may be opportunities for collaboration.

The instructions for the activity suggest suitable plant materials but you should let the children try anything they think might work. Obviously they should use those parts of the plants with the colours they want, rather than the whole plants (boiling onion skin rather than whole onions!). It may help to know that extracts of delphinium, pelargonium, pansy, peony, and petunia are all used as food colours (as is beetroot). Lichen extracts have been used for generations for dyeing Scottish tartans, acids and alkalis being added to produce a range of colours – see 'Additional activities' below.

A colourful world   **63**

A good source of ideas may be the folklore of the children's parents and grandparents – onion skins and Broom (Genista) flowers are still used for dyeing Easter eggs! You may have to refuse offers from home of Annatto (extract of seed coats of a tree), Cochineal (beetle extract), or Capsanthin (extract of paprika), because these are ready-made extracts. A very good source-book for the work is Thurstan, D. *The use of vegetable dyes*. Dryad Press, 1986.

Before you begin it will be a good idea to emphasize the need to keep the extracts for later use, and to check that everyone is wearing overalls.

PROBLEM 2: DO ALL FABRICS DYE THE SAME?

PAGES
128 to 129

This is another problem which had to be solved by early craft dyers. The children will need to concentrate hard to keep track of the samples right through to the end of part B, and it will be a good idea to read both parts with the children before they begin.

They will need three pieces of each fabric, coded by snipping in an agreed way. The pieces will be treated as follows:

Fabric X Piece 1 Set aside for later comparison with washed sample;

Piece 2 Dyed and dried;

Piece 3 Dyed, dried, washed (see part B) and compared with 1.

Fabric Y As above.

The samples should be rinsed (part A, step *3*) until no more dye comes away. Probably the best way to dry them is to hang them on a small 'clothes line' over a radiator. The small plastic clothes pegs sold for hanging up Christmas cards are ideal for the purpose (plain paper-clips will leave rust-marks).

You should find that wool takes up dyes better than other natural fabrics; and that natural fabrics are better than synthetic ones.

The last question at the end of part B is included as a link to the next problem and is intended to be open-ended. At this stage any answer is as good as any other. For instance, the suggestion that the dye should be 'glued' on sounds silly but, at this level, it is not a bad description of the action of a mordant. Incidentally, the mordants are also used to prepare canvasses for painting and for the application of gold leaf.

PROBLEM 3: HOW CAN YOU MAKE DYES STICK?

PAGES
129 to 131

We expect that, by the time they reach this investigation, the children will have established that wool is very good at picking up dyes, but that much of the dye washes out (the colour runs). So we dispense with the other fabrics and focus on improving the dyeability of wool.

Treat the five samples as follows:

Piece 1	–	–	–
Piece 2	mordanted	dyed	washed
Piece 3	mordanted	dyed	–
Piece 4	–	dyed	washed
Piece 5	–	dyed	washed

It is most important that the children should try the design challenge, at least in discussion and on paper. The important point to emphasize is that the comparative test of the mordants should be 'completely fair'. That is, quantities and conditions should be carefully controlled (using measurement) so that all things are equal for all three. This is what modern scientists mean when they talk about 'objective' comparisons. The children may have heard of *Which?* reports which involve such objective testing. Factors such as the cost and availability of the raw materials should also be taken into account.

PROBLEM 4: HOW CAN YOU MAKE DYE PATTERNS?

PAGES
131 to 133

Again, the problem was a real one for early technologists, not least because their palette of colours was often limited. The patterns that they were able to produce affected the saleability of the fabrics.

Block printing and Batik have been raised to the level of high art in some parts of the World, and you may have children in the class who were born in those parts or whose parents came from them. If so, they will be happy to bring in exhibits, but it is better to leave this to the end rather than to risk damping the children's enthusiasm for their own efforts.

Additional activities

WORKSHEET 40 'TEST YOUR OWN DYES'

If time allows, you can organize project work which gives the children a taste of a crucial element of product development – that of testing and evaluation (including costing, market research, and consumer research). Worksheet 40 will give you a start.

DYES AS INDICATORS

With a range of plant extracts to hand, it would be easy to introduce the children to the techniques of using coloured solutions as indicators of acidity/alkalinity (acidity/basicity actually, but the term 'alkali' or even 'antacid' is more serviceable at this level). Red cabbage and plum-coloured wallflowers are famous for the range of colours which they show with solutions of differing pH.

A good way to begin is to give each child a small piece of acid drop and a saltspoon of stomach powder, each on a small square of greaseproof paper. They have to compare the tastes of the two samples and describe the differences. Tasting is so valuable and relevant here that it is worth suspending your 'no tasting in the lab' rule, but emphasizing that the samples must be tipped onto the tongue from their special wrappings and not touched by hand.

Discussion of the children's descriptions of the two tastes will lead to your dissolving the two samples in separate small test-tubes of water and explaining that scientists divide solutions into two types. The ancient names for these are acids (Latin: *acidus*: sour) and alkalis (Arabic: *al-qali*: ashes of saltwort). There are many sorts of acid and alkali such as those in the reagent bottles in the laboratory – the names on the bottles are primary observational data for the children at this stage.

Some acids and alkalis are harmful and taste testing is out, so we need another method to test whether a new substance (a sample of 'spirit vinegar' – acetic acid – for example) is acid or alkali. In the 1600s the great English scientist Robert Hooke gave us the answer: use coloured plant extracts. Probably the most famous is an extract of a lichen called Roccella. The extract is called litmus.

How far you continue with this extension will depend on what the children have done before, how much time you have, and what they will be expected to do in later years.

COLOURFUL FOODS
Worksheet 41 'Do a food dye survey' gives the children a list of food dyes with 'E numbers' and suggests that they look for them in the ingredients lists of the foods they eat. You may like to introduce the worksheet as a later stage of a more general study of food colouring. This could begin with an assignment to see how many different coloured foods can be observed; or with an exhibition of coloured foods. The important question to ask is why the goods are coloured as they are. Would they be less appealing if they were differently coloured? Would they taste different?

The first six of the food colourings listed on the worksheet have an important feature in common – they are all made from coal tar. At the time of writing the use of E123 and E124 is prohibited in the USA, all six are prohibited in Norway and used under restriction in Sweden, Finland, Austria, Greece, and Japan. In his book: *E for additives* (Thorsons, 1984), Maurice Hanssen has this to say about one of them: 'Susceptible people, especially those sensitive to aspirin, and asthmatics, are sensitive to tartrazine. Reactions include urticaria (skin rashes), rhinitis (hayfever), bronchospasm (breathing problems), blurred vision, and purple patches on the skin.'
'It has recently been suggested that tartrazine in fruit cordials may be responsible for wakefulness in small children at night.'

Hanssen's notes on E110 are as follows:
'An azo dye to which some people have an allergy reaction. Important risk of allergy especially in people showing aspirin sensitivity,

producing urticaria (skin rash), angioedema (swelling of the blood vessels), gastric upset and vomiting.'

Similar comments can be made for E123, E124, E133, and E155.

On the other hand the E141 group are derived from chlorophyll which has no known adverse effects in its natural form. The same is true of E160(b), and E160(a) is carotene, E160(c) capsanthin (a paprika extract), E160(d) lycopene (tomato extract). The rest of the E160 and E170 series have no known adverse effects. However, E150 attracts the following comment: 'The safety of caramel has long been questioned. The number of types now available has been reduced to six to meet all the needs of the food industry and work is being carried out to find the safest form. Caramel produced with ammonia has been shown to cause vitamin B deficiency in rats. (Spector, R. and Juntoon, S. *Toxicology and Appl. Pharm.*, **63**, 172–178, 1982.)'

CHAPTER 5

An electrical world

Introduction

The teaching of current electricity to pupils in the 11 to 13 age range presents many problems. The topic is too central and important to be ignored, yet the evidence is that it is poorly understood by most pupils. (See, for example, Shipstone, D.M. 'A study of children's understanding of electricity in simple d.c. circuits.' *European Journal of Science Education,* 1984, **6**, 185–98.)

Some concepts, such as those of conductors and non-conductors, and of circuits, are not too difficult, although confusion arises with respect to the latter because with many real-life applications, with bicycles, cars, and torches, the circuit cannot be readily identified. When we move on to the idea of electrical current these problems become manifest. Pupils tend to hold a sequential model with the current tackling each obstacle in the circuit in sequence before staggering back to the battery in a state of exhaustion. If a lamp precedes a resistance it will be brightly lit; if it follows the resistance it will only be poorly lit. With such a model the sequence within a circuit is believed to be important. Understanding of potential difference is even more inadequate than that of current.

In the light of such evidence of pupils' understanding, we have made no attempt to deal with the ideas of current and potential difference. The importance of electricity to modern living is emphasized. Ideas about conductors, non-conductors, and circuits are introduced. We do try to tell them something about the nature of electricity, in order to satisfy curiosity and demystify the topic, without describing the nature of an electric current. These ideas should provide a good base for later development when the concepts of current and potential can be met.

Summary

Target
Read and discuss pages 39 'An electrical world'; 40 to 41 'Much more than an invisible servant'; 42 to 43 'The story of electricity' (picture story); 44 to 46 'What is electricity?' and 'How big are atoms?'

Images
Scientists' early interest in static electricity. Recognition that thunderstorms may involve this. Galvani's chance discovery. Development of batteries and their use by Davy and Faraday. Edison's work.

Skills
Handling electrical circuits. Observing.

Ideas
Dependence on electricity in modern society. Uses of electricity. Concept of the atom. Existence of sub-atomic particles.

Exploring effects of electricity. Using electricity – electrical devices.

42 'Circuit symbols and circuit diagrams'
43 'Test yourself: reading ammeter scales'
44 'Puzzle circuits'
45 'Spot the disaster points'
46 'Spot the disaster points: Answers'

Reader pages

PAGES
39 to **46**

The chapter provides the first opportunity in the scheme for studying electricity. It is a chapter about technology rather than about science, emphasis being placed on the usefulness of electricity, the great variety of devices we have developed to make use of it, and, by implication, our great dependence on this 'invisible servant'. The various effects of electricity (by which we know it despite its invisibility) are introduced by looking at devices which exploit the effects. The picture story sketches the history of our knowledge of them. The final section hints at the complexity of scientists' theoretical models of electricity. These models set upper limits on the sizes of atoms and it is possible to give a mind-boggling glimpse of atomic (and sub-atomic) scale. On the understanding that the models are imaginary anyway, we can also offer a simple 'electron gas' picture of electricity.

Activities pages

PAGES
134 to **142**

The main aim is to give the children experience of as many working electrical devices as possible, and to develop their skill in wiring them up and investigating the way they work. So, following an introductory problem the work consists of two circuses: one focusing on the exploitation of the effects of electricity and one on the generation of electric currents. The introduction allows for consolidation of primary school work on electricity.

To help with this, Worksheets 42 and 43 support the study of circuit symbols and circuit diagrams, and give practice in ammeter scale reading; and Worksheet 44 introduces the idea of a 'short circuit', and provides some simple circuit wiring puzzles. Worksheets 45 and 46 are intended to be used after the circuses. They allow a not over-serious, common-sense exploration of the dangers of electricity and of good safety practice.

Background to the reader pages

PAGE
39

Picture 1 shows a Victorian kitchen without any electrical appliances whatever. The photograph was taken by James Simkins of Brook-lands, Solihull, on 2nd July 1892. (Notice that the room was not tidied

An electrical world **69**

up before the photograph was taken!) In fact, light bulbs first went on the market in Britain and the USA around 1878. A few rich people had electric light powered by private generators – though probably not for the kitchen. Even before then, from the early nineteenth century on, electric arc lights were used to light large buildings or public places, or in lighthouses. The system was similar to the arc welding described later in the chapter, but the arc was struck between two carbon rods. The first public electricity supplies along wires from a power station were set up in Godalming, then London and New York in 1882. However, electrical appliances other than lamps mostly arrived in the early years of the twentieth century.

Picture 2 reminds pupils of the many domestic electrical appliances available today. Here is a list of modern electrical appliances, with the equivalent device that would have been used in a Victorian household (including some items which are not strictly kitchen equipment).

Electric heater: solid fuel fire or stove, oil heater.

Electric cooker: coal or wood fired 'range'. Gas ranges existed in the late nineteenth century, and electric cookers in the early twentieth century.

Electric kettle: ordinary copper or tinplate kettle to put on the stove.

Electric coffee maker: there were various non-electric devices: drip pots and stove-top percolators. Generally coffee was made in a jug.

Refrigerator: icebox. Fresh ice was delivered weekly, or brought from an underground icehouse in the garden. Mechanical refrigerators had existed since the 1830s, but they were not made small enough for home use till the early 1920s.

Freezer: none. The only way to achieve a temperature below zero in the home was to mix ice and salt, as in an old fashioned ice-cream maker. Again, large commercial freezers existed from the 1860s. Domestic freezers arrived in the 1930s.

Washing machine: there were semi-mechanical devices. The 'dolly tub' was a large bucket with a central agitator slightly like that in a twin tub – but worked by hand. The ancestor of the front loader was the 'washing box', an octagonal wooden drum turned by hand. Professional laundries had big steam-powered washers. The first home clothes washers arrived in the early 1920s. They were turned by electricity, but heated by coal.

Spin drier: mangle.

Dishwasher: none.

Electric mixer, liquidizer, food processor: nothing with power assistance – though there were power mixers in large bakeries and other food preparation works. However, the Victorians had an interesting range of hand-powered slicing and chopping devices, as may be seen in old advertisements and catalogues.

Extractor fan: open window.

Vacuum cleaner: carpet sweeper – pushed by hand – or broom. The first vacuum cleaner was built in 1901. It was a large device powered by an oil engine and mounted on a cart. It was for hire. A horse would bring it to the house. Cleaning would be done with a long hose passed in through the window. Shortly afterwards, the first home vacuum cleaner was introduced. It was worked by two people: one guided the nozzle and the other pumped a bellows to create the draught. The first electric vacuum cleaner dates from about 1925.

Electrical clock: clockwork clock.

Portable TV, radio, cassette player: do-it-yourself entertainment.

MUCH MORE THAN AN INVISIBLE SERVANT

PAGES
40 to **41**

In most places electricity is the most expensive form of energy available in the home, but a compensation is the ease of using it.

Only a small fraction of the heat obtained from fossil fuels is actually turned into electricity in a power station. Most of the waste is removed by the large volumes of warm water which come out of the steam turbines. Usually this is cooled down in large cooling towers, releasing the heat to the atmosphere. In some places – though seldom in Britain – the water is piped to a large housing estate to heat the homes. Small CHP (combined heat and power) systems can also be used in individual homes. Powered by converted car engines, they give electricity and heat several radiators at far less cost than conventional methods.

Other ways of generating electricity on a large scale for distribution, and in use at present, are:

Hydroelectric power from dammed rivers. There is a tidal power station in the estuary of the river Rance in France.

Nuclear power. The reactor produces heat, which boils water to drive steam turbines. There are environmental worries about such power plants and the disposal of nuclear waste.

Alternative methods have been suggested. These include the following.

Wind power: there would have to be very many, very large wind turbines to produce even a fraction of our needs.

Wave power: large arrays of buoys would be installed offshore with generators worked by their up and down motion. No full-scale installations have yet been built.

Solar power: current silicon cells are too inefficient and expensive to make this worth while on a large scale. Even if they were much improved, they would have to cover a huge area, which might be practical in sunny desert regions. There is also a plan to put huge arrays of solar panels in space, where sunlight is brighter, and to beam the power to earth in the form of microwaves. The arrays would have to be constantly steered to keep them facing the Sun, and the beam would have to be very accurately aimed at the receiving station on the ground to avoid cooking innocent bystanders.

Arc welding is done with a rather low DC voltage push – some sets run off car batteries – but a high current flow, typically 30 amps, which gives a good thick, hot arc. The temperature of the arc may reach 20 000 °C. The workpiece is connected into the circuit by a clip and cable to the welding set. When a steel rod is used as an electrode, the heat melts the rod and the current carries the droplets from it on to the workpiece. The metal from the melting electrode acts as a filler to thicken and strengthen the joint. In this type of welding the electrode is at positive polarity – the anode – and the workpiece negative – the cathode. This causes the steel rod to be heated more than the workpiece, so there is plenty of molten steel, and also drives the droplets towards the weld. A filler is not always necessary. For more delicate welds without filler, a tungsten electrode is used which does not melt. The polarity of the circuit is reversed, or sometimes AC is used. Other metals than steel can be welded in this way. Some metals are difficult to weld because an oxide film forms on the surface. Aluminium, for example, is welded in an atmosphere of argon, the cheapest inert gas. In one system the gas is piped to the electrode and flows out around it during welding. Further protection against oxidation is provided by using a chemical called flux.

The filament of a modern light bulb is of tungsten, which has a very high melting point, 3410 °C. The globe is filled with argon at low pressure. Even a tungsten filament would burn up in air. The light bulb was developed during the 1870s by Thomas Alva Edison in the USA and Joseph Swan in Britain. There is disagreement about who made an effective bulb first, or when. Early bulbs had a carbon filament made of bamboo cut into a strip and charred. The globe contained not argon but a partial vacuum, so that the filament burned up rather quickly. Carbon filament bulbs produced a lot of heat and not much light. You can still buy modern ones for uses where heat is needed.

Neon and fluorescent tubes belong to the group of discharge tubes, in which electricity driven by a high voltage flows across a gap between two electrodes through a gas at low pressure. Household fluorescent tubes have a starting circuit – the little round box fitted into the base of the lamp. First this heats the cathode, then the heater is switched off and a momentary high voltage sent along the tube to make it 'strike'. If it doesn't catch at once the cycle is repeated, which is why these lights flash when they are turned on. They are more efficient than tungsten lights. An 80-watt tube gives as much light as four 100-watt bulbs, and considerably less heat. The tube is filled with mercury vapour at low pressure, which glows with a bright blue-white light, plus argon to help starting. The argon glows first, so for a second after switching on the glow is pinkish. The mercury vapour gives some light, but more comes from the fluorescent coating. Mercury light is bluish white with a strong ultra-violet component, so the tube has a fluorescent coating that glows reddish white to balance the output. You can buy tubes with different mixes of fluorescent substances. The most popular type is called 'warm white'. Clothes shops use 'colour matching' tubes which approximate daylight.

Streetlights too are often of the mercury vapour type, but the vapour is at a higher pressure, about 1 atmosphere. This gives a stronger light, but it is very strongly blue. Older mercury streetlights gave a light almost completely lacking red, so that lipstick looked black. Modern ones have a fluorescent coating that gives a more natural effect. Stadium floodlights are of a special mercury type containing a metal halide, such as sodium iodide or mercury iodide, which further improves brightness and colour. Many streetlights are of the sodium type. They are filled with neon with a little solid sodium metal. They start off glowing red, then the sodium vaporizes and they give a strong yellow light. Older, low pressure sodium lights are almost monochromatic yellow. There are also newer high pressure ones that give a yellowish white light. Neon tubes, used for coloured signs, have no heater and need to run at 2000 V. Only the red tubes actually contain neon. Tubes of other colours use argon and mercury, with fluorescent substances and coloured glass to give the desired colour. Other kinds of discharge tubes do not give a continuous light, but a sudden brilliant flash. They are used in lighthouses, aircraft beacons, and camera flashlights. The gas inside is usually xenon.

Quartz halogen lights, used in car headlamps, are not discharge tubes. They have a tungsten filament inside a quartz tube containing iodine vapour. Under those conditions the tungsten filament can be heated until it is white hot without it breaking. Any tungsten which vaporizes reacts with the iodine and is then redeposited onto the filament. Quartz is used as it resists both the heat and chemical attack from the iodine.

Aluminium is produced from the red ore bauxite, which is about 50 % alumina (aluminium oxide). The ore is refined to pure alumina. This cannot be electrolytically refined as it is, because its melting-point is over 2000 °C and it is a non-conductor. It is mixed with cryolite, sodium aluminium fluoride which melts at 1000 °C, after which the alumina dissolves in it. Refining is done in heavy metal pots – the correct technical term – with a carbon cathode and anode. The anode is consumed in the reaction, so it is in the form of a large block which is gradually lowered into the pot. The reaction is:

$$2Al_2O_3 \quad + \quad 3C \quad \rightarrow \quad 4Al \quad + \quad 3CO_2$$
alumina $\quad\quad$ carbon $\quad\quad$ aluminium $\quad\quad$ carbon dioxide

Two thirds of the electricity is used in keeping the mixture hot, the rest in electrolysis. It is economic to refine aluminium only where there is abundant cheap electricity, usually near a hydroelectric power station.

The levitating magnetic train uses a linear motor. This is best understood by comparing it with an ordinary revolving motor, which has a circle of electromagnet coils forming a stator, the stationary part of the motor, around the central rotor. Imagine the circle cut and unrolled into a flat strip, with the original inside surface now on top.

Then imagine the rotor reshaped into a flat slab and placed on the line of coils. If current is passed through the coils the slab will be pulled along the stator. There is a type of electric motor, the 'cage' induction motor, in which all the electric wiring is in the stator, and the rotor consists of a cage with heavy copper or aluminium bars and end rings, with no wiring at all. The cage is made to revolve by switching the stator coils on and off in sequence. If you transfer this principle to the linear motor, the moving part can be free of wiring, so that if it is used in a train, there need be no connection between the train and the track. The stator coils are laid all along the track, angled so that they push the train upwards, to make it hover a few centimetres above the track, and along, to propel it. The coils are also arranged to give a slight inward push to keep the train from straying off the track. This is the technically ideal design for a levitating train, but is very expensive to build because of the cost of the large coils installed all along the track. The world's first levitating train carrying fare-paying passengers, serving the National Exhibition Centre at Birmingham, is of a cheaper type with some of the wiring aboard the cars, so that power has to be picked up by contacts touching the track. It is a low speed train; faster ones will have to be of the first type. Linear motors are also used in daisywheel typewriters and computer printers.

The escalator was developed independently by two people, Jesse Reno and Charles Seeberger, during the 1890s. The first practical model, of the Reno type, was built in Paris in 1900, shortly followed by one in New York. Reno's design was more like a conveyer belt than an escalator, without steps; Seeberger's had steps. The modern type, combining features from both designs, dates from 1921. Stepless 'travelators' are used today in places where no steep slopes have to be climbed. Travelators of the future may use linear motors, which would allow the track to go round curves. All current designs have ordinary revolving motors driving an endless band of track with or without steps. Each step runs on wheels resting on rails at each side of the track. On the sloping part of the escalator the rails are just below the track, pushing the steps up and out. On the flat sections at the top and bottom the rails are several centimetres lower, allowing the steps to fold down.

Electronic keyboards use an electronic oscillator circuit to produce an electrical signal with a frequency corresponding to the pitch of the note selected by pressing a key. The signal is modified electronically to give a particular timbre. Advanced keyboards have computer control which allows the sound of real musical instruments to be simulated. If any of your pupils are computer enthusiasts, they may have tried making their computer play music by using a BASIC program rather than a readymade program on tape, disk or cartridge. Any pupil who has done this will have an excellent knowledge of the waveform of different sounds and should be able to help you explain things to the class.

An electric guitar has steel strings, each of which runs over an electromagnet. The vibration of the magnetized string creates an oscillating current in a pickup coil, which is taken to an amplifier and loudspeaker. The sound can be modified electronically to change its timbre, in extreme cases giving a most unguitarlike effect.

An ordinary loudspeaker has a broad flexible cone with an electromagnet at its centre. A varying electrical signal passed to the electromagnet moves it and makes the cone vibrate, passing the vibration to the air – that is, producing a sound. If you have an old loudspeaker, hand it round, as the best way to understand how it works is to look at it. There are also loudspeakers with a flat membrane moved by an electrostatic effect. These are expensive hi-fi speakers.

Radio is too complicated to explain fully at this stage. A simple explanation is as follows. A radio transmitter produces a powerful alternating current at a certain frequency. When this is passed to an appropriately shaped transmitting antenna, it makes the antenna radiate electromagnetic waves at the same frequency. When these arrive at the aerial of a receiving set they cause electricity to oscillate with a pattern similar to the original signal. The receiving set can be tuned to receive a signal of a particular frequency, helped by the fact that its aerial is approximately the right length – a set which can receive several wavebands has a separate aerial for each one. So far we have only been talking about the main frequency of the broadcast, which is called the carrier wave. Live music, for example, is turned into an electrical signal by a microphone. This signal is modulated (superimposed) on to the carrier wave. The receiving set picks up the modulated carrier wave and electrically separates the message (DC) part of it from the carrier (AC) part. It amplifies the message (DC) signal, sends it to a speaker, and there is your music.

Television uses a radio signal. A television camera picks up an image and scans it electronically. The scanning device moves across the picture in 625 lines every 1/25 second (figures for Britain and most of Europe). As the scanning spot passes light and dark areas on the picture, it responds to their brightness by changing the voltage of an electric current. In the case of colour television there are three simultaneous scans for the amount of red, blue, and green in the picture. Thus the picture is converted into an electrical signal, which is broadcast in exactly the same way as a sound radio signal. A separate signal for sound is added to the carrier wave. The receiving set is essentially a radio which separates the picture and sound signals from the carrier wave. The picture signal is passed to a cathode ray tube whose electron beam scans the screen in exactly the same pattern of lines and varying brilliance as in the camera, so that the picture is recreated. Black and white sets have a single electron beam, and the inside of the screen is evenly coated with a fluorescent substance. Colour sets of the conventional type have three beams, one for each colour, firing from different points through a mask perforated with thousands of tiny holes. At the points where the beam from each gun strikes the screen there are dots of fluorescent substance which glow with the appropriate colour.

THE STORY OF ELECTRICITY (picture story)

PAGES
42 to **43**
The first mention of the effect of rubbing amber is by Thales (624–548 BC), a Greek living at Miletus in Asia Minor. Our word electricity comes from the Greek *elektron*, amber. Possibly the first example of the use of current, rather than static, electricity comes from Parthia, an ancient kingdom in what is now north eastern Iran. An object dating from the third century BC may be a battery used for electroplating jewellery – or it may not. Magnetism was known in ancient times, since one kind of iron ore, lodestone (magnetite, Fe_3O_4) is naturally magnetic. There are lodestone deposits at Magnesia in Asia Minor, hence the word magnetism. Magnets were not used until the compass was invented in China, before AD1000, and introduced into Europe by the Arabs around 1100. Before then magnetism was feared – sailors thought that if they sailed near a lodestone mountain it would pull the nails out of their ship.

William Gilbert (1540–1603) investigated both electricity and magnetism, publishing the results in *De magnete* (On the magnet) in 1600. He invented the word electricity. He conjectured that static electricity and magnetism were related, though for no better reason than that they work at a distance. He showed that other substances than amber can be statically charged.

Otto von Guericke (1602–1686) made a sulphur sphere in an attempt to simulate the magnetism of the earth. Instead, it became statically charged when rubbed. Since von Guericke did not clearly distinguish magnetism and electricity, he thought he was on the right track.

Early experiments on static electricity revealed that there were two kinds. One was the kind produced by rubbing glass. This was called vitreous electricity. The other was produced by rubbing amber. It was called resinous electricity. Two objects charged with different kinds of electricity would attract each other. If charged with the same kind they would repel each other. We would now call resinous electricity a negative charge, and vitreous electricity a positive charge.

These modern terms were invented by Benjamin Franklin (1706–1790), the American statesman, writer and scientist. He realized that electricity was one 'stuff', and that the two kinds of charge were produced by an excess or a deficiency of it. Since electricity is invisible, there was no way of telling which state was which. Franklin guessed wrong. The error persists to this day, which is why electrons conventionally have a negative charge. Franklin began his work on electricity in 1746. The famous kite experiment proved that lightning was an electric discharge. He invented the lightning conductor in 1753.

Luigi Galvani (1737–98) was a professor of anatomy at Bologna

University. There are several versions of the story about his wife and the frogs' legs (see *Teachers' guide 1*, pages 30–1). According to one, she was preparing them on a zinc plate when her steel knife slipped so that the blade was touching both a leg and the plate. Therefore there were two dissimilar metals touching the frog's leg, creating a simple cell. The metals were in contact with each other, short circuiting the cell so that a current flowed (see below). The current stimulated the motor nerves in the leg, causing it to kick.

Alessandro Volta (1745–1827) had been working on the detection of weak static charges when he heard of Galvani's accidental discovery. He began a series of experiments on stimulating the sense organs by bringing them into contact with various metals. He discovered that there was an effect when two different metals were used, and that there had to be a liquid – or something containing a liquid, such as part of the body – between them. Thus he invented the cell. At last it was possible to produce a flow of electricity, rather than the static electricity. Volta produced quite high voltages by connecting a lot of cells in series in a stack – hence the name 'pile', which is still the French for a battery. In the argument between him and Galvani, both were right in a way. Volta could produce electricity with his metals, though a liquid was also needed. And Galvani had discovered that electrical processes are at work in the body, without the intervention of metals (at least in visible form – we now know that sodium and potassium ions play an important part in electrical conduction in nerves).

Electrolysis involves the opposite process to that of the cell. Two conductors (called electrodes) are inserted in a liquid and connected to a source of current such as a battery. This forces a chemical reaction to take place in the liquid. The result may be the discharge of gases from the liquid – the electrolysis of water breaks it up into hydrogen and oxygen. If the liquid is a solution of a metal salt, metal ions will migrate through the liquid and settle on the negative electrode (cathode). This is the basis of electroplating. A metal object to be gold-plated is hung on a wire in a solution of gold chloride. The object is one electrode. The other electrode (anode) is a piece of gold, which is eaten away by the reaction to keep the amount of gold in the solution constant.

William Nicholson (1753–1815) was probably the first person to observe electrolysis, but he did not take the investigation much further. Humphry Davy (later Sir Humphry; 1778–1829) used the technique for many chemical investigations. The man who began as Davy's assistant and later became an even greater scientist, Michael Faraday (1791–1867), worked out the pattern statements we know as the laws of electrolysis. Davy's electrolysis of molten potash was similar to today's process by which aluminium is made from molten alumina.

Hans Christian Oersted (1777–1851) proved that electricity and magnetism were unified by his chance discovery, thus confirming the long-suspected connection. Devices using the electromagnetic effect that Oersted discovered include the following.

The galvanometer and its modern descendants, the voltmeter and ammeter. The original type of galvanometer was a compass set inside a narrow coil of wire standing on edge at right-angles to the needle.

The electric motor, transformer and generator, all invented by Faraday.

The electromagnet, invented in 1823 by William Sturgeon (1783–1850) and improved in 1829 to make a practical device by Joseph Henry (1797–1878) in the USA.

The relay, a switch worked by an electromagnet so that a small current can be used to turn on a large one, also invented by Henry.

The electric telegraph, developed 1837–41 by Charles Wheatstone (later Sir Charles; 1802–1875) in Britain, and simplified to the familiar type 1837–43 by Samuel Morse (1791–1872) in the USA.

The microphone, also invented by Wheatstone.

The loudspeaker, invented in 1857 by Herman Helmholtz (1821–94) in Germany, as a scientific device for the study of sound.

The telephone, developed 1872–6 by Alexander Graham Bell (1847–1922) in the USA.

Thomas Alva Edison (1847–1931) was expelled from his school in Milan, Ohio before he was ten. The teacher remarked that his brain was addled. Educated by his mother and his own efforts, he set up a chemical laboratory at home. He got a job selling sweets and newspapers on a train. By the age of twelve he had a laboratory and a printing press set up on the train, and was printing his own paper. On the railway he learned telegraphy, which set him off as an inventor. His first invention, 1868, was an electric vote-counting machine for Congress. Others were the teleprinter, improvements to the telegraph including a way of sending several messages at once down the same wire, improvements to the typewriter, and the modern type of telephone microphone. He also advised Henry Ford in 1896 that a car powered by a petrol engine was a commercial proposition. Many of his inventions were really improvements to existing devices to make them practical. Oddly, he invented the electronic valve but could think of no use for it – it was developed in 1900 by J.A. Fleming (1849–1945) – and he thought that his phonograph would be useful mainly as an office dictation aid.

Guglielmo Marconi (1874–1937) was fascinated at the age of 20 by the work of the German physicist, Heinrich Hertz (1857–94), who had shown that energy could be transmitted through the air in the form of electromagnetic radiation. Within three years he had a transmitter that could send messages to a receiver over 14 km away. In 1901 he sent a message across the Atlantic. The first broadcast was '...', 'S' in Morse code.

The first public sound broadcast was hard on the heels of Fessenden's demonstration, and was made from Brant Rock, Massachusetts on 24 December 1906. The first regular service in the USA was in 1920, and in Britain in 1921. The British station, 2LO, was started by Marconi himself, but within months this had been turned into a public monopoly, the British Broadcasting Company (later Corporation).

The first practical television system was devised in 1923 by Vladimir Zworykin, who worked for RCA. Like a modern television, it used a camera with the image projected on to a light sensitive surface, and a receiver with a cathode ray tube, but the scanning was done mechanically so the picture was of low quality. However, the system of John Logie Baird (1888–1946), produced in 1926 and often supposed to be the world's first, was also mechanically scanned. Zworykin patented the iconoscope, a television camera working on the modern fully electronic principle, in 1923, but did not get it working properly at once. By 1935 another Russian emigré, Isaac Shoenberg, had developed a practical version for EMI in Britain. The first regular BBC broadcasts were made the following year and continued until interrupted by the war. The system was the 405-line black and white one which was kept in Britain until 1985. Zworykin himself and RCA started America's first regular television service in 1939. The first regular colour broadcasts were in 1953 in the USA, and 1964 in Britain.

WHAT IS ELECTRICITY?

PAGE 44

It was Leucippus, born around 490 BC, who first asked the question about how far you could go on cutting something in half. His pupil Democritus, born about 470, thought that you would eventually reach the smallest possible piece. He called this piece *atomos*, Greek for uncuttable. He reckoned that each element had its own kind of atom. The number of elements was uncertain, but later Empedocles (*c.* 490–*c.* 430) and Aristotle (384–322) proposed that there were four – earth, water, air, and fire.

In 1661 Robert Boyle (1627–91) attacked these theories in *The Sceptical Chymist*. There might, he said, be any number of elements. An element was simply a substance that could not be split into simpler substances. For those that could be split he invented the term compound.

Several scientists, notably Louis-Joseph Proust (1754–1826), established that elements combine in fixed proportions to form compounds. In 1803 John Dalton (1766–1844) explained this by attributing it to the combination of fixed numbers of atoms.

In the last quarter of the nineteenth century a revolution began in experimental and theoretical physics. The revolution, which continued unabated for more than fifty years, had at its centre two new investigational techniques. One was the production of ultra low gas pressures (good vacuums) in glass tubes which came to be called Crookes' tubes. Electricity at extremely high voltage was passed through the tubes and produced coloured glows, luminous streaks and luminescence of parts of the tube walls. The other was the observation and measurement of the line spectra of the light from gases made luminous at a rather less low pressure in similar tubes.

In 1895 Wilhelm Röntgen accidentally discovered that the wall of a Crookes' tube was giving out invisible rays. He had spotted that fluorescent substances in the next room glowed if and only if the tube was switched on. Much later the Röntgen rays came to be called X-rays. Physicists soon realized that as well as the rays thrown out by the walls of a tube there were others 'shining' down its axis from the cathode. They could direct the rays onto fluorescent targets, and apply electric and magnetic fields to see if the rays changed direction. Soon, with a great imaginative leap, they decided that the axial rays consisted of particles, some positively charged and some negatively charged.

Then, most imaginatively of all, they decided that these were the constituent particles of atoms. Atoms had always been seen as the ultimate in solidity, integrity, and incorruptibility, so the new ideas were not accepted easily and there was great controversy; but the new model of the atom gradually gained ground.

The characteristic line spectra of luminous gases came to be seen as a source of information about the internal structure of atoms. As better spectrometers revealed greater complexity in the spectra, the theoretical models were altered to suit, and the atom became a more complex entity. For centuries it had been a uniform solid ball; for a while it became a currant bun (negative electrons studded in a mass of positively charged particles); then it was a miniature solar system with electrons orbiting around a tiny central nucleus. Next it was realized that the nucleus had to be made up of more than one kind of particle and the electrons had to be restricted in the orbits which they could occupy. They were allowed to change orbit only by making totally unpredictable jumps, absorbing or emitting radiation as they did so. Following the use of a better spectrometer which revealed that some spectral lines were double, the electrons of the model were made to spin as they followed their orbits.

Then, from around 1927, a remarkable change took place. All of the familiar concrete images were rejected and the structure of the atom became simply unknowable. The models used to explain the spectra became exclusively mathematical.

Nowadays, if we say that *we can imagine* an atom to be a spherical swarm of incredibly tiny particles surrounding a tiny central nucleus, we are proposing a fuzzy, simplistic model which will explain some simple phenomena. If we say that an atom *is* electrons orbiting around a central nucleus, we are getting further from the truth rather than closer to it. The truth is that we cannot say what an atom is like, so the closer our presentation is to that of a fairy tale the better!

HOW BIG ARE ATOMS?

However, suppose we accept the spherical swarm picture. We can at least say how small the swarm would have to be to explain our large scale observations. This is where our Vertical Assembly Building full of salt comes in. To work out our comparison we had first to ask how big is an atom in a sodium chloride crystal – or how big the smallest electron swarm in the crystal is.

The answer is not simple. According to theory, the atoms are ionized so the swarm extends throughout the crystal! However, practical results and theory would have us believe that the smallest building block of the crystal is a so-called 'unit cube' made up of 14 chlorine ions and 12 sodium ions tightly packed around one sodium ion. This knobbly cubical electron swarm has a volume of just 21.43×10^{-30} m^3.

A cubical salt grain of side 0.2 mm (full stop size say) has a volume of 8×10^{-12} m^3. So the number of unit cubes in the crystal must be $8 \times 10^{-12}/21.43 \times 10^{-30}$ or about 3.7×10^{17}.

Now the VAB is on record as having an internal volume of 3.6665×10^6 m^3. You must take our word for that as you have done for the volume of the unit cube. So you could get $3.6665 \times 10^6/8 \times 10^{-12}$ salt grains into it assuming that no space was wasted! That amounts to about 4.5×10^{17} salt crystals.

Of course, if you wanted to push the model over the top you could argue that, as there are 27 assorted atoms in every unit cube you would need 27 VABs full of salt to get as many grains as there are atoms in just one grain!

Notes on the activities

PAGES 134 to 142

This chapter, like the last, has more to do with technology than with science – we turn from the 'low tech' of natural dyestuffs to the 'high tech' of electrical devices. Though all of the devices were discovered and developed by scientists in the course of their normal work, they were made into practical, marketable products by technologists.

Our aims are first to develop the children's knowledge of the operational effects of electricity – that is, of electrical devices; and second to introduce them to the ways in which electricity can be generated.

At this stage we have little interest in developing theoretical models of the nature of electricity, though we have talked about it on pages 44 and 46 of the reader chapter, and have included questions in the activities which give an opportunity to discuss it.

For us, classical circuit board work would be a distraction from the main thrust which is to let the children experience as many working electrical devices as possible. We would rather that the circuit boards were left until later years when the children are better able to handle the difficult abstract ideas to do with electric currents and their conservation. However, we realize that you may wish, in this first session on electricity in the secondary school, to consolidate work which the children have done in their primary schools. Worksheet 44 'Puzzle circuits' is intended to help with this (see further notes under 'Additional activities' below).

Finally, the activities continue the development of the children's scale reading skill with a new instrument, the ammeter; and introduce them to a new range of standard laboratory equipment, and the skills involved in using it.

PROBLEM 1: WHAT CAN ELECTRICITY DO?

Circuits, components, and communication

PAGES 134 to 135

Some of the skills involved in using the new equipment are quite difficult – connecting up circuits with the right pairs of terminals connected together, checking the circuits by tracing them through, and delicately adjusting controls for instance. The nature of electricity: mysterious to all, and threatening to some, does not help. For such reasons we have chosen to start with a gentle familiarization session supported by two worksheets. The first explains circuit symbols and circuit diagrams, and the second is a self-test of ammeter-reading skill. Next, a short section of the main text warns the children of the need for care in connecting ammeters 'the right way round', and another introduces them to power packs. It will be a good idea to work through these sections with the children, making clear that the power packs they will be using are, like torch batteries, insufficiently powerful to hurt them.

In introducing the circuit diagrams worksheet, you may like to point out the importance for good scientific communication of having an internationally agreed set of circuit symbols. Those which we use today have evolved from actual sketches of the components – the symbol for a battery reflects the actual shape of Volta's original 'pile', and until relatively recently that for a bulb showed a curly filament in a bulb-shaped enclosure. Today's versions owe more to the need to make life simpler for people who have to draw a lot of circuits, than they do to representation – the symbol for a resistor, recently changed from a zig-zag line to a simple box, is an example.

We have given just one example of the translation from a real circuit to a circuit diagram. You may be tempted to set up others, but it will be difficult to do so without pre-empting some of the excitement of the circus.

THE ELECTRICAL EFFECTS CIRCUS

PAGES 135 to 138

The structure of the circus is based on the well-known way of organizing the study of electricity – by classifying its observed effects and studying each separately. We have five categories:
1 heating effect;
2 lighting effect (not necessarily associated with heat);
3 magnetic effect;

4 moving effect (usually produced by magnetic effects but worthy of a separate category);
5 chemical effects (splitting and synthesizing).

You could say that electricity has a sound (sounding?) effect, and we considered including a loudspeaker in our circus. However, this would have meant introducing alternating current, an unnecessary complication at this stage. The same is true of the radio effect.

Some teachers like to add 'electronic effect' to the list, but this seems illogical. Electronic devices: switches, amplifiers, oscillators, and rectifiers are best seen as components which operate on currents, rather than being made to operate by them.

The circus is introduced by a few words which tell the children to draw diagrams and make notes (what they did and what they saw) before leaving each exhibit. Also to leave it as they found it. You may like to emphasize the latter point – much of the excitement and benefit will be lost if the exhibits are working when the children come to them. The following additional details of the exhibits should be useful.

Investigation A : Electric heating

PAGE
136
The coils are made from 25 cm of 26 s.w.g. bare nichrome wire. The ammeter has a range of 0–5 A. It will be a good idea to put the equipment on a heatproof mat. The children should find that the current is (roughly) doubled when the second coil is added. In fact, if the current was exactly doubled the power output would be doubled, but the children will observe no more than a big increase in heat and that will be good enough. In discussion at the end you may like to demonstrate the effect of using two coils in series. You will need a terminal block with three holes instead of two. The current will be roughly half its value for one coil, and the power output of each coil will be reduced to a quarter. 'Less heat than one coil on its own', will be a good conclusion. You could ask for suggestions for comparing the heat outputs by *measuring*.

Investigation B : Electric lighting

PAGE
136
Ideally, the bulb should be 12 V, 12 W, the variable resistor 10–15 ohms with a current rating of about 5 A, and the ammeter range 0–5 A. If you have to use components with other values, you will need to try them out in advance to make sure that moving the slider of the variable resistor has an appreciable and interesting effect on the brightness of the bulb. You might like to warn the children that the coil of the resistor may get quite warm. In their notes the children should be able to suggest that the resistor reduces the amount of electricity going through the bulb; and if you use more of the resistor you let less electricity through. At the end you can explain the construction of the resistor and ask how the circuit might be used in everyday life. Stage lighting equipment and some household dimmers use such circuits. Volume controls on radio sets use a different (potentiometer) arrangement.

An electrical world   83

Investigation C : Electromagnet

PAGE
137
Suitable wire for this would be 26 s.w.g. PVC-covered copper wire. The power pack will need to be capable of handling up to 8 A at 1 V. It will be very tedious if the pack continually trips its safety cutout or blows its fuse! Even if the children have visited exhibit A they will be surprised to find that their coil gets hot and may be alarmed when it does so. Picking up identical tacks or paper clips one by one to make a chain is a good way to evaluate the electromagnet, and increasing the number of turns will increase the number which can be held up. The advantages of an electromagnet over a 'permanent' magnet: it can be switched off and on, its strength can be varied (both from a remote control), and it does not 'wear out' with time. It does however use expensive electricity, and produces waste heat.

Investigation D : Relay

PAGE
137
A relay consists of an electromagnet which can operate one or more springy switch contacts. The so-called 'Post Office' type is best here – the larger the better so that its construction can be seen. If it has a protective cover, this should be removed. (See picture 9.) It is important to use impressively long wires (at least the length of a side bench) to operate the relay coil – they are more fun and make clear the usefulness of the device. You will need to experiment with a power pack beforehand, to find the voltage which is sufficient to make the relay 'pull in'. The relay was invented in 1835 by Joseph Henry, an American science teacher and great inventor, to solve the problem of 'voltage drop' in telegraph lines. As the lines were extended, a point was reached at which their resistance was so great and the current they passed so small that it would barely operate a receiver. At this point a relay was inserted. Powered by an additional battery it passed on the morse code signal to the next length of line, and so on until the required length of line was reached.

Investigation E : Electric motor

PAGE
138
You will probably have one of the modular units in which a motor is fitted to a baseplate which also carries a double pole double throw switch. The leaves of the switch are connected to the motor, and the two contact pairs are connected respectively to the power supply and to an array of light bulbs. The purpose of this arrangement will be made clear in the notes on problem 2, investigation D below. To avoid confusion here the bulbs should be disconnected so the switch acts only to operate the motor.

It is well worth encouraging the children to collect sufficient results and to plot the graph of lifting time against load. If they increase the load in too great steps they soon will find that the motor stalls. If they make the increments too small they will need to take many readings before they reach the interesting upper part of the graph (and no-one else will get a chance to try it!). You may need to discuss this with them and work out a compromise.

Investigation F : Electroplating

If a power pack is used here it is essential that it provides 'well smoothed' direct current. You will need to experiment in advance to find a suitable voltage which produces a good deposit without liberating bubbles of gas at the anode (probably less than 4 V). Alternatively you could use a 4.5 V dry battery in series with a suitable load resistance such as two torch bulbs in holders (1.25 V, 0.25 A) or a 4.7 ohm carbon resistor. The ammeter should have a range of 0–1 A. During the discussion at the end you may like to show the children some examples of metal plated articles.

PROBLEM 2:
HOW CAN YOU GET AN ELECTRIC CURRENT GOING?

After the great electrical discoveries of the early nineteenth century, this too was a real problem for the scientists and technologists to solve. It has continued to be so ever since with emphasis on the efficiency of the method and the size of the current produced.

Our investigations are intended to form another circus. The short introduction begins with a reminder of the very important idea, presented on reader page 46, that the electricity is there in all of the metal parts of a circuit – the problem is to get it moving to form a current. This is particularly clear in the first four investigations in which there is nothing resembling a battery.

Again the children are asked to draw diagrams and make notes before they leave each exhibit, and to leave everything as they found it. It is important to note that we are asking the children to do no more than observe, report, and make pattern statements if possible. At this stage we do not expect them to explain what happens – there will be plenty of time for that in later years.

The following information about the individual exhibits may be useful.

Investigation A : Using heat

A suitable arrangement would consist of a 15-cm length of 22 s.w.g. bare copper wire joined by twisting to a similar length of 22 s.w.g. eureka wire, so that the junction sticks out and can be heated. The free ends should be connected to a digital microammeter or a centre zero microammeter (eg. 50–0–50 μA). You may like to experiment beforehand by connecting the wires (which together form a thermocouple) to a spot galvanometer on its most sensitive range. You should get a noticeable deflection simply by holding the junction in your fingers.

A simple way to cool the junction (and reverse the current) is to put a drop of alcohol on it. A more dramatic alternative is to spray it from a can of the coolant used to 'freeze' electronic components before soldering them into a circuit.

Investigation B : Using light

A silicon solar cell mounted on a base together with a low inertia electric motor has become a standard piece of apparatus in science labs. You could replace our torch with a small desk lamp, which would be more economical but less fun. After the children have tried the coloured filters it will be a good idea to offer to replace the electric motor with a digital ammeter so that they can make a quantitative comparison. They will probably find that the solar cell is more sensitive to the red end of the spectrum than to the blue.

Investigation C : Using magnetism

PAGE 140

Suitable wire for the coil would be 26 s.w.g. PVC covered copper, and the ammeter could have a range of 2.5–0–2.5 mA. The children should find that the pointer moves one way when the magnet is pushed into the coil and the other way when it is pulled out. The faster the magnet is moved the greater the current. The effect, which is called electromagnetic induction, only occurs when the magnet is moving relative to the coil (you could hold the magnet still and move the coil).

Investigation D : Using a motor as a generator

PAGE 141

If you start electricity moving through an electric motor, the motor will run (its axle will spin). Most people are surprised to find that if you spin the axle of a motor by hand it will generate an electric current. Then it is no longer a motor but a generator or dynamo. You will probably have the apparatus assembled as a modular unit, sharing a baseboard with a double pole double throw switch. The leaves of the switch will be connected to the motor. One pair of contacts will be connected to the power supply to make the motor run. The other pair will be connected to one or more bulbs, which are to be switched in when the motor is freewheeling and working as a generator. The motor will be connected to a heavy flywheel which will keep it running when the power is switched off. The motor (as generator) and its flywheel will slow down more quickly if more bulbs are connected to it. It is sufficient for the children to see this and report on it.

There will be plenty of time for explanations in later years. If you are pressed you can say that if there are more bulbs, the generator has to keep more electricity moving to light them, and this makes the generator harder to turn. So the flywheel slows down more quickly. It is probably wise not to give an explanation involving energy, as that is likely to create confused ideas which will give the pupils problems in their later school work.

Investigation E : Using a chemical reaction

PAGES 141 to 142

A torch bulb (1.25 V, 0.25 A) will be suitable for this circuit. The bulb will go out after only a short time. This is not because the chemicals are exhausted, but because of the formation of gas bubbles on the electrodes. The phenomenon, which is called polarization, is reduced in commercial cells and batteries by the more complex construction and materials. It is particularly important that the children leave the exhibit exactly as they found it.

Investigation F : Using a reversible chemical reaction

Here the apparatus amounts to a model of a 'secondary cell' (similar to those in a car or motorcycle battery). It is most important that the power pack should supply 'well smoothed' direct current. If it is set at 6 V, a suitable bulb would be rated at 6 V. The children will need to think carefully about what they are doing and follow the instructions exactly. The longer the model battery is 'on charge', the longer it will keep a current going and light the bulb. As in the previous investigation, the performance of the battery is limited by the simplicity of its construction. Again, it is particularly important that the children leave the apparatus as they found it.

Additional activities

ADDITIONS TO THE CIRCUSES

Both of the circuses can be extended with many interesting exhibits, but, as we have mentioned before, there is a need to bear in mind what the children will do in future years and restrict your additions to those which are appropriate to the limited aims of this stage. We would not advise the inclusion of exhibits which involved the use of alternating current, but an electric bell and buzzer will be interesting (if you can stand the noise), and a reed switch with a transparent capsule. You might borrow from the sixth form laboratory a discharge tube and its EHT power supply (placed well out of the reach of the children) to demonstrate the production of light other than by a hot filament. It will be a good idea to encourage the children to bring in their own electrical toys, perhaps to make an exhibition.

You might extend the 'generation circus' by adding investigations of electromagnetic induction such as that in which a length of wire connected to a sensitive meter is moved between the poles of a permanent horseshoe magnet. You could borrow a thermopile from the sixth form laboratory. We suggest you think twice about accepting the loan of a shocking coil. At the end you might cut open a spent torch battery to compare the complex construction with our model cell.

WORKSHEET 44 'PUZZLE CIRCUITS'

Short circuits are a nightmare for circuit designers and circuit builders (not to mention science teachers!), so it is worthwhile spending a little time explaining them as we do here.

In the diagrams which have to be completed for puzzles 2 and 3 the components are arranged in a peculiar staggered way for the children to join up with pencil lines. The aim is to make it equally likely that the result will be a series circuit as a parallel circuit. In the series circuit the components are joined end to end with a link back to the left hand bulb. This is the circuit in which the bulbs will be lit to half brightness. In the parallel version the two ends of the bulbs are connected independently to the ends of the battery. These bulbs will be fully lit.

The work could be extended by drawing on the activities described in Nuffield Secondary Science *Theme 4 : Harnessing energy*, pages 81 to 85. The circuits described are relatively simple examples of those which we use in our everyday lives.

WORKSHEETS 45 AND 46 'SPOT THE DISASTER POINTS'
We believe that it would be wrong to leave this first encounter with electricity without considering the dangers of mains electricity (a much bigger push than a battery – can get enough current going in your body to kill you) and sensible safety precautions in using it. The worksheet is intended as an unpompous way of doing this. It would not be difficult to convert it into a useful poster for permanent exhibition on the laboratory wall.

CHAPTER 6

The restless Earth

Introduction

Geology tends to be neglected in school sciences courses, which is a pity as the subject brings many benefits. Pupils are often interested in topics ranging from volcanoes to dinosaurs and are easily motivated. Geology has connections with chemistry, for example, in extracting metals from their ores; with biology in the study of fossils; and with many aspects of physics.

A further benefit to be gained from the study of geology is that it opens up opportunities for studying the local environment. The history of a community, both rural and urban, can be related to the underlying geology and the resources it provided. Although the precise form of a local study cannot be spelled out for each specific area in a general book of this nature, we stress the opportunity provided for making links with colleagues in history, geography, or social studies departments. In these contexts the application and social significance of science can be appreciated.

Summary

Target
Read and discuss pages 47 to 49 'The restless Earth'; 50 to 51 'From rocks to riches' (picture story); 52 to 54 'Sorting out the rocks'.

Images
Scientists disagreeing about origin of rocks. Observations and pattern recognition leading to foundation of scientific geology. Process continued recently with discovery of plate tectonics.

Skills
Observing, recording, and patterning. Making models.

Ideas
The Earth is perpetually undergoing change, owing to tectonic activity and weathering. Range of important materials obtained from rocks. Importance of identifying rocks. Making sense of the local geology.

Activities
Looking at rock types. Investigating different soils. Extracting copper from malachite. Making crystals. Making replica rocks and fossils.

Worksheets
47 'Make an "Age of the Earth" strip chart'
48 'Make your own fossils'
(It is suggested that teachers might make a worksheet to explore the geology in the school locality.)

Reader pages

**PAGES
47 to 54**
The chapter opens with the important idea that the rigidity and stability of the ground under our feet is an illusion – at least from a perspective of millions of years – and demonstrably so if you live in an

earthquake zone or volcanic region. Alfred Wegener's theory of continental drift is explained, and shown to be capable of explaining a number of modern pattern statements. The picture story follows; it describes resources which can be obtained from the earth. The historical and social importance of such resources is emphasized. The nature of rocks provides the next focus of study, and an account of how early geologists worked is followed by a brief introduction to modern ideas about rocks.

Activities pages

PAGES
143 to 149

The work begins with the further development of the children's observing and recording skills in a new field of observation: that of the Earth's rocks. The prime motive is not to identify and classify but simply to observe well; classifying can come later in an open-ended way. If the classification into sedimentary, igneous, and metamorphic types is introduced, its theoretical basis and its unsuitability for identification should be emphasized.

The second problem introduces soil as a most important natural material. A sedimentation test is carried out on local soil, and the results compared with standard criteria for different types. The children are challenged to design ways of sampling and studying the grades of particles produced in the test. A new skill is introduced with the testing of the acidity of soils – a Universal Indicator colour chart provides pH values. Next the children act out an ancient piece of research designed to solve the problem: 'How can you (best) get metals from their ores?'.

Problem 4: 'How are rocks formed?', provides the opportunity to make model 'sedimentary rocks', and to compare the sizes of crystals produced from a solution by different rates of cooling. The work provides a practical illustration of that on reader pages 53 to 54. There are two worksheets, the first giving the information needed for making an 'Age of the Earth' strip chart; and the second providing instructions for making plaster of Paris 'fossils'.

Background to the reader pages

PAGES
47 to 49

Pupils may have heard about the eruption of Mount St Helens, in the Cascades range northeast of Portland, Oregon, in 1980. The volcano had been dormant for 450 years. It gave notice that something was going to happen – there were considerable earth movements and a large bulge formed on one side of the mountain – so cameras and measuring instruments were set up. People were warned to evacuate the area, so there were few casualties. One of them was the vulcanologist in charge of the instruments. It was a large eruption which reduced the height of the mountain from 2945 m to 2560 m, sending millions of tons of dust into the air which blocked sunlight and reduced the average temperature over much of the world for several months. Far more catastrophic was the 1902 eruption of Mont Pelée in Martinique, which killed everybody in the nearby town of St Pierre (population 26 000) except a condemned prisoner deep underground in the town dungeon. This was a particularly violent eruption in which a cloud of burning gas (known as a *nuée ardente*) swept rapidly down the slope of the volcano, incinerating everything in its path. In 1883 Krakatoa, an island volcano in the Sunda Strait between Java and Sumatra, literally blew up and disappeared. The 41 m high tsunami, or tidal wave, caused by the eruption killed at least 36 000 people, and the dust from the eruption remained in the atmosphere for several years. Picture 3 shows a tidal wave striking the Royal Mail steam ship *La Plata*. This picture was first published in the *Illustrated London News* in 1867.

Earthquakes are even more destructive. The worst one in recent years was at Tangshan in Hebei province, China, in 1976. Over 200 000 people were killed. The worst earthquake on record was also in China, in Shensi province in 1556, and killed 830 000. In comparison, the famous 1906 earthquake in San Francisco killed only 452 people, and the strongest ever British earthquake, around Colchester in 1884, killed one. The most severe earthquakes and volcanic eruptions occur in subduction zones, which are one of the phenomena associated with continental drift (see below).

Alfred Wegener (1880–1930) has the odd distinction of having built a correct theory on hopelessly faulty premises. Measurements made by geographers at several times in the nineteenth century seemed to show that Greenland and Europe had moved 1.6 km farther apart in 100 years, that the North Atlantic was widening by 3.5 m a year, and the Pacific narrowing by 1.8 m a year. In fact the movement is a few centimetres a year, far too little to register by the crude measuring techniques of the time, and the apparent shift was due to mistakes in measurement. But it led Wegener to realize that the continents were shaped as if they had once fitted together in a single mass. This primeval continent came to be known as Pangaea (Greek for all the earth). In 1915, when Wegener advanced his theory, there was no way of properly surveying the deep ocean floor to see, for example, if the Atlantic was spreading and where it was spreading from.

Now we know that the continents move on continental plates which extend some distance from the shore. Molten rock may be added along the junction between the North American and European plates. Molten lava rises from inside the Earth and forms a ridge called the mid-Atlantic rift which stretches south from Iceland, occasionally breaking the surface at the Azores, Cape Verde Islands, Ascension, St Helena, and so on. The ridge is volcanic and new islands are sometimes formed by eruptions, for example Surtsey off the south coast of Iceland in 1963. But the volcanic activity of spreading zones like this is far milder than that at subduction zones, where two plates are moving together. For example, the Pacific plate is colliding with the west edge of the North American plate and is being forced under it. The deep ocean trenches are places where one plate is bent down to go under another. When the lower plate has been forced down far enough into the hot interior of the Earth it melts, and turbulent masses of lava can rise to the surface and break through the upper plate several hundred kilometres in from the edge. The position of Mount St Helens and the other volcanoes in the Cascades range is an example. Where two plates collide, the upper plate tends to wrinkle, building mountains. Notable examples are the Andes along the west coast of South America, and the Himalayas where the Indian plate is pushing into the south of Asia. Plates need not collide head on. On the Californian coast two plates are sliding past each other. The boundary is the San Andreas Fault, where the ground on each side is moving several centimetres a year, causing quite obvious distortions to roads and other structures running across the fault. The movement is not smooth, as the rocks grind together and sometimes stick solid for years at a time. Then they suddenly unstick, causing an earthquake such as the one at San Francisco. Geophysicists can measure the strain on the rocks, and report that California is overdue for another and stronger quake.

The recognition of tectonic plates and their movement came from geophysical surveys of the Atlantic Ocean in the 1960s. As a molten rock cools down, those particles in it which are magnetic, principally the iron oxide *magnetite*, settle into position aligned with the Earth's magnetic field. The Earth's magnetic poles not only undergo continuous drift but at intervals totally reverse. The geophysical surveys found the rocks closest to the mid-Atlantic ridge had the magnetic minerals orientated towards the magnetic poles as they now occur. Moving out from the centre of that ridge, two strips were identified with the minerals possessing the reverse orientation, indicating that the rock had cooled when the poles were the other way round. Further from the centre again, two more strips were found with the minerals in the current orientation. That pattern of alternate strips was repeated many times.

The only plausible explanation for that pattern was that the crust was split along the mid-Atlantic ridge, and fresh rock was coming to the surface along that split and cooling there to add to the Earth's crust. This continuous process causes the crust to grow along that line, so that the Atlantic becomes wider and the American and European land-masses further apart.

FROM ROCKS TO RICHES (picture story)

PAGES
50 to **51** These pages describe the resources obtainable from the Earth's crust and at the same time tell of the development of our culture and civilization.

The early period of human history is interspersed with the ice ages. There were at least four of these, very roughly 575 000, 450 000,

200000 and 100000 years ago, with warmer periods between. The ice finally (or for the time being) receded 12000 years ago from northern Europe.

The earliest stage, the Stone Age, is divided into three periods. The transition from one period to the next depends on the state of culture of particular people; some are still in the late Stone Age today.

Lower and Middle Palaeolithic (1.75 million–100000 BC)
In this period, the Old Stone Age, the first crude flint tools were made. The early men who used them reached Europe, including Britain (from Africa via Asia – at this time Britain was still joined to the Continent by a land bridge, so they simply walked in) about 500000 years ago.

Upper Palaeolithic (100000–12000 BC)
Modern man arrived in Europe by the same route as earlier races. These people made cave paintings, stone sculptures, and finely formed flint, bone, and antler tools, and painted the famous Lascaux cave around 18000 BC. A rather more primitive culture called Cresswellian was dominant in Britain at this time.

Mesolithic (12000–3000 BC)
The people of this period, the Middle Stone Age, set small flints in rows in handles to form implements such as saws and sickles. They lived in huts on rafts at the edge of lakes. About 5000 BC the land bridge subsided and Britain was isolated.

Neolithic (3000–1800 BC [in Britain])
In the New Stone Age people made polished flint tools. They were the first real farmers and town dwellers. The first British culture is called Windmill Hill, after a fortified town they built in Wiltshire. Later settlers from Europe built huge stone circles and tombs.

Bronze Age (1800–550 BC [in Britain])
The first people in Britain to use metals were the Beaker people (named for their pottery drinking cups), who may have arrived from the Continent. There were many other cultures, some of whom traded with peoples across the Channel. The Wessex culture buried the dead in barrows (mounds), some of which contain Egyptian pottery beads and articles from eastern Europe.

Iron Age (from 550 BC [in Britain])
About this date the Hallstatt people arrived from 'France'. They were not much different from a late Bronze Age people except that they had iron tools. About 300 BC a higher culture called La Tène arrived. They were influenced by the Greeks, as can be seen from their elegant jewellery and pottery. Around 150 BC the Belgae invaded. These people were partly Romanized, and were efficient farmers who exported grain to the Continent. The first Roman invasion was Julius Caesar's brief expedition in 55 BC. Claudius arrived in AD 43 and the Roman conquest began.

Remains of Roman activity abound in Britain. They mined lead from near Charterhouse in the Mendips and examples of their use of lead can best be seen at Bath. Open-cast iron-ore mines dating back to Roman times, known locally as *scowles*, can be examined in the Forest of Dean, not far from the exposure of Roman road surface at Blackpool Bridge. The Romans used slag from iron smelting to surface the road from London towards the iron rich area of the Kent and Sussex Weald. A section of that road can be seen near the village of Holtye between East Grinstead and Tunbridge Wells.

The remains of the Roman gold mines at Dolaucothi in mid-Wales, between Lampeter and Llanwrda, belong to the National Trust and can be visited (fee payable).

The price of gold varies considerably over a period of time and it might be worth checking the current price per ounce, which is given each day in the financial section of newspapers. The value is such that it proves economic to mine rock with a very small (well below 1 per cent) proportion of gold in it. (In contrast an iron ore would not be worth extracting even if it contained 5 per cent of the metal.) Gold is extracted by crushing the rock and then dissolving out the gold in a soluble complex formed with potassium cyanide solution.

In recent years, there have been a few tin mines in operation in Cornwall but their economic viability is precarious, being dependent on the prevailing World price for the metal. Remains of tin mines can be found all over West Devon and Cornwall. Most of the World's tin now comes from Malaysia, Indonesia, Thailand and Bolivia.

The story of North Sea oil and its discovery and exploitation should need no amplifcation. The oil companies produce lavish booklets, maps, and so on which are available free of charge to schools.

The study of earthquake shock waves to learn about rock formations provides an example of techniques yielding data not readily available from direct observation. An initial survey by such methods suggests which areas of a sea-bed should be studied more closely. In these areas, exploratory drillings would then be made to confirm the presence of an oil reservoir of a viable size. Without the initial geophysical survey, much expensive and time-consuming drilling would be unproductive.

Underground salt deposits of sodium and potassium chlorides and so on are found in Cheshire and East Yorkshire. Their presence causes the chemical industry to site many plants near the Mersey and Humber rivers.

In any area it is worth examining old houses to see the materials employed in their construction. Ordinary houses tell you more about the local geology than churches or castles, as these often were built from stone brought in from outside the immediate area. Until the completion of the railway network in Britain at the end of the last century, transport costs made it prohibitive to build ordinary houses with anything other than local materials. Various types of stone were used, including flints collected from the chalk areas; bricks were made from local clay. The variety of materials gave rise to the local characteristic styles, such as the yellow limestones of the Cotswolds and the flint faced walls of Sussex. Outcrops of the same type of rock can be traced right across Britain. For instance, the Jurassic limestones of Bath can be traced south through Dorset or north through the Cotswolds into the Midlands, as seen in towns such as Stamford or Lincoln. It may well be that two or three distinct geological zones, demonstrated by different building materials, can be found in the school catchment area.

Pupils may find the Latin names of fossils baffling. It may be better to worry less about precise names and concentrate attention on the features of the specimen. From the details of the specimen itself and the matrix in which it is found we can learn a lot about the organism without using technical jargon. The availability of fossil or mineral specimens varies from area to area, but there is scarcely anywhere in Britain outside the big cities where worthwhile specimens of one sort or another cannot be collected. There is a problem in cities as one cannot readily gain access to the underlying geological formations. Field trips to countryside areas or museum visits may have to be substituted.

SORTING OUT THE ROCKS

PAGES
52 to **54**
In the eighteenth century, building a canal was an arduous task. All the digging was done by hand except for the blasting of solid rock in cuttings, and drainage and dredging which were done with steam engines. Earth was removed by horses pulling carts along tramways. The worst problems were not cuttings, which were simply very hard work, but earth embankments which kept spreading and settling, and above all leakage. The canals were lined with puddled clay, that is, clay stamped down by foot, in an effort to make their linings waterproof. It was a perpetual problem to keep canals filled, since much water was also lost each time a lock was used.

Abraham Gottlob Werner (1750–1817) became professor of mineralogy at Freiburg in Saxony in 1775. He classified the rocks of the Harz mountains, a principal mining area, in a perfectly sensible way, and his Neptunian theory – named for the classical god of the sea – was not entirely wrong, as sedimentary rocks are formed in this way. However, he was so convinced of the rightness of his views that he ignored all evidence to the contrary, concentrating only on his native Harz mountains. Although these include much granite, an igneous rock, there is no formation that obviously contradicted his views. In fact granite is often traversed by parallel vertical cracks which give the illusion of sedimentary strata turned on their side. In other parts of Europe there are many features of obviously volcanic origin, including unmistakable extinct volcanoes. (See picture 6.) Werner's assertion that volcanoes were caused by burning coal seams came easily to him, for almost certainly he had never seen a volcano.

James Hutton (1726–1797) advanced the opposing view, which was called the Vulcanist theory, after Vulcan, the god of volcanoes. He did realize that not all rocks were directly made by volcanoes, but that some were sedimentary, formed from eroded fragments of the original igneous (volcanic) rocks. We now know that there is a third kind: metamorphic rocks, which have been first laid down, then altered by volcanic heat and violent earth movements. Examples are gneiss, marble, and slate. Hutton's views were the basis of the modern science of geology.

William Smith (1769–1839) began to study rocks in 1794, when he was appointed engineer to the Somerset Coal Canal. In 1815 he published a geological map of Britain, followed from 1819 to 1824 by detailed maps of each county.

Igneous rocks include coarse grained granite and fine grained rocks such as basalt and obsidian (black volcanic glass, without any crystal structure). Granite consists mainly of white or pink feldspar, interspersed with sparkling black mica and transparent quartz. Related rocks include bits of other minerals. In volcanic areas there may be fresh lava (pumice is lava full of gas bubbles).

Sedimentary rocks include chalk (as well as any flints in it) and limestone. Both these rocks are forms of calcite, while flint is a form of silica. Sandstone is compacted silica sand bound with clay, ironstone (mostly iron carbonate) or limestone. Conglomerate is a similar substance formed of sea-rounded pebbles; breccia is formed of jagged fragments. Clay, though soft, is classed as a rock. Its composition varies, but it consists of varying amounts of silicates of aluminium and iron. Mudstone and shale (similar, but with visible layers) are compacted clay.

Metamorphic rocks include gneiss and schist, transformed from rocks of the granite type; marble, transformed limestone; quartzite, transformed sandstone; and slate, transformed shale. The transformations are caused by heat and pressure which can bring about chemical changes.

Rocks are also classified by their age. The table shows geological ages, with some of the life forms which appeared in that age and are to be found as fossils in these or later rocks.

The opportunity for a study of the local environment and community as an extension of this chapter on geology has already been mentioned. Surveys can be made of building materials used for older houses, land use in farmed areas, the development of local industries, the road and railway pattern, and so forth. Quarries can be studied, old maps examined, and specimens collected. Pupils usually enjoy such work and recognize its relevance to themselves.

Useful information can probably be obtained from the reference section in the local public library. There are a good number of guides to local geology available in bookshops and most areas of the country

Name	Age	Life forms and events
Pre-Cambrian	600–4600 million years	from the formation of the Earth about 4600 million years ago to the formation of the first multi-celled organisms about 600 million years ago
Palaeozoic Cambrian	500–600 million years	marine invertebrates
Ordovician	425–500 million years	early fish, molluscs
Silurian	400–425 million years	land plants, corals
Devonian	345–400 million years	insects, molluscs, early trees
Carboniferous	280–345 million years	spiders, amphibians, early reptiles
Permian	230–280 million years	land reptiles; final assembly of the super-continent of Pangaea
Mesozoic Triassic	180–230 million years	dinosaurs; opening of the Atlantic Ocean
Jurassic	135–180 million years	*Archaeopteryx* mammals
Cretaceous	60–135 million years	early flowering plants, hardwood trees; extinction of dinosaurs at end of period
Cenozoic Eocene/ Palaeocene	40–60 million years	monkeys
Oligocene	25–40 million years	gibbons; collision of India with Asia
Miocene	11–25 million years	apes; formation of Himalayas
Pliocene	2.5–11 million years	*Australopithecus*
Pleistocene	500000 years– 2.5 million years	oldest stone tools (1.8 million years); *Homo erectus* (1.5); use of fire (0.5); neanderthals (0.1)
Holocene	younger than 50000 years	modern Man

The geological ages of rocks, with some of the events and life forms which appeared in that age.

are covered to some extent. The Ordnance Survey geological map of your area should prove invaluable. A visit to a local museum or quarry might prove profitable.

More information (including some on fossils) is given in a simple form in Evans, I.O. *The Observer's book of geology*. Frederick Warne (frequently republished). For ancient cultures and archaeological remains, consult Wood, E.S. *Collins field guide to archaeology in Britain.* Collins, 5th edn, 1979. More able pupils should be capable of using this book themselves.

Pupils can be encouraged to build up collections of geological specimens. According to the locality, pebbles from the beach, fossils, minerals (many of these being crystals), and rocks can all be collected. These can be identified, arranged, and in some instances polished to make decorative stones. In this way both individual and school collections can be built up.

Notes on the activities

PAGES
143 to 149 Reader Chapters 6 to 9 have a common theme which is that of the planet on which we live: its rocks, its water, and its atmosphere. The four activities chapters reflect this theme but have another important feature in common: a return to emphasis on the basic techniques and skills of the professional scientist.

This chapter focuses on the skills of observing, recording, patterning, and communicating, as applied to a new range of phenomena: those to do with the rocks and minerals which form the outer layer of the planet. It also provides valuable illumination of the process of mental modelling; that is, it provides some small examples of the scientists' work of explaining the world of observation by making mental models of events which cannot directly be observed. Here the mental models are those which scientists have thought up to explain the origin and formation of the Earth's sedimentary and igneous rocks. They are introduced as the children make physical models of the imagined events.

PROBLEM 1: WHAT ARE ROCKS LIKE?

PAGES
143 to 144 There will be plenty of time in future years for the children to carry out specific tests on rock samples, and to use keys to identify them by name. At the present stage the motive is simply to apply their developing skills of observation and recording to a new set of natural objects, namely samples of rocks.

We want their study of the samples to be as open-ended as possible, placing full responsibility on the children to make their observations thorough and comprehensive. So we do not tell them what to look for, simply to look carefully 'seeing those things which they might otherwise miss', and sharing their observations with their classmates. We emphasize their responsibility by dividing them into groups and letting them have only one sample at a time. Then, in part B, we ask them to get together and report back. The result is to be a catalogue of descriptions refined in discussion with you.

During the discussion you will find it useful to suggest some categories for the descriptions such as the following.

Colour: is it plain or multi-coloured? How many colours? Is there a main colour?

Feel: is it rough or smooth? Is it silky or glassy or resinous (like toffee?)

Texture: does it have grains or is it all the same right through? How big are the grains? Are they the same size or different sizes? Can you see crystals? Do any of the grains sparkle? Is the sample lumpy? Does it have layers? Does it have veins or bands of different colours?

Hardness: how easy is it to scratch with a nail? (See also *Pupils' book 1* activities page 105 and *Teachers' guide 1* page 27).

We have chosen the types in our list to give a good range of these features and, with one eye on the reader pages, to make sure that sedimentary, igneous, and metamorphic rocks are well represented. It may help you to have the following descriptions (given here in alphabetical order).

Basalt: dark-coloured, very fine grained, may be studded with large lumps and may be glassy. (Igneous rock – produced by volcanic action, cooled very quickly.)

Conglomerate: multi-coloured lumps with a plain background ('matrix'). (Sedimentary rock – laid down in a stream bed or at end of glacier.)

Clay: usually plain mid-brown to deep brown, almost smooth but not silky. (Sedimentary rock – usually laid down in deep water.)

Gabbro: smooth, dark with many large interlocking crystals usually feldspar (white or pinkish) and augite (dark green to black), may be banded. (Igneous rock – formed by the slow cooling of magma (molten rock) well below the surface.)

Granite: smooth, light multi-coloured, (speckled) with many crystals ranging in size from very small to very large. (Igneous rock – formed by the slow cooling of magma (molten rock) well below the surface.)

Limestone: rough, fine grained, plain, usually light greys and browns, may have fossils or the granular particles called ooliths buried in it, soft compared with sandstone – chalk is one variety of limestone. (Sedimentary rock – normally laid down on the floors of ancient seas – though often found uplifted to form today's hills.)

Marble: smooth, very fine grained, light-coloured with darker veins and bands. (Metamorphic rock – usually from limestone reheated and subjected to stress by earth movement.)

Obsidian: glassy, very dark-coloured. (Igneous rock – thrown out of volcano and cooled very rapidly indeed.)

Rhyolite: flinty, smooth, light-coloured, may have veins or bands. (Igneous rock – volcanic lava which cooled and hardened very close to the parent volcano.)

Sandstone: rough to very rough, fine grained, plain (but may have bands) yellow, light greens, light to red browns, harder than limestone (grains are mainly quartz). (Sedimentary rock – laid down in ancient flood plains, deltas, and beaches.)

Schist: smooth, fine textured, light-coloured with fine banding, may show shiny planes of mica. (Metamorphic rock – produced in different varieties by a great range of conditions of temperature and pressure.)
Shale: silky smooth, grey or black, multi-layered and flakes easily. (Sedimentary rock – laid down in ancient swamps and inland seas.)
Slate: smooth, usually plain dark grey but sometimes light to mid-green, hard but can be split into its obvious layers. (Metamorphic rock – formed by the action of heat and pressure on clay rocks including shale.)

We hope that it will be possible for you to show the children some microscopic slides of such rocks (see part B step 2). It is an interesting and valuable experience and shows another important application of microscopy.

The grouping activity in step 4 of part B is probably best done with the whole class together around one bench or in several large groups with you acting as a peripatetic referee. The instructions tell the children that they must be able to give reasons for grouping the rocks in particular ways. It will be useful to point out that when they state their reasons they are making pattern statements.

A good question to ask is: 'How useful would your classification be for making a key?' (see *Pupils' book 1* pages 158–9, and *Teachers' guide 1* page 153). It is worth noting that such keys are based on classification according to physical and chemical properties, and not on the theoretical classification into sedimentary, igneous, and metamorphic types.

PROBLEM 2: WHAT ARE SOILS LIKE?

PAGE
144 to 146

Soil has been called 'the most important material on our planet', and the more one thinks about it the less surprising the statement becomes. Directly or indirectly, almost all our food arises from it (fish being the notable exception), all the non-oceanic ecosystems have their bases in it, and the plants which maintain the oxygen-carbon dioxide balance of our atmosphere grow in it.

Part A : Sedimentation test

PAGE
145

The sedimentation test is well known and long used in the early years of secondary school, and there is a tendency for its simplicity and familiarity to obscure its value. Not only does it show that soil is a complex material with identifiable components; it can be used in a semi-quantitative way to classify soils into three types. Picture 4 reflects the convention regarding the three soil types as follows:

Sandy: sand 75–100%; silt 25% or less; clay 25% or less.
Loam: sand 50–75%; silt nil; clay 25–50%.
Clayey: sand about 30%; silt about 30%; clay about 30%.

It is important to note that our purely geological analysis leaves out an extremely important component of good agricultural soil. This is humus: the complex material produced by the action of microbes on plant and animal debris. The children may notice a thin layer of bits floating on top of the water in their sedimentary columns. This consists of plant debris rather than humus.

Part B : How do sand, silt, and clay differ?

PAGE
145

You could say that part B is a professional extension of the sediment-ation test. The children are being asked to use their scientific skills to interpret a table of standard numerical values; and to use the new information in the design of an investigation. The design presents two problems: how to obtain samples of the particles from the different layers; and how to measure their size. The text gives a hint of the solution to the second problem. If the children have followed Year 1 of the course they may have measured the field of view of a microscope (Worksheet 16). You could revise the method with them now.

The question which needs to be answered is: 'What is the smallest grain I can see and measure with my microscope?' An average school microscope on low power has a field of view of a few millimetres and it is fairly easy to estimate the size of an object down to a tenth or twentieth of the field of view. So the convenient lower limit for particle size is about a fifth of a millimetre or 200 microns; so we can explore the sizes of sand grains. We would need to increase the magnification ten times to take us into the silt range.

Not all suggestions for sampling methods can be tried out in practice. 'Brainstorming' for ideas might produce: 'Could you freeze the column?', 'Could you dry it?', 'Could you do a sedimentation test in molten wax?', 'Could you pick up a sample with a pipette – without disturbing the layers?', 'Could you replace the column with a series of sieves?' (the method used by powder technologists to grade powders and by soil technologists to grade soils). The experience of generating multiple solutions and discussing them is at least as valuable as trying any one of them – though it would be nice to do so.

Part C : How acid is our soil?

PAGE
146

Many keen gardeners have tested the acidity of their soil at some time, and have added lime to reduce it. Gardening manuals give advice on the kind of soil which particular plants 'like'. Questions about soil acidity/alkalinity are answered by using indicator solutions; and you may have introduced the children to these as an extension of Chapter 4 of these activities. If not you may like to do so now, using plant extracts first, then moving on to Universal Indicator.

At this stage the children should see pH values as no more than the numbers used to label the different colours on the indicator chart. In this sense the indicator is acting as a standard for measurement. 'The pH is 7 because it goes sea green', rather than 'it goes sea green because the pH is 7'.

It would be interesting to collect and test samples of soils from local gardens and nurseries, making a careful note of the sites of the samples and the names of plants which were growing nearby.

The restless Earth   **101**

PROBLEM 3:
HOW DO WE GET METALS FROM THEIR ORES?

PAGES
147 to 148

We believe that people discovered how to extract metals from their ores probably in Sumeria, probably around 4000 BC, and probably by chance. Perhaps beads of copper were discovered in the ashes of a fire which had been burning on a hearth of copper-bearing rock. As soon as people realized the full significance of the discovery they must have begun looking for solutions to the question asked in problem 3.

Here and now the children are able to act out the early research beginning with an experiment which is doomed to fail. It is important that they do roast the ore on its own if only to remove the misconception that, if there is metal in the ore, it will melt and run out when heated. Of course, it does not work that way: the metal is tightly joined up to other substances in the rock. The carbon is needed to cause a reaction which tears the metal free.

Provided that the malachite is finely divided and intimately mixed with a large excess of carbon, tiny beads of copper will be obtained. It will help if the children pick up the Bunsen burner by its base and heat the heap strongly from above. Explanation of the result is best left for future years. For the time being the method, the observations, and the excitement of finding the copper are sufficient in themselves.

One extension of this activity is to demonstrate that the beads produced can conduct electricity.

PROBLEM 4: HOW ARE ROCKS FORMED?

PAGES
148 to 149

The chapter ends with the making of some models which illustrate key features of our theories (our mental models) to do with the formation of the rocks.

Part A : Making sandstone (sedimentary rock)

PAGE
148

Instructions are given for making three types of 'sedimentary rock': sand and plaster, sand and salt, and sand and sugar. Preferably the sand should be deeply coloured. Saturated solutions of sugar and salt are needed. To get the best results, the samples should be allowed to dry in a warm place for about a week, so some forward planning is necessary.

In the interim the children have to decide (step 5) how they will test the strength of the model rocks, and discuss their suggestions with you. You will need to emphasize that the tests should be 'objective'. All things must be exactly equal for all the samples. For example, if you choose to drop a ball bearing onto one you must drop the same ball bearing from the same height onto another. Ideally, all the samples should have the same dimensions, but this is difficult to achieve without a great deal of trial and error.

The children are asked to observe through a hand lens the broken edge of a sample. The comparison with their earlier observations or rock samples will be striking. You can tell the pupils that we have used sugar because it is convenient to do so, and you would not expect to find a stratum of sugar in a sedimentary rock. Having said that, you do find deposits of halite (rock salt) and gypsum (calcium sulphate rock). You might like to try other saturated solutions such as copper sulphate.

Part B : Making crystals (igneous rock)

PAGE 149

With the exception of 'instant cooled' volcanic glasses such as obsidian, igneous rocks are largely distinguished from each other by the size of their crystals. Here we are making a model of the *process* of crystal formation with the aim of arriving at the pattern statement: 'the faster the cooling the smaller the crystals'. The investigation is straightforward and the children should quickly see the pattern. You might like to extend the work into the well-known and well-documented activity of growing crystals from 'seeds' suspended on thread in saturated solutions.

Additional activities

WORKSHEET 47
'MAKE AN "AGE OF THE EARTH" STRIP CHART'

This is an activity in which the children can work in quite large groups. Apart from those responsible for the cutting and marking up of the strip, there is a need for artists to draw pictures of the organisms mentioned. You will need to have ready a good selection of reference books for this; and an overhead projector with acetate sheets will be useful for enlarging or reducing drawings (probably the latter).

WORKSHEET 48 'MAKE YOUR OWN FOSSILS'

Fossils are the traces of once-alive plants and animals. They do not have to include any part of the original organism, though shells and bones do sometimes survive turned into stone (petrified) by chemical action, and a whole woolly mammoth was excavated from a glacier in Russia. Often, the organism has been surrounded by a material which has hardened; the organism has decayed; and a cavity has been left as the fossil. Equally often the cavity has been filled with a new material to form a cast – as is the case in our method.

Should you wish to extend the study of fossils into a project, reproductions are available from most major laboratory suppliers.

CHAPTER 7

Water, water, everywhere

Introduction

Water makes an obvious topic for a science course at this level, not least because a wide range of practical investigations can be undertaken.

A feature of this chapter is the emphasis laid on the social and economic importance of an adequate supply of water. Much of the World's population is not certain of such a supply – witness the starvation in parts of Africa. In other countries, such as Bangladesh, it is the threat of extensive flooding that concerns the population. Even when water is abundant, it has to be effectively managed to prevent flooding and ensure the purity of supplies.

Although the properties of water tend to be taken for granted, the abler pupils might pursue the evidence that it is an extraordinary liquid and that it is precisely these properties which underly its utility.

A slight variation has been made with the format of this chapter. The picture story has been replaced with a large diagram illustrating the water cycle.

Summary

Target Read and discuss pages 56 to 57 'Water for life'; 58 to 59 'The water cycle' (double page spread); 60 'Investigating the water cycle'; 60 to 61 'Living with water'; 62 'Water: an extraordinary liquid'.

Images Scientists investigating parts of the water cycle such as underground movement of water, and modifying it such as seeding clouds to help rain formation. Using water.

Skills Techniques of evaporating, filtering, and distilling. Calibrating.

Ideas Water essential for life. Removal of water to preserve things. Social and economic effects of drought. Distribution and use of water. Water purification. Properties of water unusual.

Activities Measuring dirtiness of water. Purifying water. Separation of a solute from a solution. Identifying water.

Worksheets 49 'A floating test for liquids'
50 'Make a golf-ball submarine'
51 'What makes steel rust?'
52 'Do you live in a hard or soft water area?'

Reader pages

The chapter opens with a series of captioned pictures which make clear the importance and usefulness of water, the most abundant single substance in the biosphere. The themes of the pictures are picked up and elaborated later: water as an essential component of living cells; as a solvent; as a habitat; as the medium which balances the temperature of the biosphere and keeps it within suitable limits for life; as part of the great 'weather engine'; and as a source of power. The picture story pages are used for a large diagram which illustrates the recycling of water to meet our daily needs. The final section sets out to show scientists and technologists in action, studying and exploiting both the behaviour of water in the biosphere and its physical and chemical properties.

Activities pages

An important aim of the work is to introduce the children to some outstanding items on our agenda of basic skills and techniques: filtering, evaporating, and distilling. These come later; we begin with a discussion of the 'things which can make water dirty'.

This gives opportunity for the development of the notion of purity of substance, and the distinction between suspensions and solutions. One simple test of dirtiness – that of turbidity – is presented as a design exercise (with broad hints from a cartoon!). Problem 2: 'How can you make muddy water clear?' leads to a three-part development of the technique of filtration; and an abortive attempt to filter out copper sulphate leads to those of evaporation and distillation.

Next, a short article provides for an introduction to a series of investigations of the properties of water. The investigations are not described in the text but details are given under problem 4 below. The results are used to develop a battery of tests for identifying water. These may include the use of the simple home-made hydrometer described on Worksheet 49. Three further worksheets are provided: one gives instructions for making and investigating a 'golf-ball submarine'; one supports an investigation of hardness and softness of water; and one sets up a puzzle investigation related to rusting. The puzzle is designed to give opportunities for exercising the skills of observing, making pattern statements, modelling, and making predictions.

Background to the reader pages

The theme of the sets of pictures on the first page is the importance of water, the need for it, and its uses.

The kidneys (picture 1) clean waste products from the blood by absorbing them through the thin walls of long, narrow blood vessels. Sewage plants clean water in a more straightforward way. (See below.)

Picture 2 reflects the importance of water to organisms. When food is dried, some of the natural enzymes in it which are left over from when it was alive are prevented from working, as are any bacteria already present or invading later. Not all the enzymes are completely inactivated: for example, they make dried fruit go brown (orange-coloured dried apricots are bleached with sulphur dioxide, then dyed) and may cause fat in the food to go rancid (which is why dried milk has to be skimmed first). Enzymic and bacterial activity is only suspended, and when water is added, both restart. Trees take huge quantities of water out of the soil through their extensive root systems. Some trees, such as swamp cypresses and mangroves, need so much that they will grow only in wet places.

One way of obtaining salt from underground deposits is by leaching it out. Water is pumped into the deposits to dissolve the salt, and the resulting brine is evaporated to recover it. This saves digging, but a great deal of heat is needed to evaporate the water. In hot countries the brine can simply be run into shallow ponds. Elsewhere the water is evaporated by heating it in a partial vacuum, which lowers the temperature at which water boils. Washing is another way of removing solids with water, in this case aided by detergents – substances which when in aqueous solution attract particles of grease and separate them from the material being washed.

A water wheel is a simple turbine. Most kinds are simply pushed round by the force of flowing water. More complex turbines have shaped blades which exploit dynamic or pressure effects. A steam turbine is an axial flow turbine – the steam flows parallel to the rotor shaft. The rotor is ringed with rows of blades, each of which works in the same way as an aircraft wing.

WATER FOR LIFE

PAGES
56 to 57

Animals and plants that live in dry areas have developed many strategies for survival. Many of them, such as the Australian frog shown in picture 5, encase themselves in mud to prevent evaporation and go into a dormant state. Even some fishes do this, such as various species of lungfish. These creatures, found in Africa, South America and Australia, have simple lungs so that they can breathe air. Some creatures survive only in an inactive form: insects as eggs or larvae, and plants as seeds. Other plants have tough exteriors enclosing a store of water, for example cactuses. The baobab tree, of which several species are found in tropical Africa and Australia, has a huge, bottle-shaped trunk in which it stores water. Eucalyptus trees, of which there are many kinds in Australia, send roots to a great depth in search of water.

Water is vital to living creatures because the chemical reactions that sustain life take place in aqueous solution. Even the electrical signals in the nerves depend on water. Nerve impulses are made possible by a reaction involving sodium and potassium ions in solution. Sodium and potassium levels have to be kept constant for this to work, and the body maintains them exactly. However, if you lose a lot of salt (sodium chloride) in perspiration, ill effects can follow unless the supply of salt is replenished. Severe diarrhoea causes a loss of fluid and sodium and potassium salts, all of which must be replaced by a rehydration mixture.

Dirty water – and cleaning it up

Cholera used to kill thousands in London. It was caused by bad drainage. Sewage contaminated drinking water. The cause was unknown: people ascribed it to all kinds of agents from rats to 'bad air'. As described in *Pupils' book 1*, in 1849 Dr John Snow (1815–58), investigating an outbreak of the disease in Soho, London, traced it to the public pump in Broad Street (now Broadwick Street). He took the handle off the pump and the disease stopped spreading. This was one of the greatest steps in proving that disease is caused by germs. Later on in the nineteenth century, London was given a proper sewer system – an enormous task.

At this time sewage was purified to some extent by using it to irrigate agricultural land – hence the expression 'sewage farm'. The plants broke down the sewage to extract nitrogen. From about 1900 onwards, some of the solid matter was removed from it first by adding a salt of iron or aluminium and some lime, which converted the salt into a hydroxide of the metal. This precipitated out, carrying a lot of the solids with it. The next improvement was the biological filter, a large bed of porous clinker or slag on to which the sewage was sprayed. The surface of the porous material becomes covered with bacteria which break down the sewage. A more efficient method discovered in 1916 is to add activated sludge – partly treated sewage full of live bacteria – to the incoming sewage and blow air through it in an aeration tank. The solid matter is broken down by the bacteria and settles to the bottom of the tank, becoming activated sludge which is added to further sewage. In the most modern works, the sewage is first screened to remove large solid lumps, which are burnt or broken up and put back. Then it is passed down channels to allow any grit to settle out, and into a sedimentation tank where some of the solids settle. These are removed, and may be treated with chemicals, or broken down by anaerobic (non air-breathing) bacteria in an airtight digester, which produces methane that can be used to power machinery in the sewage works. Both processes yield an inoffensive fertilizer. The liquid from the sedimentation tank is treated in a biological filter or with activated sludge. It may be given a final purification in a sand filter.

As an example of the minerals that give water a taste, here is a recipe for synthetic Vichy water – one of the stronger flavoured mineral waters. To 1 litre of water add:

20 mg potassium bicarbonate
32 mg sodium chloride (common salt)
16 mg sodium sulphate (anhydrous)

10 mg sodium phosphate (anhydrous)
480 mg sodium bicarbonate
240 mg tartaric acid

The resulting water will be slightly fizzy as a result of the reaction between the last two ingredients. It can be made more fizzy by putting it into a soda water maker. This will further improve the flavour with the sweetish taste of dissolved carbon dioxide.

Kidneys contain long, narrow tubes, intricately coiled to fit into the 11×4 cm organ (the size of a human kidney). The tube walls are semi-permeable, allowing dissolved substances but not blood cells to filter through slowly. The outer parts filter waste products from the blood. The inner parts selectively reabsorb vital elements. The final waste product is urine, which goes to the bladder. Kidneys are considerably more efficient than is necessary, and you can live a perfectly normal life with only one. If both kidneys fail and no transplant is available, their function can be rather crudely imitated with a dialysis machine, which filters the blood through cellophane.

THE WATER CYCLE

PAGES
58 to **60**

The water cycle goes on inexorably and is very hard to alter. Human action can reduce the rainfall in an area. If forests are cut down there is less evaporation from the ground, and therefore less cloud, so regions downwind of the former forest will become drier. Destruction of forests has contributed to the prolonged drought in parts of Africa.

Although the water cycle may appear to the pupils to be obvious it has only been understood through the application of such scientific processes as observation and experimentation. The use of dyes to trace the movement of underground water provides an example of the former process; rain-making experiments, involving seeding clouds with crystals, provide an example of the latter.

LIVING WITH WATER

Water power

PAGES
60 to **61**

The first water mills were in use around the eastern end of the Mediterranean in the first century BC. Vitruvius (born *c*.70 BC) described them in detail. In the oldest type, the wheel was horizontal and was turned by a stream of water directed against the edge by a chute. The millstones were mounted directly on top of the vertical axle, so no gears were needed. A few wheels of this kind are still to be found in parts of Scandinavia, the Balkans, and the Near East. Vitruvius also described the two kinds of vertical wheels that were to become the usual European types: the undershot wheel driven by water flowing under it, and the overshot wheel where the water is channelled over the top. The Romans used undershot wheels to raise water for irrigation by means of buckets mounted around the edge of the wheel, angled so that they scooped up water at the bottom and tipped it out into a trough at the top. Such a wheel could lift only a small fraction of the water flowing under it. There is a Roman water-raising wheel at Hama in Syria which is still in use, although of course the wooden parts have been renewed many times. Water-raising wheels became common in southern Europe and the Middle East.

The pumped storage system at Dinorwig in North Wales, opened in 1983, is the largest in Europe. All the works are in underground excavations to avoid spoiling a scenic area. When the lake at the top is full, it holds over 6.6 million tonnes of water and can deliver it at up to 400 tonnes a second for five hours (the rate of delivery slows as the lake empties). The water flows into a 1695–m sloping tunnel, then straight down a 439–m shaft, 10 m wide, to a 700–m tunnel, lined with reinforced concrete to resist the huge pressure. The tunnel divides into six, each branch leading to a turbine. The turbines are housed in the machine hall, a tunnel over 40 m high (as tall as a 16–storey building) and 23 m wide. They generate a total of 1320 MW. It takes four units of power to pump the water up for every three units recovered when it runs down. Losses are caused mostly by friction in the tunnels. Dinorwig was built to meet sudden peaks in demand, such as occur on cold winter evenings when there is a commercial break in a popular television programme, and millions of people switch on their electric kettles to make a cup of tea. It can run up from a standstill to full speed in 10 seconds.

Water supplies

In western countries each person typically consumes 200–250 litres of water a day, of which just over 1 litre is drunk and the rest used for washing, flushing lavatories, and so on. Industry uses far more water for cooling and washing in all kinds of processes, and to make steam in power stations. Water supply comes from reservoirs fed by clean rivers, and from deep bores into underground water deposits which are filled by water seeping in from above. Keeping water in a reservoir purifies it to some extent, as sediment settles and sunlight destroys harmful bacteria. A little copper sulphate is added to keep down algae. The water that is piped to the consumer goes through various stages. If the water is from a very clean source, it may only need filtering slowly through a big sand filter, but most water needs more treatment. First it is screened to remove floating debris, then filtered through activated carbon (charcoal treated to improve its porosity), chlorinated, passed through a very fine stainless steel microstrainer, and treated with iron or aluminium salts and alkali (see the section on sewage treatment above) to remove any particles that have been missed. Next it is filtered through sand, and sometimes anthracite. Then it is sprayed through a jet to aerate it and again chlorinated to polish off any surviving bacteria. Lastly, most of the chlorine is removed with sulphur dioxide and the water is pumped into the mains. In countries where water is short, supplies are sometimes boosted by desalinating sea water. This is done by various processes, all of them expensive.

WATER: AN EXTRAORDINARY LIQUID

PAGE
62

Despite its understandingly commonplace image, water is a very special substance. All of its properties are either unique or at the extreme of their range for liquids. It is unique in the way it expands and decreases its density during freezing. So ice floats on water (leaving an unfrozen survival zone for aquatic organisms below – crucial in the development of life on Earth). It is liquid over the range of temperatures most suitable for supporting life, with a high freezing-point of 0 °C and a high boiling-point of 100 °C.

Its so-called specific latent heats are high – it needs a great deal of heat to melt it and considerably more to make it boil. This allows its function as the medium of heat exchange in the great atmospheric engine of climate and weather systems. It has a very high specific heat capacity – a great deal of heat is required to raise its temperature. This means that it can tolerate large inputs and outputs of heat whilst changing its temperature relatively little. This gives the oceans their function as the temperature buffers of the biosphere.

It has high surface tension – the phenomenon in which every part of the surface of a liquid seems to be pulling against every other part. This effect accounts for the powerful way in which it creeps into fine spaces (such as capillary tubes and blotting paper pores) and the way in which the surface can support light objects and organisms such as insect larvae and water boatmen. (Detergents operate by reducing the surface tension.)

Finally it is chemically neutral, as indicated by a purple colour with litmus solution and a sea green colour with Universal Indicator solution.

Notes on the activities

PAGES
150 to **155**

Major aims of this chapter of activities are to introduce the children to the basic techniques of evaporation, filtration, and distillation and to develop their skill in using them. A worksheet offers the opportunity for calibrating and using a simple instrument: the drinking straw hydrometer. The context of the work is provided by the reader pages: an exploration of the nature and properties of water. There are opportunities to develop the children's conceptions of purity of substance and of the distinction between suspension and solution.

An ideal way to begin would be to take the children on an excursion to a sewage works. Water authorities are usually happy to entertain such visits and children find them enjoyable, stimulating, and memorable. Their understanding of what happens at the works will be helped by their experience of the microbiological activities of Chapter 3, as will the discussion which follows their return to the laboratory. The further discussion initiated by the first part of the activities text (see below) will follow naturally.

PROBLEM 1:
HOW CAN YOU MEASURE THE DIRTINESS OF WATER?
Part A : What is dirtiness?

Before you can get to grips with the problem you have to decide what it means to say that water is 'dirty'. If you wanted to be extreme you could argue that the water in the glass in front of you was dirty if it contained anything other than, simply, water – if it was other than completely *pure*.

Even the water authority scientists would not go that far – the water we drink is allowed to contain tiny amounts of a whole range of substances and organisms, but they have to be kept within carefully specified limits. Most people would say that the water was dirty if it contained harmful, unpleasant, or unpalatable things (but then some would mention cola, and beer . . .). In such terms your discussion will help to develop the children's ideas of purity of substance.

This would be a good point, cryptically, to put a few drops of tap water onto a clean watch-glass and put this in a warm place. You will need it for problem 3, part B.

The development of the concept of purity of substance will continue as the children think about classifying 'things that can make water dirty'. Initially, four good categories would be solids; liquids; gases; and organisms. In further discussion you can bring out the distinction between suspended solids and dissolved solids ('those which disappear into the liquid'); and between liquids which mix ('disappear into the water') and liquids which do not. If the children have visited a sewage works they will probably have suggested 'smells' rather than gases. In discussing this you might like to mention that most clean water has lots of oxygen gas from the air dissolved in it – that is what the fish utilize. There will be more about this in the next chapter.

Part B : Measuring turbidity

If the children have followed Year 1 of Nuffield Science 11 to 13 they will have met one method used by the scientists to test for purity – chromatography. This year they have met three others: microscopy, culturing in a nutrient medium, and the use of indicators. Other more esoteric techniques include conductivity testing (for dissolved oxygen for instance), and mass spectrometry. The turbidity test is interesting and valuable because it allows a good quantitative measurement of a very simple kind of dirtiness.

Should you choose to do it, you will need to prepare in advance for the children's 'self-designed' investigation. You will need a large quantity of your local soil or 'dirt', preferably dry. One quarter fill with water one of the measuring cylinders the children will use, and put it on top of a bold cross marked on a sheet of paper. Stir in dirt, a measured teaspoonful at a time until you can no longer see the cross. You will have the volumetric composition of your first sample of dirty water. You could repeat this with the measuring cylinder half full, three quarters full, and full, to get the compositions of three other samples. The problem is that the samples may be so different that anyone can see at a glance which is the most dirty!

An interesting alternative would be to get one of the classes in the year (draw lots) to work out the details of the investigation for the other classes to try. We do not think that the designers would feel disadvantaged.

PROBLEM 2:
HOW CAN YOU MAKE MUDDY WATER CLEAR?

Part A : Investigating straining

PAGE 151 We would hope that you can set this investigation as a micro-project for homework. If you have to do it in class, it would be best to do it as a co-operative demonstration. You could add some interesting dye to your sample of dirty water.

Part B : Filtration

PAGE 151 The children will enjoy learning this trick of the trade. Not all the children will find it easy. A good tip is to hold the filter paper cone in place in the funnel with the tips of your fingers while you pour a few drops of the solution down the *opposite side*.

Part C : A model sewage plant filter

PAGE 151 Like part A, this part lends itself better to homework or to demonstration than to a class practical. Of course if you genuinely want to compare the filter paper method with the percolation method you will have to use the same sample of dirty water.

PROBLEM 3:
HOW CAN YOU SEPARATE COPPER SULPHATE AND WATER?

Part A : Filtering copper sulphate

PAGE 152 A suitable way to explain the fact that copper sulphate goes straight through the filter paper is to say that when the copper sulphate dissolves it breaks up into incredibly tiny bits about the size of atoms (which we talked about on reader page 46); and that they are so small that they go straight through the holes in the filter paper. We suggest that you do not attempt to talk about molecules and ions at this stage.

Part B : Evaporating

PAGE 152 If you put away a watch-glass with a few drops of water on it during the discussion of problem 1, this is the time to take it out and show the obvious traces of dissolved solids. If you have to prepare the watch-glass now you will have to heat it over a Bunsen flame to save time. Alternatively, everyone can watch what happens to a few drops placed on a clean slide on a hot overhead projector stage. The text tells the children to explain in writing the marks on the glass using the words 'dissolved' and 'evaporated'. Ask a few to read out their explanations for the others to discuss.

Part C: Evaporating copper sulphate solution

PAGES
152 to 153

The class investigation is straightforward and the children will obtain the pretty blue crystals of copper sulphate back again. Provided, that is, that they stop heating while there are still signs of water left in the basin. If they continue to heat they will produce either white anhydrous copper sulphate or, if they really overheat the basin, some black copper oxide.

Part D: Condensing the water vapour

PAGE
153

The last step in the sequence answers the question: 'How can we save the water as well as the copper sulphate?' It is important that the children try out the method themselves. It is equally important that you should discuss the results with them and show them a water condenser. If there is time it might be a good idea to introduce the term 'distillation' and tell the children something about its importance in science and technology.

PROBLEM 4: HOW CAN YOU TELL THAT IT IS WATER?

Part A: Investigating water

PAGE
154

The short article and written exercise in the text are intended to introduce the series of investigations listed below. A good way to organize the work would be to put out three sets each of the five investigations. Divide the children into three sets of five pairs (say). At the end, one pair from each set will have done each investigation and they can report back to the others.

If you want all of the children to do all of the investigations you will have to allow for three sessions with periods of sitting reading and writing in between (whilst you restore the apparatus to its initial state!)

Investigation 1 The apparatus consists of a test-tube filled to the very top with boiled and cooled water, and closed by pushing in a bung fitted with a length (about 30 cm) of glass tubing. The water rises up the tubing, and a strip of graph paper numbered from the bottom is taped along the tube behind, and above and below, the meniscus. The test-tube is placed in a beaker of water with a thermometer. Also required is a bowl containing freezing mixture (ice and salt mixture). The children have to note the temperature of the water in the beaker, and then immerse the beaker in the freezing mixture. They have to report on the behaviour of the water level as the temperature falls.

Investigation 2 Put a measured 50 grams of cracked ice into a beaker on a tripod over an unlit Bunsen burner. Put 50 grams of boiling water from a kettle into an identical beaker also over a burner. Equip both beakers with thermometers. Provide a stopclock. The children have to light both burners and compare the time taken to melt the ice in one beaker with that needed to boil away all the water from the other (stop heating whilst there are still a few drops left). You could ask them to take the temperatures at regular intervals, but this is not essential. The thermometers are there to establish the melting-point and boiling-point for later discussion.

Investigation 3 The apparatus consists of three beakers each equipped with a thermometer and half filled with a different liquid: water and, for example, glycerol and glacial acetic acid. Also required is an electrically heated water bath at 50 °C. The children have to transfer the three beakers to the water bath and measure the time for the liquid in each (stirred constantly) to reach 50 °C.

Investigation 4 *a* The apparatus consists of a series of capillary tubes of different bores and labelled with their bore diameters. The children have to stand up the tubes in a beaker of water and report on the results.
b Fill a shallow dish with water and float a loop of thread on its surface. Provide a dropping bottle of detergent solution. The children have to put one drop of detergent into the middle of the loop and report on the result.
c Float a razor blade on the surface of the water in a beaker. Without touching the razor blade the children have to study it, and the water surface around it (perhaps with a hand lens). Then they have to put one drop of detergent on the water surface beside it.

Investigation 5 The apparatus consists of a rack of test-tubes, a beaker of water, and labelled dropping bottles of Universal Indicator solution, litmus solution, and perhaps one more indicator such as methyl orange solution. A little acid or alkali should be added to the solutions so that the initial colour does not indicate neutrality. Cobalt chloride paper is also provided. The children have to test water with each of the indicators and with cobalt chloride paper.

The properties of water
These are discussed in the notes on page 62 of the reader.

Part B : Tracking down the water

PAGE
155
Following the previous discussion, the children should be able to suggest some tests for the 'mystery liquids'. Examples of suitable liquids would be saturated salt solution, dilute acids and alkalis, alcohols including glycerol, and turpentine. When the children have tried out their tests it will be a good idea to introduce them to the drinking straw hydrometer (Worksheet 49 'A floating test for liquids') as a simple home-made instrument. There is no need to get involved with density and specific gravity at this stage. It is sufficient to say that we use water as a standard substance to calibrate the instrument, giving the floating point in pure water the value 1. It would be nice to give the children Worksheet 50 'Make a golf-ball submarine' for homework.

Additional activities

DEALING WITH DIRTY WATER
If a visit to a sewage works is not possible you should be able to borrow a film on the subject from the local film library. A telephone call to your local water authority will probably yield a package of interesting printed material. Small groups could develop a collage or poster based on this information and on the graphics on reader pages 58 and 59.

WORKSHEET 51 'WHAT MAKES STEEL RUST?'
This worksheet offers an exercise in observing, patterning, mental modelling and making predictions. The subject of rusting provides a link with Chapter 9.

WORKSHEET 52
'DO YOU LIVE IN A HARD OR SOFT WATER AREA?'
The children will enjoy the activity which provides a good exercise of their developing skills and is relevant to their everyday lives. There are two kinds of hard water: so-called 'temporary hard' and 'permanent hard'. You can prepare a sample of the former by bubbling carbon dioxide gas into limewater until all trace of cloudiness disappears; and a sample of the latter by dissolving magnesium sulphate (Epsom salts) in water. Temporary hardness can be removed by boiling, but permanent hardness requires some form of ion exchange (as in a water softener), or by adding chemicals such as hydrated sodium borate (borax).

. . . into thin air

Introduction

This topic introduces some challenging issues in science methodology. How can you study something which cannot be directly observed in any simple way? The study of gases therefore involves an extension to established processes.

The idea of air being a mixture leads on to some consideration of the particular properties of oxygen.

One unusual feature of this chapter is that in writing about the atmosphere we have introduced some weather science which highlights the role of pattern and prediction in science processes.

Summary

Target Read and discuss pages 63 '. . . into thin air'; 64 'How do we know it is there?' and 'What do we know about it?'; 66 to 67 'The story of air' (picture story); 68 to 69 'The air and the weather'; 69 to 70 'Scientific forecasting'.

Images Scientists studying air and combustion, pursuing some false trails on the way such as seeing air as an element, or the phlogiston theory of combustion. Observing patterns in the weather systems leading to forecasting.

Skills Observing. Measuring. Patterning. Making predictions based on patterns.

Ideas Effects demonstrating existence of air – pressure, winds, flight, etc. Components of air. Oxygen. Nature of the atmosphere. Atmospheric pressure and weather systems. Weather forecasting based on pattern recognition.

Activities Effects of weather. Forecasting weather. Observing and measuring cloud cover, wind speed, visibility etc. Making a wind vane, anemometer, barometer, hygrometer, and rain gauge.

Worksheets 53 'Weather records table'
54 'Cloud chart'
55 'Wind force chart'
56 'Making weather instruments A'
57 'Making weather instruments B'
58 'Making weather instruments C'
59 'Studying factory-made instruments'

Reader pages

The chapter is the first of two which concentrate on the air which surrounds us. Here we are more interested in the physical nature of the air and atmosphere; in the next chapter we will look at its chemical nature, particularly that of its most important gas, oxygen. The opening section provides a good illustration of the difference between seeing and observing: it looks at the evidence for believing that the air is there, which we never normally consider. A review follows of our knowledge of the nature of the air and the structure of the atmosphere. The importance of the component gas oxygen is mentioned. The cartoon pages sketch the history of this knowledge and, as they describe the chemical study of the air, begin to provide a link with Chapter 9. The final section concentrates on the great movements of the air which cause our weather. The processes of observation, measurement, and patterning, and the making of predictions from pattern statements (forecasting, of course) are well represented and link directly with the activities.

Activities pages

The work starts with a written activity and discussion of the question: 'Why does the weather matter? (and 'Why is it important to different people?'). The collection of weather data is described and organized with the help of worksheets. These provide a table for the entry of data, as well as information charts on clouds and wind force. Simple data collection can start at once as a medium to long term activity.

Whilst this is going on, a number of simple measuring instruments can be constructed and put into operation, and the design of some commercially available ones can be studied. Making pattern statements about the data comes next, leading up to the final stage: making predictions (forecasts) from the patterns. These latter stages give valuable opportunities for the use of computers. Folklore of the weather is an interesting additional topic which can be inserted at almost any stage in the work, and this is extensively described in the following notes.

Background to the reader pages

HOW DO WE KNOW IT IS THERE?

A hurricane is a violent revolving storm similar in nature to one of the ordinary depressions which sweep over Britain but far more intense. Like them it revolves anti-clockwise in the northern hemisphere and clockwise in the southern hemisphere. In fact, the word hurricane is used only for storms generated in the tropical regions of the Atlantic and moving towards the Caribbean region and the east coast of North America. The word comes from the Carib word *huracan*, since it was in the Caribbean that hurricanes were first observed by Europeans. Very occasionally a hurricane does reach Europe, but by the time it arrives it has lost most of its power and is no more than a severe storm. In the East Indies and the China Sea a hurricane is known as a typhoon. The wind speed in a hurricane may exceed 220 km per hour, which is the upper limit of the highest number, 17, on the Beaufort scale. The centre of the storm moves quite slowly at 15–25 km per hour. At the centre – 'the eye of the storm' – the air is still, and its pressure extremely low.

The wing of an aircraft has a convex upper surface and a relatively flat lower one. As the wing slices through the air, air passing over the convex top has to take a longer path than air going underneath. This increases the speed at which the air moves relative to the upper surface. Increasing the speed of any fluid lowers its pressure, so the pressure above the wing falls. The unchanged pressure under the wing forces it up, lifting the aircraft. This effect also helps to lift hang gliders, despite the fact that the bottom of the wing is concave and not flat. The air flowing over the top still takes a longer path.

A parachute appears to be a simple braking device, slowing the parachutist by air resistance, but the effect is not as simple as that. When a parachute is used in that way, for example trailed behind a landing aircraft to slow it, it operates unstably and swings about in the turbulent airflow. When used by a parachutist it slips through the air sideways and there is a smooth airflow across the upper and lower surfaces. It therefore acts like a wing. Holes and slots in the fabric enhance the effect. The parachute can be steered by pulling the cords. Modern parachutes are square and almost as manoeuverable as hang gliders.

The supply used by divers is normally compressed air. At great depths, the pressure can cause nitrogen (the most abundant gas in air) to dissolve in the blood to such an extent that the diver suffers a form of poisoning, nitrogen narcosis. Deep divers use an oxygen–helium mixture. Nitrogen narcosis is not the same as the bends, which is caused by coming up too quickly from deep water, so that the sudden reduction in pressure causes air dissolved in the blood to form gas bubbles.

The air pressure under a hovercraft is not particularly high, about $3000 \ N/m^2$ above normal air pressure ($101\,325 \ N/m^2$) to raise a 100-tonne craft to a height of 30 cm. That is why a hovercraft can travel over water without sinking in. The pressure in a car tyre is about 200 times greater. Under the hovercraft, the air is directed inwards through angled slots around the edge of the flat bottom of the hull. A flexible skirt around the edge of the hull helps to retain the cushion.

WHAT DO WE KNOW ABOUT IT?

The composition of air at sea level is on average:

nitrogen   78.08 %
oxygen   20.95 %

argon	0.93 %
carbon dioxide	0.03 %
neon	0.0018 %
helium	0.0005 %
krypton	0.0001 %
xenon	0.00001 %

plus varying amounts of water vapour, dust and pollutants (hydrocarbons, sulphur dioxide, nitrogen oxides, etc.).

The gases are not chemically combined (though carbon dioxide is itself a compound), and can be separated by cooling and fractional distillation. During cooling, first the water vapour freezes and is removed. At $-79\,°C$ the carbon dioxide freezes and is removed. Then the air is cooled to below $-240\,°C$, so that all the gases in it are liquefied except the helium, which would not liquefy until $-269\,°C$. The helium is removed. The liquid air, which is pale blue, is gradually allowed to warm up. As each gas in the liquid reaches its boiling-point it boils off and is collected.

Things that burn in air burn violently in pure oxygen. Liquid-fuelled rockets exploit this fact. Generally they run on liquid hydrogen and liquid oxygen. The boiling point of oxygen is $-183\,°C$, but that of hydrogen is $-259\,°C$, and the fuel must be kept at this temperature while the rocket is waiting to be launched.

HOW MUCH IS THERE?

The atmosphere is breathable up to a height of about 9 km, the height of Mount Everest (8847 m), which an exceptionally fit man who has acclimatized to high altitude can just climb without oxygen. This is also the height at which ordinary airliners fly, so if the cabin becomes depressurized the occupants will survive if the aircraft promptly descends to a more comfortable altitude. In Concorde, which flies about 15 km high, they would not be so lucky. The atmosphere retains the same proportion composition up to about 100 km, but above this its atoms are increasingly ionized owing to ultraviolet radiation and X-rays from the Sun. The effect prevents most of these dangerous rays from reaching the ground. The ionized region – the ionosphere – reflects short radio waves, so that they can travel around the World. Nitrogen extends only to about 150 km. Above this the oxygen is mostly monatomic, that is with single atoms, not O_2 molecules.

Auguste Piccard (1884–1962) had the idea of hanging a sealed, pressurized aluminium cabin below a balloon so that he could ascend to a height at which there was not enough air to breathe. In 1931 in Germany he reached a height of 15780 m, and slightly bettered this the next year in the USA. His purpose was scientific observation of the atmosphere and the cabin carried measuring instruments. The height record for an unmanned balloon rising of its own accord is 30784 m. (The Echo balloons sent into low orbit in the 1960s were carried up by rockets.) Piccard later turned to exploring the deep ocean in a bathyscaphe, reaching a depth of 10912 m in 1960.

THE STORY OF AIR (picture story)

PAGES
66 to **67**

The ancient Greek philosopher Anaximenes (*c*.570 to *c*.500 BC) believed that air was the fundamental element of the universe, and that liquids and solids were simple compressed air. Empedocles (*c*.490 to *c*.430 BC) was the first to suggest that air was one of four elements, an idea which was solidly established by Aristotle (384–322 BC) and became the accepted view for almost 2000 years.

Jan Baptista van Helmont (1577–?1635) was a physician, alchemist, and mystic. He investigated carbon dioxide, which he called *chaos sylvestre* because he obtained it from burning wood. The words 'gas' and 'chaos' sound almost the same in Flemish, where g is pronounced kh. Carbon dioxide was studied more thoroughly by Joseph Black (1728–1799), who called it 'fixed air'.

John Mayow (1640–1679) realized that breathing and combustion are in many ways similar. He suggested that there was a combustive principle in air which also turned blood bright red. He called it 'fire air', a better name than oxygen (see below). Had he lived longer he might have obtained pure oxygen a century before Priestley and Lavoisier.

Georg Ernst Stahl (1660–1734) was largely responsible for one of the great wrong turnings of scientific discovery: the phlogiston theory. Phlogiston (from the Greek *phlogistos*, inflammable) was the substance in things that made them burn. When they burned the phlogiston came out of them. In the light of contemporary knowledge it was quite a reasonable guess – except that it had been known for half a century that metals gain weight when they burned, a fact established by Robert Boyle (1627–1691). So it was necessary to claim that phlogiston had negative weight. Despite this the theory persisted until the end of the eighteenth century.

Henry Cavendish (1731–1810) was as near mad as makes no difference. His pathological reclusiveness, however, ideally suited him to research, which he pursued with fanatical devotion. He was helped in this by a large allowance from his relative the Duke of Devonshire and, at the age of 40, a legacy of £1 million. His experiments included work on electricity and measuring the force of gravity. He was the first to measure the density of gases. The lightness of hydrogen led him to suppose at first that he had found phlogiston, but he went on to discover that when hydrogen was burned it formed water, so it was clearly a different substance.

Joseph Priestley (1733–1804) invented fizzy drinks when, having dissolved carbon dioxide in water under pressure, he tasted the result – a usual testing procedure at the time. Soda water was highly fashionable for a time as a drink and a supposed medicine. The gas produced by heating mercuric oxide he called 'dephlogisticated air' because in 1777 Daniel Rutherford (1749–1819) had called the gas that was left when something had been burned in air and the carbon dioxide absorbed – so that what remained was mostly nitrogen – 'phlogisticated air'.

Antoine Lavoisier (1743–1794), among his many investigations, heated gypsum to drive off the water and weighed the water. He also burned a diamond, showing it to be composed of carbon. A man who constantly made precise measurements could scarcely be expected to believe that phlogiston weighed less than nothing. He repeated Cavendish's hydrogen experiment and gave the gas its name, meaning 'water producer' (from Greek *hydōr*, water and *gennaein*, to produce). He also gave oxygen its name, meaning 'acid producer' (Greek *oxys*, sharp or sour), because he believed that it was the active principle of acids. Later this was shown to be wrong by the discovery of hydrochloric acid (HCl), but it was too late to swap the two names round. Lavoisier, a member of the *Académie des Sciences*, barred Jean-Paul Marat from entry to the academy for the good reason that the thesis Marat presented was worthless. Marat later became a revolutionary leader. No wonder that Lavoisier was guillotined.

Sir William Ramsay (1852–1916) first separated the inert gases from air by chemically combining the oxygen, then the carbon dioxide and finally the nitrogen with appropriate substances. He studied the gases spectroscopically in 1894. In 1898 he obtained the inert gases separately from liquid air by fractional distillation.

THE AIR AND THE WEATHER

PAGES
68 to **69**
As a thunderstorm approaches the air becomes increasingly ionized. Not only leeches but also humans often notice this. This is probably how Dr Merryweather's apparatus worked (if it did).

WEATHER SAYINGS

1 'Those who are weather wise are rarely otherwise.' A pattern statement, but is it a true one? How could you do an experiment to attempt to falsify it?

2 'Red sky in the morning, shepherds' (sailors') warning; red sky at night, shepherds' (sailors') delight.' Light is scattered by dust particles in the atmosphere. The light at the blue end of the spectrum is scattered most, hence the blue colour of the sky. Red light is less vulnerable to scattering, and penetrates the atmosphere more effectively. In the morning or evening, when the sunlight has to traverse much more of the atmosphere to reach our eyes, so much of the blue end is scattered out that what remains is the red end alone. Most of the weather in Britain develops from the west, so people living there can usually look to the west to see what they are about to get, and to the east to see what they have had. A spectacular sunset with intense oranges and reds and with broken cloud between you and the horizon could be an indication of clear skies and high pressure on the way. A similarly spectacular sunrise could mean that the high pressure and clear skies are moving away to be replaced by low pressure, higher winds, and rain clouds. With years of experience of sunsets and sunrises, shepherds and sailors can learn to tell the difference between a good red sky and a bad red sky.

3 'Trace in the sky the painter's brush, then wind around you soon will rush.' The first sign that a warm front (see below) is moving towards you is the development overhead of cirrus clouds like sweeps of thin white paint ('Mares tails'). You know that a moving depression is not too far away, so it is reasonable to expect the wind to increase and to show rapid changes in direction when the ground level front arrives, say in about 20 hours.

4 'First rise after low foretells stronger blow.' At the very centre of a depression or of an anticyclone there is a region of complete calm, but this is surrounded by a circulation of high winds. As a depression moves away the air pressure will rise and the winds can be predicted to blow harder.

5 'When a cow tries to scratch its ear, it means the rain is very near.' This is an American example of the scores of sayings (pattern statements) connecting the behaviour of animals with changes in the weather. Another example: **'When the peacock loudly bawls, soon we'll have both rain and squalls.'** Perhaps animals are sensitive to the changes in pressure, temperature, and humidity which indicate the approach of bad weather (perhaps their coats itch when the humidity increases) and perhaps not. As scientists we can apply the rule that a pattern statement must be falsifiable and suggest a test such as: 'If rain does not shortly follow the scratching by a cow of its ear then the statement is not true.' Then all we have to do is to observe the cows and wait for them to scratch.

SCIENTIFIC FORECASTING
Weather stations are still useful despite the pictures available from satellites. Satellites show cloud, from which the position of high and low pressure areas and fronts, and general wind speed, can be deduced. Weather stations on the ground or at sea report in greater detail on local temperature, wind speed, pressure, and rainfall. All information is fed into a powerful computer which compares the pattern with many records of similar weather in the past.

Sir Francis Galton (1822–1911), a cousin of Charles Darwin, was the first person to understand the pattern of anti-clockwise depressions and slower moving clockwise anticyclones – a word he invented. Linking areas of equal pressure with isobars makes the circular shape of depressions visible, while the closeness of the lines shows the steepness of the pressure gradient and thus the wind speed.

Galton was not the first to realize that fingerprints are individual (it was Jan Purkinje [1787–1869]), but he devised a way of classifying them to make identification easier. He was also a statistician, arguing that intelligence in a population follows a normal distribution curve.

Notes on the activities

PAGES
156 to 160
The aims of this chapter of activities continue the emphasis on the further development of basic skills. Here the skills are those of observing, measuring, patterning, and, most importantly, using pattern statements to make predictions. Opportunities are offered for long term study; for computer analysis of large amounts of data; for the construction, calibration, and use of a number of simple measuring instruments; and for the study of professionally designed ones. The work closely reflects the concept development of the reader pages.

PROBLEM 1: WHY DOES THE WEATHER MATTER?

PAGE
157
If your class includes children who were not born in Britain they may be able to tell the others that in some parts of the World there are almost no changes in the weather. With the exception of rare and often dramatic changes, the climate can be expected to remain more or less constant for many months at a time. You can leave this idea hanging, and return to it later to emphasize the important point made at the beginning of the introduction to problem 2: that most of the trouble with the weather is caused by unexpected (and frequent) changes.

The introductory text to problem 1 sets up an activity the aim of which is to establish the importance of the weather (and the way it changes) to a wide range of people. The activity has an underlying aim which is to help the children to understand that not everyone is the same as they are, and that other people are affected in quite different ways. That is to make the point that opinions such as: 'Snow's terrific – we can go sledging or stay indoors with the central heating on', are not likely to be shared by a farmer searching for his sheep or a stranded motorist! In order to achieve this aim it is most important that the children should divide into small groups to discuss the importance of the weather in the lives of a wide range of people. Appoint a secretary for each group and have them report back to a plenary session. You might extend the discussion by asking the children what they want to be when they grow up, and how those jobs might be affected by the weather.

The text suggests that the children should collect pictures similar to the examples given, and make posters to show the importance of good and bad weather. A good way to organize this would be to set up a weather noticeboard for the duration of work in the chapter. The contributions which accumulated could be used for poster-making at the end.

PROBLEM 2:
HOW CAN YOU FORECAST THE WEATHER?

Weather lore

PAGE
158
Problem 2 must have taxed people's skills and intellect as long as there have been weather and people to suffer its vagaries. Weather lore is a rich and exceptionally extensive reflection of this. There are thousands of such pattern statements as 'Red sky at night, shepherds' delight'.

You could introduce the work on the problem by asking the children whether they know of any such sayings. If they do, it will be interesting to record the sayings with a view to seeing if they work. The children can do this later while they are collecting data. If they do not, which is quite likely with modern children, you could tell them some. The notes on reader pages 68–9 give examples and explanations.

FIRST COLLECT YOUR DATA!

(Please refer briefly to our notes on problem 3 below before reading on.)

You could continue by reading through with the children the strategy for making pattern statements on page 158. The first step is to collect data; Worksheet 53 provides a table for this, and the text explains how to make entries in it. The following additional notes should be useful.

MAKING THE ENTRIES

The children can begin making entries in category A right away without instruments, and can make provisional entries for categories B to F. The question will arise as to how frequently recordings should be made. This is a decision best made by you in consultation with the class. The useful minimum is three per day (breakfast, lunch, and supper times), but the more the better of course. Perhaps you can devise a schedule so that each child is responsible for just one set per day, but different children have different times (although their estimates, for instance of cloud cover, may differ).

A Cloud cover

A good way to tackle this is to hold your arms out at right angles to embrace a quarter of the sky (two eighths upper and lower), estimate the cover, turn to embrace the next quarter, and so on. The sky is covered unless it shows clear blue.

B Cloud type and height

This is supported by Worksheet 54 'Cloud chart'. Two entries are needed: looking west ('where the weather usually comes from'), and looking east ('where it's going to'). The official symbols are quite good representations of the different types. If you can see both high and low clouds, enter both. Posters showing different types of cloud can be obtained from BP Education Service, Britannic House, Moor Lane, London EC2Y 9BU (telephone 01-920 8000).

C Precipitation

It is important to write 'none' if that is the case.

D Visibility

Even on the coast and hills, mist and fog are quite rare in Great Britain. If they are able to observe fog, the children can enter the name of the furthest thing they can see through the fog and their observing point, and find out the distance later. If the air seems particularly clear, that should be noted too.

E Wind speed

Worksheet 56 gives instructions for making an anemometer. Until that is ready, Worksheet 55 'Wind force chart' will help in estimating the speed.

F Wind direction

It will be worth while making the wind vane described on Worksheet 56 – the direction is not easy to establish. Of course you will need to know the compass directions. Later on, it will become clear that you need the directions both of the upper and lower winds in order to make local forecasts. That of the upper winds can only be found from observation of the high ('streaky') clouds, and these are not always present or visible. Turbulence around hills, buildings, trees, and so on causes local variation in the wind at ground level, so it can even blow in the reverse direction from the main current.

G Air temperature

The text warns that the thermometer must be kept out of direct sunlight (which would push the reading up). It should also be kept out of rain because evaporation of moisture on the bulb would lower the temperature. The distinctive white boxes with louvred walls called Stevenson screens provide an ideal environment for thermometers. Your school may have one of these.

H Air pressure

Worksheet 57 gives instructions for making a simple but sensitive barometer. Until that is available you will need to use a factory-made one (probably an aneroid type).

I Water vapour

Instructions for making a simple hygrometer are on Worksheet 58. Until that is ready you may have to leave blanks in the table. However, some schools do have factory-made hygrometers.

J Changes

This is a crucial entry. It should describe any changes *since the last set of readings was taken.*

K to N

24-hour readings of rainfall, maximum and minimum temperatures, and sunshine are important for two reasons. First because they give you an idea of what has been happening during the night; and secondly because they build up into a body of data which may one day be able to be used for long term forecasting. If the children have followed Year 1 of Nuffield Science 11 to 13 they will have studied such data and attempted to make pattern statements about it (*Pupils' book 1* page 157 and *Teachers' guide 1* pages 145–6).

FORECASTING 1:
THE WAY YOU, THE TEACHER, WOULD DO IT

The best way of forecasting weather is to make use of the weather maps on TV and in the daily newspapers.

The notes below will be easier to follow if you have in front of you the illustrations on reader page 70.

Most of the major changes in the weather of the United Kingdom are produced by the tracking across the country (or north or south of it) of low pressure areas called depressions. A depression shows up on a weather map as a series of concentric irregular ellipses. In simple terms, it is a great inverted whirlpool of air. That is, the air is moving in a very similar way to the water over a plughole but upside down – the air rotates *anti*-clockwise and flows *up* the middle of the depression to spread out when it reaches the tropopause. The air moving round the periphery of the depression does not usually have a uniform temperature. In the simplest case, a great curving wedge of slightly warmer air extends outwards from its point near the centre.

The leading edge of the wedge is called a *warm front* and its intersection with the ground is shown on a map by a line with bumps on it. The trailing edge of the wedge is called a *cold front* and its intersection with the ground is shown by a line with spikes on it. The wedge rotates (anti-clockwise) around the depression like a huge pointer.

There is one further complication: the leading and trailing faces of the wedge (the fronts) are not vertical. The warm front leans forwards rising to 8 or 9 km altitude over a distance of about 800 km. The cold front leans back, rising 8 or 9 km in about 500 km. Thus the wedge is wedge-shaped both in plan and in end elevation.

Now most weather changes at a particular town (say) occur as a front moves over the town. If you can forecast the approach of a front you can forecast the weather. It is likely to deteriorate when the ground level part of the warm front reaches you, improve for a while as the bulk of the wedge passes over, and deteriorate again when the cold front reaches you. The weather maps in newspapers will show you where the fronts were at a certain time. If you know that a typical speed for a wedge is about 40 km per hour (25 mph) you can work out roughly when the fronts will hit you.

FORECASTING 2: THE WAY THE CHILDREN CAN DO IT

The children will want to be able to forecast bad weather or, if it is already bad, will want to forecast when it will improve. We hope that they will be able to make a series of pattern statements about small changes leading up to the major change (for instance, the arrival of rain). They need a statement about winds, one about pressure, and so on.

For example, if they stand facing the wind, the depression will be on their right. If the upper winds, shown by the direction of the streaks of cirrus cloud, are from right to left the wedge has not yet arrived and the signs are bad. It turns out that, if the upper winds are towards them (parallel with the lower) they are within the wedge – the weather may be good but the cold front is still to come. Finally, if the upper winds are from left to right the cold front has passed and the weather should be better until the next depression arrives. So we might get the pattern statement: 'Whenever the upper wind is across the lower wind, from the right as you face the lower wind, bad weather is on the way.'

The children may be able to make statements which reflect the following information (though you are very unlikely to want to tell them all this).

Clouds Cirrus clouds directly overhead and very high indicate the leading edge of the sloping warm front. Their streaks will lie roughly parallel to the edge (across its direction of movement). The front at ground level will be about 80 kilometres or 20 hours away. You will probably see some cumulus clouds low overhead at the same time. As the ground level front moves towards you the sequence of clouds overhead will be cirrus, then cirrostratus (a thin veil giving the sun a halo), then altostratus, and nimbostratus as the front arrives. Under the wedge the sky could be clear or densely overcast with a layer of stratus. If clear you may be able to see nimbostratus coming towards you and marking the cold front.

When this has passed, the sequence will be altostratus with cumulus low down, then cirrus possibly with cumulonimbus (thunder tower clouds) giving showers, followed by clear skies.

Pressure When the leading edge of the warm front reaches you (the ground level front still being up to 20 hours away), the pressure will start to fall, slowly at first then faster as the front arrives. When it has passed the pressure will rise again. It will probably stay fairly steady for a while within the wedge. Then it will fall and rise again as the cold front arrives and passes.

Temperature Since the wedge is a mass of warm air, you can expect the temperature to rise a little as the ground level warm front passes and to fall a little after the cold front.

These are examples: the children should be able to make pattern statements about humidity and visibility too.

An excellent reference is: Watts, A. *Instant weather forecasting.* Adlard Coles, 1985.

It would be an interesting and valuable activity to develop a computer program which reads in the data and looks for connections between particular sorts of changes. Easy as it is to suggest, we do realize that this is a demanding and time-consuming job for a real computer enthusiast!

PROBLEM 3:
MAKING YOUR OWN WEATHER INSTRUMENTS

PAGE
160

The construction, calibration, and use of the instruments are of great value in terms of the skills and process objectives of the whole scheme. The children will enjoy making them and will be able to do so while they are collecting their data. Instructions are given on Worksheets 56, 57 and 58.

A good plan would be to divide the children into groups, giving each the responsibility for one of the five instruments. Collaboration with the school CDT department could be explored.

WORKSHEET 59
'STUDYING FACTORY-MADE WEATHER INSTRUMENTS'

The worksheet presents the children with a challenge – to find out how some beautiful, purposefully-designed instruments work. It is important that they see it as a challenge to reach a point where they can explain the instruments to you and not vice versa.

Additional activities

It will be clear from the foregoing that the chapter of activities can expand or contract to last as long as you wish. Elements of the activities described, from cloud-spotting and cloud poster-making through instrument construction to computer forecasting can be selected to cover the full ability range.

However, should you be looking for additional activities, one is to collect and display a long sequence of the weather maps from daily newspapers, adding your own comments on the weather you experienced. The school geography department may obtain synoptic charts from the Met. Office on subscription.

Another activity is to carry out an 'accuracy survey' of your local forecasts as obtained by ringing the number in your local telephone directory.

CHAPTER 9

Fire!

Introduction

Although this chapter centres on the study of fire, the nature of the phenomenon and its management and prevention, the chapter covers more extensive ground. It provides an opportunity to explore the effects of heating materials in some detail, such effects including both physical and chemical changes.

Combustion is essentially seen as one example of oxidation. Other instances in which oxidation occurs more slowly, as with iron rusting, or more quickly, as with the use of explosives, are also examined. The idea that burning involves oxygen links directly with the study of air and oxygen in Chapter 8.

Summary

Target   Read and discuss pages 71 'A picture puzzle?'; 72 to 73 'Joining up with oxygen'; 74 to 75 'Making fire (picture story); 76 'Very slow burning?'; 77 to 78 'Very fast burning?'.

Images   Fire crucial to humans. Attempts to understand fire. Discovery of phosphorus and sulphur. Development of matches.

Skills   Observing. Measuring. Patterning. Modelling.

Ideas   Combustion as one example of chemical reaction with oxygen. Use and control of fire. Rusting of iron also involving reaction with oxygen. Explosion being very rapid combustion.

Activities Heating materials. Classifying changes observed when things are heated. Change in mass on heating. Study of the heating of copper under various conditions.

Worksheets 60 'Investigating the effect of heat on potassium manganate(VII)'
61 'Investigating the gas from heated potassium manganate(VII)'

Reader pages

PAGES
71 to 78

As mentioned earlier, the chapter focuses on the most important component of the atmosphere, the highly reactive gas, oxygen. A picture puzzle and its explanation introduce the different forms which oxidation can take: the yellowing of paper, rusting, burning, and exploding. The nature of flames and burning are briefly discussed.

The picture story describes some of the interesting inter-connections in the history of fire-making. For example, the production of fire could be said to have led to the accidental discovery of smelting, which led to (among other things) the availability of iron for use in tinder boxes. The development of fire as an investigational tool by the Arabs led to its use by the alchemists in their search for the philosophers' stone, and on such a search phosphorus was isolated and later used to make matches. Of course, history is not quite as simple as that, but important scientific and technological processes are sketched.

The final section sets out to show scientists, the processes of science, and pure chance all at work in the development of our knowledge of rusting and exploding.

Activities pages

PAGES
161 to 165
The work begins with a circus which is very similar to that of Chapter 1 of Year 1 ('Heating things and observing the results': see *Teachers' guide 1* page 35, and *Pupils' book 1* page 107). This year we are particularly interested in the changes in mass which may occur on heating. Page 161 shows pupils how to draw up a table for the entry of results.

The important discussion which follows the circus gives the opportunity for the development of a higher level skill than observing, measuring, and making pattern statements. This is modelling: suggesting explanations derived from imaginary models of the events observed during the circus, and making predictions from the explanations.

Two alternative pathways are now open: Worksheet 60 provides for a careful investigation of the action of heat on potassium manganate(VII) (and the introduction of the technique of collecting gases over water); the main text leads to the heating of copper in the absence of air in a variety of ways. Next, copper is heated again whilst air is passed over it from one gas syringe to another. The children are able to watch something which is invisible but takes up space disappearing as it combines with the copper!

Finally, Worksheet 61 returns to potassium manganate (VII), offering careful study of the gas liberated when it is heated.

Additional activities can include the demonstration of explosions (see notes below), a lecture from the Fire Officer, and an investigation of rusting.

Background to the reader pages

A PICTURE PUZZLE?

PAGE
71
Liquid fuelled rockets use either liquid hydrogen or kerosene as a fuel. Oxygen for the reaction has to be carried in liquid form. The reaction is fierce: the five engines of the main stage of the Saturn V which sent the Apollo mission to the Moon burned 13400 kg of fuel and oxygen every second to give nearly 35 million newtons of thrust.

Rust is a particular problem in cars. Mild steel rusts very quickly. The formation of the oxide layer lifts off the paint so that moisture can seep under it and spread the rust. Defences against rust include anti-rust primer; this contains a metal such as zinc which forms an electrolytic cell with the steel and the water, in which the zinc is consumed rather than the steel. Sometimes the steel body is galvanized (dipped in molten zinc) before it is painted.

The 1.5 litre turbocharged engine of a Formula 1 racing car develops at least 600 hp (450 kW) according to how high the turbo boost is set, and has a fuel consumption as low as 3 or 4 miles per gallon (70 to 93 litres per 100 km) though this is being improved by restrictions on the amount of fuel that can be carried during a race, forcing drivers to keep the boost turned down.

Explosives work by the conversion of a relatively small volume of solid into a large volume of gas in a very short time. To be effective it must be in a confined space. Gunpowder, apart from being smoky, is a 'low', comparatively slow burning explosive. If a high explosive were used the cannon would blow up.

Paper yellows with age as a result of oxidation. The main constituent of paper is cellulose, a carbohydrate. Modern paper, except for some high quality kinds, is made from wood pulp and is bleached by chemical reduction, using sulphur dioxide or a bisulphite. The traditional papermaking process used linen rags, giving a paper that is more resistant to oxidation. Old books will outlast most modern ones. Medieval manuscripts made of calf-skin last even longer.

JOINING UP WITH OXYGEN

PAGES
72 to 73
Carbon in the pure state is allotropic, that is it can exist in more than one form. (Picture 7a and b.) In graphite (pencil lead) the atoms are arranged in a hexagonal array forming flat sheets with weak links between the sheets, so that they can easily slide over each other. That is why graphite is slippery and used as a lubricant. Soot is the same allotrope as graphite, but the crystals are very small. In diamond the atoms are arranged in a tetrahedral lattice – each atom is joined to four other atoms spaced equally around it in three dimensions. This gives diamond great strength and unequalled hardness.

Carbon is not the most abundant element in the body. By weight, there is more oxygen, because of the large amount of water in the body. But it is the most abundant by weight in dry matter, and it is present in almost all body tissues. The only exception is the calcium phosphate of which the hard parts of bones and teeth are made – but in fact bone is intimately mixed with protein, which does contain carbon. Carbohydrates are compounds of carbon, hydrogen, and oxygen only. Most have long, complex molecules made up of units of simple sugars. There is not much carbohydrate in the body, apart from any food that is being digested. There is glucose, a simple sugar, in the blood as a store of energy; and glycogen, a complex carbohydrate, in the liver to top up the level of glucose. Proteins and lipids (fats etc.) are composed of carbon, hydrogen, and oxygen with smaller amounts of other elements, the main one in proteins being nitrogen.

Carbon monoxide is given off when substances are burned in such a way that the carbon cannot combine fully with oxygen to make carbon dioxide.

The amount of oxygen that combines with the natural gas in a Bunsen flame is regulated by the revolving air valve at the base of the tube. Coal is largely composed of carbon. Natural gas and crude oil are hydrocarbons, compounds of hydrogen and carbon only: for example methane is CH_4. Crude oil is a mixture of hydrocarbons from propane, C_3H_8, through octane, C_8H_{18}, to tars with very large molecules.

Gunpowder was discovered in China over 2000 years ago. There it was used for fireworks. The Arabs brought it to Europe after AD 1200 and soon turned it to use in warfare. The earliest type of cannon was actually more like a mortar: an iron bucket full of stones with a small touchhole at the bottom. This was propped up on the ground so that it tilted towards the enemy and set off. The first European to discover the formula was Roger Bacon (1220–1292), who recorded it as a Latin anagram in 1245 in his *De secretis operibus artis et Naturae* ('On secret works of art and Nature'). Proper, though small, cannon were in use in Europe from 1320. Gunpowder, also known as black powder, is today made from 75% saltpetre (potassium nitrate), 15% charcoal (carbon), and 10% sulphur. It is still used in fireworks and blank cartridges, and sometimes for blasting.

Firework colours come from various metallic salts: strontium and lithium for red, barium for green, sodium for yellow, and copper for blue. White fire is produced with compounds of potassium, antimony, arsenic or sulphur, or with magnesium metal. Actually some of the compounds contain carbon, but it is not the active principle in producing the colour. The rocket flame does not involve carbon if the rocket is fuelled with liquid hydrogen. Kerosene is a hydrocarbon fuel.

MAKING FIRE (picture story)

PAGES
74 to 75

You can make a fire drill that will work – with a lot of effort. Drill a shallow hole in a pair of wood blocks. Sharpen both ends of a wooden dowel, as thick as a pencil, to a point. Make a bow out of bamboo and string. Wrap the string once round the dowel. Set the dowel upright between the blocks with one point in each hole. Move the bow rapidly back and forth till the dowel catches fire from the friction.

Copper was used before the discovery of smelting, since the metal occurs in a few places in the 'native' state, that is as pure metal, and is easy to hammer to shape. It is not known exactly when or where copper was first smelted. In about 3000 BC bronze was discovered. This alloy of copper and tin (which occur together in some ores) is easier to cast than copper.

Copper ore is of various types: sulphide ores (copper glance, Cu_2S, and copper pyrites, $CuFeS_2$) and oxide ores (cuprite, Cu_2O). The former are more common.

Iron was discovered later than copper although iron ores are very common, because the metal's melting-point is too high for simple furnaces. It emerges as a spongy 'bloom' which has to be heated again and hammered flat to make a bar of metal. The first users of iron were the Hittites. The carbon content of iron varies, and early metalworkers had little control over it. If iron has a lot of carbon in it, as cast iron does, it is hard and brittle. Wrought iron has very little, and is soft. Steel has a small amount, and is tough and springy. The Romans were able to make steel on a small scale by heating wrought iron with charcoal. Its principal use was for sword blades.

Geber (c.721 to c.815) was the first scientist to question the old Artistotelian doctrine of the four elements. He chose sulphur because it seemed to him to be the archetypal combustible substance, and mercury because it seemed the archetypal metal. His practical achievements included making sal ammoniac (ammonium chloride), white lead (basic lead carbonate), acetic acid (made by distilling vinegar) and weak nitric acid.

Hennig Brand (1630–?) was the first person to discover an element (phosphorus) that had not been known before the fall of the Roman empire. Although at that time the notion of an element was thoroughly confused, the discovery is still notable.

Robert Boyle (1627–1691) the great Irish scientist and co-founder of the Royal Society prepared phosphorus ten years later than Brand, in 1680. In his *The Sceptical Chymist* (1661) he stated for the first time the modern concept of an element: any substance that could not be broken down into other substances.

Early matches were highly dangerous, as they were liable to ignite spontaneously. A whole box of matches going up at once in your pocket was inconvenient! That is why most modern matches are called 'safety' matches. They can be struck only on the box. The head or the striking strip alone are not particularly flammable. 'Non-safety' matches such as Swan Vestas are much safer than old types, but they can still be struck on any rough surface. The phosphorus matches of the nineteenth century were also dangerous in another way. White phosphorus gives off a poisonous vapour which causes necrosis of the jaw – 'phossy jaw' – a disease which gravely afflicted the girls who used to make matches.

Pierre Curie (1859–1906) worked with his elder brother Jacques on the piezoelectric effect before he married Marie Sklodowska in 1895, and as a husband and wife team they went on to greater discoveries.

VERY SLOW BURNING?

PAGE
76
Stahl and the phlogiston theory were referred to in the notes on Chapter 8. Louis Guyton de Morveau (1737–1816) was a lawyer and an amateur scientist who exchanged information with Lavoisier, and

weighed rusting iron in 1772, two years before Lavoisier did. Not yet a baron (he was made one by Napoleon), he survived the revolution, and advised the revolutionaries on how to use balloons in aerial warfare – the first time this had been done.

The two forms of iron oxide are also found as iron ores: magnetite (Fe_3O_4), black and magnetic; and *haematite* (Fe_2O_3), red and the same as rust. Although some metals, such as copper, form a stable oxide surface layer, that of aluminium is porous so the metal does corrode slowly. It can be given a durable, shiny surface by anodizing, an electrolytic technique which builds up an impervious coating of oxide thicker than normal but not so thick as to hide the shine of the metal. This process should not be confused with electroplating in which the article to be plated is the cathode. The Forth railway bridge was built by Sir Benjamin Baker and Sir John Fowler between 1883 and 1889. It was the first really large steel bridge. Each main span is 520 m long, and the whole bridge weighs more than 50 000 tonnes.

Tin is being used less and less, as the high price of the metal made it uneconomic until it slumped in 1986. A thinner coating of tin is used on tinplate, and tinplate is being replaced by lacquered steel. Tin provides an indifferent protection for steel since, as soon as the plating is scratched in damp conditions, an electrolytic cell is set up in which the steel is consumed rather than the tin. With galvanized steel the zinc is consumed first, so the steel lasts longer. Both tinplating and galvanizing are done by the hot dip process – dipping in molten metal – and some items are electro-galvanized. Chromium plating is always done electrically. In fact the chromium is only a very thin layer to give lustre to a thicker layer of nickel plating underneath.

VERY FAST BURNING?

PAGES
77 to **78**
Christian Friedrich Schönbein (1799–1868) made a good financial success out of nitrocellulose at first, though one of his own factories blew up in 1847, killing 21 people. On the other hand Ascanio Sobrero (1812–1880) was so appalled at the power of nitroglycerine that he made no attempt to exploit it – though others did. The first safe smokeless powder for cartridges, still used today, was cordite, developed by Sir James Dewar (1842–1923; better known as the inventor of the Thermos flask) and Sir Frederick Augustus Abel (1827–1902). It is a mixture of nitroglycerine and nitrocellulose stabilized with petroleum jelly.

Alfred Bernhard Nobel (1833–1896) inherited his interest in explosives from his father, who invented a type of naval mine. The substance that he mixed with nitroglycerine to stabilize it was kieselguhr, a kind of clay. This clay is formed from the skeletons of diatoms – tiny, intricately shaped marine creatures – and is very absorbent on account of their lacy structure. Fuller's earth, used for cleaning because it absorbs grease, is similar. Nobel left $9 200 000 to fund prizes for peace, literature, physics, chemistry, physiology, and medicine. The first prizewinner was Wilhelm Röntgen (1845–1923), discoverer of X-rays.

Notes on the activities

PAGES
161 to 165
This is the last of the group of four chapters in which there is special emphasis on basic techniques and skills. In this chapter the skills of observation (as always), measurement (with top-pan balance and gas syringes), patterning, and modelling are well represented; and there are opportunities to introduce the techniques of collection of gases over water, and gas testing. References are made to the reader pages and it will help if the children have read these before they begin the activities.

PROBLEM 1:
WHAT HAPPENS TO THE MASSES OF THINGS WHEN THEY ARE HEATED?

PAGES
161 to 162
As is made clear on reader pages 66 to 67, this was an important and controversial puzzle for several generations of scientists. Resolution of the controversy was not made easier by the refusal of some of them to make use of the chemical balance! Today, pattern statements about the changes in mass of substances when they are heated are part of our 'unproblematic background knowledge', and we do not want to pretend otherwise in our discussions with the children. They are not setting out to solve problem 1; rather they are about to act out some of the work which led, years ago, to solutions to it. On the way they will continue to develop the knack of being a scientist.

If the children have followed Year 1 of Nuffield Science 11 to 13 they will have heated many if not all of the substances in our list (see *Pupils' book 1* pages 106–9, and *Teachers' guide 1* pages 33–5).

Heating the specimens
We have given a list of specimens so that the children will have a printed record of the names to copy if need be. We have also indicated that you will probably make a selection from the list. Ideally, all of the children (that is all of the working groups) should heat all of the specimens you provide, so that they can compare results at the end. You may have to limit the number to avoid long queues at the top-pan balance. With the same aim you could pre-weigh some of the crucibles and contents – the children would not lose much by this. Also, if each working group can have two crucibles, one can be being weighed while the other is being heated.

It is important that all of the specimens are treated in the same way.
⚠ Eye protection must be worn. Because potassium manganate(VII) tends to propel bits of the hot solid into the room when it is heated, this activity is best done by you as a demonstration.

A final point about your choice of specimens: it should, of course, include substances which gain mass (such as copper and magnesium), some which stay the same (such as nichrome wire, zinc oxide, clean dry sand, and ice – provided that you do not let the water boil), and some which lose mass (such as potassium manganate(VII) and copper sulphate crystals).

The discussion

There are two questions to be answered in the plenary discussion. The first asks which of the specimens gain mass, which stay the same and which lose mass. There is sure to be some disagreement about particular specimens, and this will be your cue to heat some of them again in test-tubes.

The second question asks why the changes in mass occur. We hope that the children's speculation on this will be informed by their reading of pages 68 to 70. You will have good opportunities to say: 'All right, let's try it', and turn to your hard glass test-tubes again. The heating of potassium manganate(VII) is particularly interesting and well worth demonstrating. The loss in its mass when it was heated in a crucible could have been due to bits of solid flying out. This is unlikely to be the reason if you use a test-tube.

A Caution: the solid potassium manganate(VII) fractures quite vigorously as it is heated, and small bits of hot solid can be propelled out of the tube. These present a hazard, particularly to the eyes. EYE PROTECTION MUST BE WORN throughout the practical session. A loose plug of ceramic wool (not Rocksil) placed in the tube should act as a filter and trap most solid particles.

You could follow the demonstration by introducing Worksheet 60 'Investigating the effect of heat on potassium manganate(VII)' (also see notes under 'Additional activities' below).

The test-tube demonstration of the effect of heat on magnesium is exciting, and coupled with the results of heating copper it provides a lead into the next problem.

PROBLEM 2:
WHY DOES COPPER GAIN MASS WHEN YOU HEAT IT – AND HOW CAN YOU TEST THE EXPLANATION?
Before starting the children on the text of the investigations, it is important to discuss the problem with them. Their memory of the reader pages may supply a ready answer to the first part, but designing a way to demonstrate it needs discussion.

'Demonstrate' is a more correct word to use here than 'test', because we are confident in our belief that copper gains mass because it combines with oxygen from the air. Our problem is to produce a set of events which can only be explained by accepting this.

The first step is to realize that if the change needs air to happen, it cannot happen if we exclude the air. The second is to devise ways of heating the copper in the absence of air. It will be interesting and valuable to discuss this with the children and obtain their solutions – perhaps more than one.

Part A:

Try keeping the air out

PAGES 163 to 164

When the children come to read our text they will find that we have given our answers to the problem and have suggested our ways of 'keeping the air out'.

We have suggested three ways. The first, which everyone can do, involves folding the copper and hammering it down so that air is excluded from the inner faces.

⚠ The second, to be demonstrated by you, uses steam to drive the air out of the tube. This can then be heated to softness so that it collapses and seals the copper. The third, also a demonstration, uses a so-called vacuum pump ('which has a powerful fan inside, to sweep the air along the tube and out of the test-tube').

In experiment 1 the copper will stay bright in those parts not exposed to the air. In experiments 2 and 3 it will stay bright and will not gain mass. A stern critic might suggest that there could have been something wrong with the copper in these cases – perhaps it was a kind which does not go black and gain mass? To deal with this criticism, one of the specimens is heated again in the open air (experiment 4).

Part B:

Letting the air in and watching oxidation happen

PAGES 164 to 165

Once we are confident in our theory about the blackening and gaining mass of the copper, we can ask questions such as 'How much of the air combines with the copper?' This leads to the demonstration which introduces gas syringes.

At the centre of the apparatus is a transparent silica combustion tube loosely packed with fragments of bright copper. Spaces are left at the ends of the tube and into these are fitted short lengths of hard glass rod (to prevent solids getting into the syringes). Ideally, the tube should be filled with black wireform copper(II) oxide which is reduced to copper in advance of the investigation by passing hydrogen over it with heating. Alternatively, fresh copper turnings can be used. You will need two volunteers to operate the syringes and, before starting heating, they will need to practise moving air back and forth from one syringe to the other. You will also need to check that the apparatus is airtight (ask the children for suggestions for this).

It is important to heat the copper at one end of the tube only. Continue heating vigorously for a couple of minutes while the air is moved back and forth. At the end of this time, the copper will have blackened and the reduction of the volume of air in the syringes will be obvious. Cool the tube with a damp cloth to counteract the thermal expansion of the air, and read the syringes. At this point you will probably notice that most if not all of the oxygen has been removed. Of course, the children will not realize this. If you want to be quite sure – the reason will be clear shortly – heat the same part of the tube for another minute or two, cool the tube and take the readings again.

If you now heat the tube at the other end, the copper should stay bright and there should be no further reduction in the volume of the air. The children will find this puzzling and will enjoy the discussion which leads to an explanation. The interesting feature of the investigation is that they have been able to watch something which is quite invisible but takes up space (oxygen gas) disappearing as it combines with the visible copper.

Additional activities

WORKSHEET 60:
'INVESTIGATING THE EFFECT OF HEAT ON POTASSIUM MANGANATE(VII)'

The investigation offers a follow up to the heating of potassium manganate(VII) under problem 1, and introduces the technique of collecting gases over water. Allowing for a few failures you should be able to collect at least one tube of oxygen per group (pair of pupils?). From their study of the reader pages the children will probably be able to name the gas and relate it to the test of relighting a glowing splint.

The initial motive for the investigation was further exploration of the effect of heat on an interesting substance; but once the gas is coming off, the method can be seen to offer a good simple way of making the gas when you need it (though potassium managanate(VII) is expensive).

At the end of the worksheet we suggest that the children should ask you to burn some substances in pure oxygen. Restrict the substances to sulphur, magnesium, and iron (wool) say. Ignite a combustion spoonful of the first two and immediately plunge into a tube of oxygen. Heat the iron to redness and do the same.

WORKSHEET 61:
'INVESTIGATING THE GAS FROM HEATED POTASSIUM MANGANATE(VII)'

The investigation is intended to give the children a taste of analysis and to allow them to exercise and develop skills which by now (and particularly if they have followed Year 1 of Nuffield Science 11 to 13) they should be taking for granted. A casual glance at the text – which is extensive – will reveal the following: the word 'density', a numerical value 1.429 mg/cm^3, and a suggestion of difficult calculations. It would be easy to jump to the conclusion that this is an investigation for more able children than those in your science group. But there is no suggestion that you should attempt to teach the concept of density and the formula: mass/volume. Here density is simply a property: the mass of a centimetre cube, which scientists have measured and tabulated for a large number of gases, and which can be used to identify the gases.

The questions at the end are intended to develop important ideas to do with sources of experimental error in handling gases.

RUSTING

The theme of the chapter as a whole is that of oxidation, and the relevance of rusting is made clear on the reader pages. If you have not already used Worksheet 51 you may like to do so now.

EXPLODING

It would be a pity to leave the chapter without demonstrating at least one example of explosive oxidation. The classical one uses a tin with a tightly fitting lid (press-on type not screw-on). A small hole is made in the lid and a hole large enough to take a length of rubber tubing is made in the bottom. The tin is filled with mains gas through the tube at the bottom (5 to 10 seconds should be long enough to displace all the air). Then the gas seeping out of the lid is lit and the rubber tube removed from the base. The gas inside the tin cannot burn because there is no oxygen; but as the gas at the top burns, air is drawn in through the bottom until . . . .

⚠ Make sure that everyone is standing well back! Eye protection must be worn.

The force of an explosion is developed because large volumes of gas are produced in a very short time and these are confined in a small space. An unconfined explosion can be demonstrated with a flour shaker full of powdered milk. Have a colleague stand on a bench and produce a 'snowstorm' of powder by shaking it out. Use a safety screen, and do not carry out the demonstration immediately underneath a light. As soon as the powder reaches the floor, ignite it, near to the floor with a burning twist of paper . . . . Such powder explosions, trapped in the confined space of warehouses, have had disastrous effects.

⚠ It is essential that the children are warned not to try out this demonstration at home. You have to make a judgment about their maturity before carrying it out.

FIRE PREVENTION

Many Fire Brigades will provide a visiting speaker and demonstrations of the dangers of fire, its prevention, and the use of extinguishers. This would be a good time to arrange such a visit which could initiate research, poster making, and project work on the subject.

CHAPTER 10 Rocket!

Introduction

This chapter provides a bridge between Chapter 9, the theme of which is oxidation, and Chapter 11 which focuses on the technology of engines (that is, devices for making things move), some of which rely on burning to work. So the chapter is as much to do with technology as with science.

This focus on technology is reflected in both the reader pages which start by considering the 'spin-off' benefits obtained from space exploration, and in the activities, for example the production of a 'reaction-propelled vehicle'.

The topic of space exploration can obviously be extended to introduce some astronomy, particularly with reference to the Solar System.

Summary

Target
Read and discuss pages 79 to 81 'Space spin-offs'; 82 to 83 'From rockets to star-ships' (picture story); 84 'The recoil pattern'; 85 'Isaac Newton and Robert Goddard'; 86 'How does a rocket engine work?' and 'Inside a rocket engine'.

Images
Rockets passed from military tools and toys to instruments of scientific enquiry. Work of pioneers from Newton onwards. Scientists looking for spin-offs from the NASA programme.

Skills
Designing. Measuring. Finding patterns.

Ideas
The idea of explosions (in last chapter) leads to controlled explosion of a rocket engine. Rocket design and principles. Variety of spin-offs from rocket research.

Activities
Making a model rocket. Patterns of rocket flight. The catapult trolley. Recoil patterns.

Worksheets
62 'Make a fizzy rocket'
63 'Make a rocket poster'
64 'Make a Shuttle display'

Reader pages

PAGES
79 to **86**
The previous chapter talked mainly about scientific knowledge and the way it was achieved. The technology which was described had resulted directly from scientific activity. In this chapter the technology is given greater emphasis beginning with a study of the 'spin-off' from the pure

scientific research of space exploration.

The picture story focuses on one device: the rocket, and follows the historical changes in its role from a magical creator of delight (or fear and panic), to a destructive weapon, then to a scientific research tool.

The final section sets out to show how scientists have provided explanations of the operation of the rocket, and how technologists have used scientists ideas to make better rockets. The section is completed with a description and explanation of a modern rocket engine.

Activities pages

PAGES
166 to 169
The work begins with the construction of model water rockets from washing-up liquid bottles. The performance of the rockets is investigated. A series of demonstrations introduces the challenge to design a small reaction propelled vehicle. Worksheet 62 'Make a fizzy rocket' adds another partial solution to those provided by the demonstrations. Next, a laboratory trolley from which a passenger can throw sandbags is used as a test rig for investigating the 'recoil pattern', and making it more of a quantitative statement. The investigation provides an exercise in the handling of multiple variables.

Worksheet 63 supplies the information needed to make a poster showing different types of modern rocket. This could form the nucleus of a 'spaceflight exhibition'.

Background to the reader pages

SPACE SPIN-OFFS

PAGES
79 to 81
The one spin-off of the space programme that everyone mentions is the nonstick saucepan. In fact it is no such thing. The plastic coating, polytetrafluoroethylene (PTFE for short, trade names Teflon and Fluon) was developed during the 1930s by DuPont in the USA, and was in commercial production in 1943. From the outset, NASA was concerned with spotting commercially exploitable discoveries and had a Technology Utilization Office as one of its departments. Silicon solar cells are a genuine spin-off, and are much used to generate power on space vehicles of many kinds – though not ones that travel a long way from the Sun, like Voyager II.

The reading machine in picture 4 has a camera which scans the page one letter at a time. The image is reproduced on a pad covered with a rectangular array of small needles. The needles corresponding to the black areas of the image vibrate, and the shape of the vibrating area can be felt and interpreted as a letter.

Very small heating elements like the ones in the goggles in picture 3 were developed for space helmet visors. One of the worst problems in space is that the side of an object facing the Sun becomes very hot and the side in shadow intensely cold. The body of a space suit such as was used on the Moon is kept at an even temperature by water circulating in small tubes. The helmet has two visors which together shield against infra-red and ultra-violet radiation and micrometeoroids (fast moving dust particles).

During the experimental flights of new space vehicles, and for health checks on long missions such as Salyut and Skylab, the bodily functions of astronauts are monitored by electrodes stuck to various parts of the body. Both the electrodes and the telemetry (data transmitting) apparatus had to be made as small and unobtrusive as possible, a benefit now enjoyed on Earth.

Quartz is a piezoelectric material: when an electric current is applied to it, it changes shape slightly. In a quartz clock or watch a rapidly alternating electric current is applied to a piece of quartz to make it vibrate. The quartz vibrates at its natural frequency – similar to the way that a tuning fork sounds a certain note – and generates a new a.c. current with this frequency. This new current drives the clock display. The best quartz clocks are accurate to 10^{-5} seconds a day, and quartz watches to $0.1 - 1$ second.

Various features of space suits can be useful on Earth. Germ-free environments can be created for people lacking normal resistance to disease. Heat-retaining blankets can be made from polyester sheet coated in aluminium, a combination first employed in space suits.

Computer diagnosis of faults in cars is done through a socket permanently installed in the car with leads running to sensors on the parts whose performance is analysed. The garage connects the computer to the sensors with an appropriate plug. The principle is based on the complex telemetry techniques used to monitor the systems of space vehicles. Unfortunately there is no universal standard design for plugs and sensors, and each make of car needs its own equipment.

For information on Sputnik 1 see below under the notes on the picture story.

Microelectronics are the most important of all space spin-offs. The original reason for trying to miniaturize electronic components was to save mass. This was particularly important for the US space programme, which at first had much smaller and less powerful rockets than the Soviets. Soviet space vehicles have always been heavier and simpler than their US equivalents. This has often been an advantage, as shown by the great durability of the Salyut space stations. In the first rendezvous between US and Soviet spacecraft (Apollo–Soyuz, 15 June 1975) the American astronauts who visited the Russians in their capsule were amazed to find that the flight was controlled by a revolving drum which touched electrical contacts as it turned, in the same way as the programme unit of a 1960s washing machine.

The 'sight switch' shown in picture 7 tracks the movement of the eyes, which can be done without touching them because of the contrast in colour between the iris and the surrounding white. Thus it is possible to switch something on by looking at it.

Computer enhancement may be used to clarify any photograph, whether it is from Voyager II looking at Uranus, a spy satellite above a military installation, a blurred picture of a crime suspect, or one of many types of medical scan using X-rays, ultraviolet, ultrasound, nuclear magnetic resonance, etc., to produce a picture. The picture must be converted into digital information, which is then scanned to detect which bits are part of a pattern (the picture) and which are random 'noise' (unwanted specks and lines). The random parts are removed, leaving the picture clearer.

Nitinol is only one of many alloys and other materials that have come from the space programme. Many alloys incorporate titanium, a light metal which can give considerably more strength for a given mass than steel or aluminium alloy. It is also heat-resistant, and is used for supersonic aircraft. The metal is both expensive and difficult to shape. Even thin panels have to be machined out of a solid block. Other materials include high performance ceramics that resist even greater heat, for example the tiles of the Space Shuttle. Synthetic rubbers have been developed to resist both heat and cold. Unfortunately a cold-resistant rubber was not used to make the joints on the solid booster rockets attached to the Space Shuttle. It is thought that the unusual cold at Cape Canaveral in January 1986 was one of the reasons why a rubber seal failed, allowing fuel to escape, and causing an explosion.

The most important single use of satellites is for relaying communications – telephone calls, television pictures, and other information – around the Earth. Most communications satellites are in geosynchronous orbit, at an altitude of about 36 000 km and travelling eastwards along the Equator. At this height the period of a circular orbit is 23 hours 56 minutes, which is the time it takes the Earth to turn once (it is 24 hours measured by the Sun because we are moving around it). So the satellite stays above the same spot on the Equator and antennae can be permanently aimed at it. However, parts of the Soviet Union are too far north to get a good view of a geosynchronous satellite, so three satellites are used, equally spaced around the same highly elliptical north-south orbit with its highest point at 40 000 km over Siberia and its lowest at 500 km on the other side of the Earth. This 'polar' orbit means that the satellite is moving most slowly when in view from Siberia. Survey satellites follow an orbit that covers the whole Earth in successive sweeps. Some military spy satellites have rockets controlled from the ground so that they can be steered into any desired orbit.

Laser reflectors were left on the Moon by the Apollo astronauts and the unmanned Soviet Lunokhod vehicle of November 1970. They were corner prism reflectors, using the same principle as a car reflector, so that they would reflect light from any angle (over a narrow arc) back exactly the way it came.

FROM ROCKETS TO STARSHIPS (picture story)

PAGES
82 to **83**

Chinese rockets were fireworks, not weapons. Their use was simply to terrify the enemy. The Chinese never developed a true military use for gunpowder, but the Arabs did. Around the time of the Seventh Crusade (1249–54) they also made the first mortar, an iron bucket loaded with gunpowder and stones. Europeans developed this into the cannon. But after the French used rockets to defend Orléans in 1429, interest in them lapsed.

In 1792 British troops in India were most effectively attacked with metal-cased, stick-stabilized rockets. Sir William Congreve (1772–1828) was comptroller of the laboratory of the Royal Arsenal at Woolwich. Congreve's rocket had either an explosive or an incendiary warhead, and was very effective if it arrived where it was meant to, which it didn't very often. The siege of Baltimore in the war of 1812 is mentioned in the US national anthem 'The Star Spangled Banner', which refers to 'the rockets' red glare'. The fins added by William Hale in the mid nineteenth century were angled to make the rocket spin, inspired by the feathers of an arrow and the spin of a rifle bullet.

In 1855 Colonel Boxer improved the line carrying rocket by adding a second stage, explosively separated from and ignited by the first. This was the first multi-stage rocket. The idea was not his own, but came from a Frenchman called Frézier.

The rebirth of rocketry in the twentieth century is largely due to the Russian physicist Konstantin Eduardovich Tsiolkovski (1857–1935), who first suggested the use of liquid fuel, artificial satellites, and space stations, and worked out the practical details of space suits and multi-stage rockets.

Rocket propulsion of aircraft was tried soon after the Wright brothers' flight by Henri Coanda, a Romanian living in France. The rockets, on either side of the fuselage, angled outwards at 45°. As the plane gathered speed the flames clung to the fuselage, setting fire to it. Coanda worked out why this had happened – it is the same fluid dynamics phenomenon that makes teapots dribble – and it is now called the Coanda effect or wall adhesion.

Robert Goddard (1882–1945) invented the bazooka, or hand-fired anti-tank rocket, during World War I. In 1919 he was already proposing to fire an unmanned rocket at the Moon, loaded with flash powder so that he could see when it arrived. After his first liquid fuelled rocket of 1926 he went on to develop many of the practical features of modern rockets. During World War II the Germans were to use his discoveries (infringing the patents).

The *Verein für Raumschifffahrt* (yes, it really does have 3 f's) was founded in 1927 by Hermann Oberth, Willy Ley, and others. In 1934 the Nazis broke up the society, which already had its sights on the Moon, and redirected some of its members into military research. Ley fled to the USA, where later he was to work on the space programme. Von Braun (1912–76) stayed and began work at Kummersdorf near

Berlin on a series of rockets called A1, A2 and so on. In 1937 work was transferred to Peenemünde on the Baltic coast, later to be subjected to much Allied bombing. Despite repeated failures, the programme culminated in the A4, better known as the V2 (*Vergeltungswaffen,* revenge weapon) of which several thousand were launched at Allied targets. At the time of the Nazi collapse, von Braun's group was working on a rocket that could reach New York, and three- and four-stage rockets for putting satellites into orbit. At the end of the war he surrendered his stock of V2s to the Americans and went with 130 of his workers to Huntsville, Alabama, where he developed the Jupiter rocket used to launch Explorer I, the Juno rocket for other early satellites, and the Redstone used for Alan Shepard's suborbital flight.

The Soviet space programme, begun by Tsiolkovsky himself in the 1930s, was continued by Sergei Korolev (1906–66). The GIRD (Group for Jet Propulsion Research) sent a liquid-fuelled rocket to a height of 5.63 miles in 1936. Sputnik 1 and its rocket, the R-7 or Semyorka ('old no. 7') were both designed by Korolev, who wanted to launch them on 17 September 1957, the 100th anniversary of Tsiolkovsky's birth. In the event they missed the date by 29 days, but still stunned the world. Sputnik 1 contained nothing more useful than a radio transmitter which sent a bleeping noise, just to show it was there. The purpose was really to show that the Soviet Union now had rockets powerful enough to launch an intercontinental ballistic missile. A subsequent launch carried a dog, Laika – which could not be brought back, and was killed. Then came satellites carrying instruments. The Soviets began a programme of scientific and military research. Korolev designed the Vostok vehicle (both rocket and capsule) in which Yuri Gagarin orbited the Earth on 12 April 1961, the larger Voshkod, and unmanned probes which surveyed the Moon, Mars, and Venus. He also worked on the first Soviet communications satellite.

America's first satellite, Explorer 1, was launched on 31 January 1958 after several embarrassing failures. The satellite was the size of a grapefruit, much smaller than Sputnik 1, but thanks to the electronic skills of James Van Allen (born 1914) it contained genuinely useful instruments. The Van Allen radiation belt that it discovered has two parts. The inner belt lies between 2400 and 5600 km above the equator and consists of charged particles emitted by the atmosphere as a result of the bombardment of cosmic rays. The outer belt, between 13000 and 19000 km, consists of particles emitted from the Sun. The doughnut shape of the belt is due to the Earth's magnetic field. Departing and returning astronauts must go north or south of the belt.

The US Apollo moon programme was initiated by President Kennedy on 25 May 1961 in response to Gagarin's exploit. Meanwhile the one-man Mercury capsule (only 2.08 m high, 1933 kg) took John Glenn into orbit on 20 February 1962 (Alan Shepard had made a brief 15-minute hop in one the previous year). The two-man, 3792-kg

Gemini capsule first flew in 1965. The first manned Apollo flight was Apollo 6 (following unmanned trials), which took Walter Schirra, Donn Eisele, and Walter Cunningham on a short hop on 11 October 1965. Less than four years later Neil Armstrong and Edwin Aldrin landed the Lunar Module on the Moon, while Michael Collins waited for them in the Command Module above. Lunar, Command, and Service Modules together had a mass of 45 000 kg and the entire vehicle with its three booster stages 2 851 150 kg, most of it fuel. The stack stood 110 m tall, just lower than the cross on St Paul's Cathedral.

On 20 February 1986 the Soviets launched the first part of a space station called *Mir* (which means both 'peace' and 'world'). Essentially it is a larger version of the earlier Salyut stations, but unlike them is meant to be extended by joining on pieces launched later. A true space station will have to be self-supporting, with plants or some devices to renew the oxygen in the air and provide food, and artificial gravity because the human body deteriorates after a few months' weightlessness.

ROCKETS AND SCIENTISTS

The recoil pattern

PAGES
84 to **86**

Isaac Newton stated his third law of motion as 'For every action there is an equal and opposite reaction', which is of course meaningless unless you know what action and reaction are, and if you do there is almost no need for the law. With acknowledgement to Ernst Mach (see *Teachers' guide 1* page 96), we would want to say something like: 'When you push against an object it seems to push back at you equally strongly' (because the idea has its basis in physical sensation); or, being more formal: 'When a force acts on an object there is a resistance either because of the inertia of the object (if it can move), or because of its elasticity (if it cannot). In effect the resistance produces a force (the reaction) equal to the initial force.' However, such statements are a long way from the world view of our eleven- and twelve-year-olds, and we want to save them for use in later years. Instead we can use a pattern statement which will make much more sense to them and which is easy to demonstrate: 'If you throw something in one direction you will tend to move in the opposite direction.' This 'recoil pattern' is useful and constructive and leaves much room for elaboration by direct investigation (see notes on the activities for this chapter).

A rocket doesn't push against anything, which is why it works in space. Jet-engined and propellor aeroplanes need air for two purposes. They do not carry a supply of oxygen and require atmospheric oxygen for the combustion of fuel. They both work by the principle of recoil, with air being thrust backwards and the vehicle forwards. The rocket thrusts its fuel backwards, so it moves forwards itself. Furthermore conventional aircraft obtain the 'lift' necessary to stay up in the atmosphere from the air flow around the wings. At very high altitudes that effect begins to diminish.

The *Solar Challenger* is a light, small, low-powered aircraft. Solar power is not feasible for anything bigger or quicker. It takes over 3 m² of silicon cells to produce 1 horsepower or about 750 watts in bright sunlight. This is an efficiency of less than 20%. The rest of the solar energy falling on the cell is lost as heat. If the *Solar Challenger* flies under a cloud it loses most of its power, and of course it can't fly at all in the dark.

Isaac Newton and Robert Goddard

PAGE 85

Newton published his laws of motion in his *Principia Mathematica* in 1687. He originally formulated them to explain the motion of celestial bodies, but they apply to any matter. Notes on Tsiolkovski and Goddard appear above.

How does a rocket engine work?

PAGE 86

The F–1 engines of the Saturn V are powered by kerosene and liquid oxygen. Kerosene gives less power than liquid hydrogen, but it was felt the amount of fuel that had to be carried, 950 100 litres of kerosene for the five engines, made liquid hydrogen impractical. The smaller J–2 engines, five on the second stage and one on the third, do use liquid hydrogen and oxygen. The liquid gas problem can be avoided entirely, at some cost in power to weight ratio, by using hydrogen peroxide as an oxidant, as was done on the V2.

The engine of the Apollo Service Module and the small thrusters for manoeuvring in space use a hypergolic fuel, that is one which ignites on mixing with the oxidizer – on the Service module aerozine 50 (a type of hydrazine) and nitrogen tetroxide. Hypergolic chemicals are also used to start other rocket engines.

Liquid-fuelled engines are usually mounted on gimbals so that they can be swivelled to steer the rocket. On the lower two stages of the Saturn V stack, only the outer four are movable. The fins on the bottom stage are not used for steering.

Solid fuel contains a mixture of fuel and oxidant: in gunpowder the oxygen comes from the potassium nitrate. Modern solid fuels for large rockets use oxidants such as a mixture of polyisobutene and ammonium perchlorate. Some military missiles, as well as the two boosters of the Space Shuttle, are solid-fuelled. The shuttle's own liquid-fuelled engines steer.

Notes on the activities

PAGES 166 to 169

As mentioned in the introduction to this chapter, emphasis is given to technology rather than pure science, and the activities reflect this. We concentrate on the design and production of a particular device, the 'reaction propelled vehicle'. However, the skills of the scientist are not neglected, and problem 4 introduces a design challenge which has as its aim the acquisition of data using those skills, and the making of pattern statements from the data. In addition, the problem offers opportunities to develop the children's understanding of strategies for handling multiple variables.

PROBLEM 1: HOW CAN YOU MAKE A MODEL ROCKET?

PAGES
166 to 167

The construction of the model rocket requires little comment. You will need to start your collection of washing-up liquid ('squeezie') bottles early. It would be convenient to obtain a range of sizes – to give you another variable to consider in problem 2. You will need further supplies for Worksheet 62 'Make a fizzy rocket'.

Water rockets have been marketed in the past as boxed toys; some laboratory equipment suppliers continue to stock them, and you may have some in your department. If so, it would be a pity to use them here rather than letting the children make their own and try to improve the design of these. The ready-made ones will come into their own in problem 2.

There are one or two small problems of operation of the home-made types which we should mention. The plastic nozzle can work loose and it is a good idea to secure it with PVC tape. Also, the hole in the nozzle can become too loose to seal the inflator tube properly. You could try bathroom sealant for dealing with that. Finally, we have heard of one teacher who chose to try out the water rockets in the laboratory rather than in the playground. This is not to be recommended!

PROBLEM 2:
ARE THERE PATTERNS IN THE WATER ROCKET FLIGHT?

PAGES
167 to 168

Part of the design of a new product is the testing of a prototype. This involves deciding on criteria of its performance. Cost and safety aside, the most important criteria for a rocket are its ability to fly straight and its range. You might begin by leading the children to suggest these criteria in discussion.

Part A

PAGES
167 to 168

The text gives instructions for investigating the connection between range and launch angle. We have suggested plotting the results on polar co-ordinate graph paper, and hope you will try this. It widens the children's experience and skills of graphical communication.

Part B

PAGE
168

Here the emphasis is on the amount of water added. Of course, this could affect the range in three different ways. More water means greater mass (and smaller acceleration for the same thrust), but the thrust lasts longer provided that all the water is expelled. More water also means that there is less air to be compressed by the pump, and this could mean a lower thrust. Even if we could work out a theory of the way in which these factors interact we would have little confidence in it. As is often the case in technology, careful, 'hands on' research offers the only solution to the problem. Once we know how the rocket performs we might be able to work out a theory to explain it.

You might like to investigate other variables such as the size of the squeezie container, the number of strokes of the pump, the size of the fins, alternative stabilizers to fins, a weighted nose cone. If you have 'factory-made' water rockets you could design an objective comparison between these and your home-made one: 'How would the *Which?* report do it?'.

PROBLEM 3:
CAN YOU DESIGN ANOTHER MODEL ROCKET?

PAGES
168 to 169

The problem is intended as an open-ended design challenge for the children. We have described the balloon rocket and the catapult rocket only as starters, and to provide at least two things the children can get on with if you want them to. As we have mentioned earlier in these notes, a good way to begin a design exercise is to have a 'brainstorming' session. Get everyone together, spend a little time making clear the starting point – in this case what the 'rocket' has to do – then ask for suggestions for achieving it. Any suggestion, however silly it may sound, is acceptable ('You can say anything you like'). It is not unknown for a silly suggestion to become a workable solution after minor modification. At all costs avoid an atmosphere in which you are looking for the single 'right' solution. Aim for at least two reasonable suggestions which you can try out.

⚠️ At this stage you must consider safety. Certain procedures should be established: all plans must be approved by the teacher before construction and trials, rockets must not be aimed at other children, and so on.

The balloon rocket
It is extremely unlikely (nothing is impossible!) that you will be able to make a balloon fly straight without finding a way to control the exhaust. This was a problem which taxed the inventiveness of the early rocket designers. The nozzles from the squeezie containers which you cut up for the water rockets can be made into serviceable nozzles for balloon rockets. Trim off the unwanted parts of the plastic moulding with a craft knife. If you use these you can also use the pump and inflator valve to blow up the balloon.

Even with a nozzle it is difficult to get a straight flight other than on a wire. Perhaps you could put a balloon inside a corrugated cardboard tube fitted with fins? Would it lift off? Making the balloon drive a wheeled vehicle is much simpler.

The catapult trolley
Almost any device with a spring which can be tensioned and released is a potential source of power here: a miniature bow and arrow, a mousetrap, a spring clothes peg, or a cotton-reel catapult. For

the last, a wide rubber band is looped around a cotton-reel so that it covers both holes, then one end is moved just to uncover one hole. A cocktail stick with sharp ends removed can be pushed into this hole and through so that it stretches the band covering the other. The band is held in the fingers like a common catapult until you want to release the missile.

⚠ You should remind the children of the warning in the text not to stand behind the catapult trolley on launching.

The text asks the children whether it is fair to call a catapult trolley a rocket. To an aeronautic engineer, rocket propulsion is reaction propulsion (throwing something in one direction to obtain movement in the opposite direction) using a stored propellant rather than the atmosphere. A rocket has to be capable of operating in space. There is a NASA design for an in-orbit propulsion system which makes use of a device like a two-bladed windmill. Thrust is obtained by ejecting pellets at high speed from the tips of the blades. (See Heppenheimer, T.A., *Colonies in Space*, Warner Books Inc., 1977, page 117.)

Worksheet 62 'Make a fizzy rocket' provides another source of ideas for the design. You may like to give this to the children as a mini-project for homework.

⚠ Dilute hydrochloric acid can be dangerous. There should not be much unreacted acid in the spray emerging from the bottle, but warn pupils to keep clear of it. Wash off spills with plenty of water. The products of the reaction, common salt and water, are quite harmless. Vinegar may be substituted for the hydrochloric acid. It is safer, but the evolution of gas would be less vigorous.

PROBLEM 4:
CAN THE RECOIL PATTERN BE EXTENDED?

PAGE
169

In an explosion, you start with one object and end up with at least two fragments going in opposite directions. In these terms the air rushing out of a balloon and driving it along is like an explosion, as is the throwing of a sandbag from a stationary trolley.

Since around 1666 scientists have known that if you multiply the masses of each of the bits by their velocities, taking direction into account, then add up the products, the total will be zero. Taking direction into account means, for example, giving bits moving in one direction a positive velocity and giving those moving in the opposite direction a negative velocity. In a collision, the total of all of the mass × velocity products before impact is equal to the total after impact.

John Wallis, one of the founders of the Royal Society, was the first to make this pattern statement. To the scientists of the day it seemed that the product mass × velocity must be one of nature's significant quantities, so it was given a special name 'momentum'.

Now, if you sit on a trolley and throw something away from you the momentum (mass × velocity) of the trolley and yourself will be equal to that of your projectile (so they can add up to zero taking direction into account). Assuming that your mass and that of the trolley is constant, the speed of your retreat will increase with both the mass of your projectile and the speed you project it at.

We would be very happy if the children could make such a pattern statement at the end of their investigation. We hasten to add that it would be a big mistake to introduce momentum at this stage.

For the children : handling four variables
In designing the investigation, the children have to deal with four variables: the mass of the trolley and its passenger (the vehicle); the mass of the projectile; the speed of the vehicle (backwards?); and the speed of the projectile (forwards?). In discussion, you will have a valuable opportunity to point out the confusion likely if all of the variables are allowed to vary at once. It makes much better sense to follow a strategy such as this.
1 Choose one variable to keep steady (mass of vehicle?).
2 Choose one variable to control (mass of projectile – one sandbag, two sandbags etc.).
3 Arrange to measure the other variables (the velocities).
In a later investigation, you can alter the value of the fixed variables and start over again.

Having chosen such a strategy, your problems have just begun! You have to find a trolley which is sufficiently free-running to recoil a measurable distance and, if you want precise results, you need to find a way of measuring its speed and that of the projectile. How far you go will depend on the suggestions of the children, on their enthusiasm, and on the range of equipment which you can muster.

Additional activities

CARBON DIOXIDE ROCKETS
In the department you may have one of the Nuffield Physics carbon dioxide capsule rockets (item 168 in the first edition). A metal bulb as used in proprietory fizzy drinks 'syphons' is secured by two plastic covered tool clips to a small wheeled trolley; or to a Perspex block with a hole drilled through so that it can run along a suspended wire. The nozzle of the bulb is pierced by a sharpened nail tapped smartly with a hammer. To be sure of puncturing the bulb, the flat of a second hammer can be held against its other end. The results are well worth the trouble and expense of setting up a demonstration with an overhead wire running the length of a corridor. Up to 30 metres should be possible.

⚠ If you try this, post guards to make sure that no-one enters the corridor while the demonstration is in progress, and do not leave the wire unattended while the corridor is filled with people.

'JETEX' ROCKET ENGINES – A WORD OF WARNING

A generation ago, Jetex engines were popular with model makers. These miniature solid fuel rocket engines were used to power all sorts of model vehicles from racing cars to speedboats. In America today you can purchase 'second generation' toy rockets which operate on the same principle and come in a range of sizes. You may have access to one of these or to an old Jetex.

⚠ Before using it you must check with your local authority: the use of such devices in school may be forbidden. Such devices can be very dangerous if improperly used.

A SPACEFLIGHT EXHIBITION

Worksheet 63 'Make a rocket poster' supplies the information you will need to make a collage to show different rocket designs. When you have chosen a common scale, you can use an OHP to project an image of each drawing onto a sheet of thin white card at the desired magnification. Trace the drawings, cut them out and stick them onto a dark coloured backing sheet (deep blue would be good).

The poster could form the nucleus of a small spaceflight exhibition, including models of spacecraft loaned by the children, and a pin board for press cuttings, photographs, and drawings.

WORKSHEET 64 'MAKE A SHUTTLE DISPLAY'

Since the Shuttle missions continue, not all the questions can be answered here. However, here are partial answers. The initial designs for the Shuttle were drawn up around 1974, and construction was fully under way in 1977. After some test glides of prototypes, the first full-scale flight was made by *Columbia* on 12 April 1981. The cargo bay was empty, and the main purpose of the mission was to test all the systems.

Highlights of Shuttle missions have included America's first woman in space, Sally Ride, who went on the first mission of *Challenger* on 18 June 1983. *Spacelab*, the European built orbiting laboratory, made its first mission on 28 November 1983. On 12 April 1985 *Discovery* made its first flight. Problems with early missions included the heat resistant ceramic tiles falling off, which could have endangered the Shuttle in the intense heat of re-entry – fortunately none fell off a critical place during a mission, and they are now more firmly stuck on. Three satellites were lost in two missions as a result of the booster rockets that were meant to take them into a higher orbit not firing. This was not a fault of the Shuttle itself, and later a crew actually repaired a faulty satellite in space.

Challenger was destroyed two minutes after launch on 28 January 1986, killing all seven on board, including the first genuinely civilian passenger, the teacher Christa McAuliffe.

CHAPTER 11

Moving around

Introduction

This chapter continues with the emphasis on technology. The development of machines to move people and materials around was central to the Industrial Revolution. Many features of our contemporary life-style, from holidays abroad to the availability of a wide range of foodstuffs, come from the application of engines.

Underlying this theme is the science concept of energy. We have extensive evidence to show that this concept is poorly understood by children of eleven to thirteen. (See, for example, Solomon, J. 'How children learn about energy'. *School Science Review*, 1982, **63**, 415–22.) The concept is too abstract. Science teaching can compound the confusion: for example, they learn in school that energy is always conserved but learn from television and newspapers that the World's finite sources of energy are being used up. That confusion is not easy to sort out – it involves understanding the nature of free energy.

To avoid such confusion we recommend that energy should not be covered as a key topic in a science scheme at this level. What we aim to do in this chapter is to provide ideas and activities which act as useful precursors for developing a sound understanding of the energy concept later on. This discussion about the treatment of the energy concept is continued in more detail in the notes on the activities.

Summary

Target Read and discuss pages 87 'Moving around'; 88 'It's a small world'; 89 to 91 'Making things move'; 92 to 93 'The heat engine story' (picture story); 94 'Technologists, scientists, and heat engines'; 94 to 95 'Internal combustion'; 96 'Spinning motion or to-and-fro?'; 96 'Making spinning motion'.

Images Much technology developed before science. Later, scientists provided explanations.

Skills Observing. Comparing. Designing.

Ideas Moving people and materials very important. Range of devices to help do this. Development of steam and internal combustion engines.

Activities Ways of making things move (movement circus). Heat from chemical reactions. Making a model of Savery's pump.

Worksheets 65 'Make a rubber band "tank"'
66 'Make an aeolipile'
67 'Make a water pump'

Reader pages

PAGES
87 to **96**

Once again, the emphasis of this chapter is more on technology than on science. Here it is the technology of engines – devices for making things move with little or no effort from their human operators. The opening section introduces the idea of a 'technological society' and shows that one of the distinguishing features of such a society is the forms of transport used for people and goods, and the distances over which they are commonly transported. The picture story is about heat engines – from the toy steam turbine of ancient Alexandria to the steam turbine of today (and with a late mention of the development of the internal combustion engine). The final section uses a series of ancient and modern devices to illuminate the various ways in which we have learned to make things move and to produce different kinds of movement.

The chapter is emphatically not intended as 'a chapter on energy', and our rationale for this is explained in the 'notes on the activities' below.

Activities pages

PAGES
170 to **177**

The work begins with a circus (or exhibition) of devices which produce useful movement. As well as observing the devices in operation, the children are encouraged to explain them in their own words (but with the help of our questions). They are invited to investigate the performance of the devices, and this gives another opportunity to develop the ability to handle multiple variables.

A series of investigations follows, the motive of which is to compare the liberation of heat during different chemical reactions, and to reach a judgment about the most potentially useful of these for producing movement. Finally a series of demonstrations introduces the key pattern statements which describe the production of movement when the atmospheric pressure is unbalanced. The children are challenged to use the statements to design a model of the water pump invented by Thomas Savery (see below). With careful thought for safety, one or more of the designs could be tried out.

Three worksheets for the chapter give instructions for making a rubber band tank (offering possibilities of a competition), an aeolipile (as mentioned in the picture story), and a simple water pump (from washing-up liquid containers).

Background to the reader pages

PAGE
87

The picture of methods of transport does not include some older devices from an earlier stage of technology: horse and cart, rowing and sailing boats, balloon (and the airship is back in fashion), bicycle; nor some other less commonly seen devices: tram, overhead cable car, flat travelator – even roller skates.

IT'S A SMALL WORLD

PAGE
88

Some luxury or high technology goods were traded in ancient times. The Romans imported among other things pepper and silk overland from the Far East, and trade continued in the Middle Ages, adding other things such as oranges and Damascus sword blades when they became available. The medieval wool trade was considerable. However, it is only in the past 200 years that improving transport has made it possible to send ordinary goods long distances at an economic price.

MAKING THINGS MOVE

PAGES
89 to 91

The plough was probably invented in Mesopotamia or Egypt around 4000 BC. It is found in several Neolithic cultures, as there is no need to use metal in its construction: at its simplest all you need is a forked branch forming the share and guiding handles, lashed to a pole to pull it along. Although the first ploughs were hand-drawn – and such ploughs are still in use by people too poor to afford draught animals – the use of oxen came early. The oldest Mesopotamian ideogram for a plough, dating from about 3500 BC, already shows a yoke for harnessing them. Around 800 BC in the Mediterranean countries an iron tip was added to the share. To deal with the heavier soil of western Europe, the Romans added a metal blade, the coulter. It is likely that the Slav people of what is now western Russia invented the mould board, a curved plank behind the share to turn the soil over. This had spread throughout Europe by the Middle Ages. Such a plough could be very large and heavy, requiring a pair of wheels and four oxen.

The way in which the Pyramids were built is still unknown, and every expert has a theory about ramps, rollers, ropes, and so on. The pulley seems to have been invented around 800 BC. There is an Assyrian relief of this date showing what may be one, and an actual pulley was found in the slightly later Mesopotamian city of Nimrud. The crane was first described by the Roman architect Vitruvius (born c.70 BC) and by Hero of Alexandria (see below). It was simply a beam fixed down at one end and raised by pulleys. Modern cranes are of various shapes. The familiar tower crane seen on building sites has a rotating horizontal boom with a counterweight on the other side of the pivot. A trolley carrying the hoisting mechanism runs along the boom. The maximum load the crane can carry decreases with the distance of the trolley from the centre, because of the increasing leverage. This disadvantage is partly overcome with the Scotch derrick crane, which may also be mounted on a tower. It has a jib hauled up and down by cables, and is stayed or secured to stop it from being pulled over. In factories, gantry cranes are often used: a bridge of steel lattice-work with wheels at each end running on rails fixed to the walls, and with a trolley running across the bridge so that every part of the floor can be reached. Transporter cranes of similar design, but with the bridge standing on legs running on rails on the ground, are used at docks. Dock cranes also include jib types, often also on rails. Medium-sized mobile cranes are often of the telescoping boom type. The boom is extended and moved by hydraulic rams. It can lift relatively small loads to tenth floor level or even higher. The heaviest shipyard cranes are over 120 m tall and lift 1500 tonnes.

Early types of waterwheel are described in the notes on Chapter 7. The best Roman water mills could develop up to 4 kW and mill 300 kg of flour per hour. By the eleventh century, water mills were also being used for other purposes: grinding oak bark for tanning leather, and powering metal and woodworking equipment – bellows, hammers, stamps, and saws. These were all reciprocating devices; the circular saw had not been invented. The wheel turned a cam against a lever to produce the required motion. Later, the Industrial Revolution brought new uses in factories, though during the nineteenth century waterwheels were largely replaced by more powerful steam engines.

The windmill was invented later, probably in Persia in the seventh century AD. The first type had sails rotating horizontally on a vertical shaft, calling for a wall to be built between the mill and the prevailing wind to direct the wind onto one side of the mill. By the time of the Crusades a vertical type had been developed, probably much like the canvas-sailed Greek mills of today, and it was this design which the Crusaders brought back to Europe. The first mention of a windmill in Britain dates from 1191. It was at Bury St Edmunds. Medieval mills were all post mills, with all the machinery installed in a wooden house mounted on a vertical pole, so that the whole thing had to be turned into the wind. Later this was made automatic by a fantail, a small wind wheel on the downwind side of the mill connected to gears which revolved the mill until the wind wheel was edge on to the wind and stopped turning. By the seventeenth century the tower mill had been developed. Only the top part carrying the sails turned, so it was much less likely to blow over in a gale. Another problem in strong winds was that if you didn't take the canvas off the sails, the mill would run so fast that it caught fire. Mills did have brakes, but they were not very effective. In 1772 Andrew Meickle, a Scottish miller, invented the spring sail, resembling a Venetian blind with spring-loaded slats which would open if the wind loading increased dangerously, and could be left open to stop the mill.

Apart from milling grain, mills have also been used for pumping water to drain land in the Netherlands and the English fens. At the beginning of the nineteenth century the first small wind pumps for water supply were built. They had about 20 steel blades, and were mounted on a steel lattice-work tower. A hinged, spring-loaded tail turned the wheel into the wind but skewed it sideways if the wind became too fast. The pump was a cylinder type worked by a crank and rods. These devices are still in use in many places.

The use of wind generators for electricity has been much discussed, but only a few have been built, mostly in Scandinavia and the USA; there is also a small one in the Orkneys. The main difficulty is that to give the output of a small power station, say 700 MW, you would need up to 50 generators with blades over 100 m across and towers over 250 m high. The environmental impact might be much worse than that of the power station.

The first water turbine other than a simple watermill was known as Barker's mill or the Scotch mill, and was invented around 1740. It was a water version of Hero's aeolipile (see below), but gave too little power to be of practical use. The design survives in the revolving lawn sprinkler. The French inventor Benoît Fourneyron (1802–67) in 1827 built a turbine with a horizontal rotor. Water fell down a long pipe from a dam into the centre and passed outwards through stationary curved blades to rotor blades around the edge. The design was later improved by turning it inside out, so that the water flowed from the edge inwards to a central rotor with a hole in the bottom. In this way the energy of the rotating mass of water was completely expended by bringing it to a standstill at the centre. There are several such designs, but the best known was invented by James Francis in Britain and James Thomson in the USA around 1850. These wheels are good for water flowing at a fairly high speed. If the water has a long fall and is moving fast, a different type of wheel is used, invented by Lester Pelton, a British mining engineer in California around 1870. This has hemispherical cups around the rim into which the water is squirted. For a large mass of water moving slowly the most efficient design is that invented by V. Kaplan in 1920. It resembles a ship's propellor inside a broad pipe. At first water turbines were used directly for driving factory machinery, but with the coming of mains electricity it was realized that they were ideal for driving generators. The first large installation was at Niagara Falls, built 1886–95. It originally had Fourneyron turbines, but they were soon exchanged for Francis ones. The modern tidal power station in the Rance estuary in France uses Kaplan turbines.

The solar furnace at Font Romeu, near Odeillo in the French Pyrenees, was built in 1970. It is at an altitude of 1800 m to take advantage of the thin air and consequent strong sunlight. The parabolic mirror is 45 m tall and consists of 8750 panels. Light is directed at it by 11 000 steerable flat mirrors on the opposite slope. The parabolic mirror focuses this onto the central furnace room. The temperature is 3300–3500 °C, and the furnace can melt a hole 30 cm across in a 1 cm thick steel plate in 1 minute. Small portable solar cookers of a similar design have been built, but they are not very practical on account of the size of the reflector and the impossibility of using them at night or on a cloudy day. However, solar water heaters, resembling radiators inside sealed glass-fronted boxes, are widely used and can be useful even in Britain. Silicon solar cells are discussed in the notes on Chapter 5.

Power stations use steam turbines, yet another design of turbine (see below).

You could say that in burning fossil fuels such as coal we are making use of the sunlight of millions of years ago – when the plants which ultimately formed the coal were alive and growing.

THE HEAT ENGINE STORY (picture story)

PAGES
92 to **93**

Hero was born in about AD 20. Hero wrote various technical works including the *Pneumatics* and *Automatic theatres*, which described power driven gadgets and toys for amusement only. This was a typical classical attitude to machinery. A slave-owning society didn't need engines, and the only machines that were at all esteemed were military ones – about which Hero wrote another book, the *Belopoiica* (dart throwing). He also wrote the *Mechanics*, about the simple lifting and hauling devices of the day. The name aeolipile means 'ball of Aeolus' – the god of the winds. In the temple door opener, lighting a fire on the altar boiled water, creating pressure that forced water into a bucket hanging on a rope running over a pulley and whose other end was wound around the bottoms of the door posts. It was usual for classical doors to be set on posts rather than hinges. As the bucket descended it turned the posts and opened the doors.

Otto von Guericke (1602–86) has already been mentioned in Chapter 5 for his work on static electricity. There was at this time a vague theory that it was impossible to create a vacuum because 'Nature abhors a vacuum'. Von Guericke set out to produce a large evacuated space by pumping water out of a barrel. It leaked through the staves. Next he bought an air pump and tried to exhaust a copper sphere. It collapsed – apparently supporting the old theory. So he made a pair of stronger copper hemispheres sealed together with a leather washer, and built his own much better air pump. An illustration to his own *Experimenta Nova* of 1672 shows that 18 horses couldn't separate them.

Around 1680, Denis Papin (1647–1712) a French-born scientist resident in London, and the inventor of the pressure cooker, built a model pump in which steam was used to lift a small piston up a tube. Weights pulled the piston down again. He was unable to develop the model into a practical engine and shelved it.

Water has been the enemy of the miner ever since the first deep mines were built. The Romans pumped their mines dry with a chain of Archimedean screws, each turned by a slave. Georgius Agricola's great work on mining, *De re metallica* (On the subject of metals) of 1556 is full of pictures of huge pumps worked by men or animals inside treadmills. Thomas Savery (1650–1715) made an engine which had no moving parts other than taps and valves. It consisted of a boiler and two oval vessels, each about the size of an oil drum. The only reason for having two was that the engine worked so slowly that the vessels had to be used alternately. The bottom of each vessel was connected by a T-junction to a pipe running up from the water to the top of the mine. Above and below the junction were one way flap valves which allowed water to pass only upwards. Steam from the boiler was admitted to one vessel by opening a tap by hand. The pressure forced up any water in the pipe above the vessel. Then water was poured over the vessel to condense the steam. The drop in pressure allowed the atmosphere to push up water from below. While this was happening, steam was let into the other vessel, and so on. Pressure had to be fairly high to lift the water and open the valves – though it couldn't lift water far enough to drain most mines – and there does not seem to have been a safety valve. At this time no one had any experience of building strong boilers. No wonder it blew up. The engine developed about 0.7 kW.

Thomas Newcomen (1663–1729), strictly speaking, invented not a steam engine but an atmospheric engine. It didn't develop its power by steam pushing the piston up, but by atmospheric pressure pushing the piston down when the steam was condensed. The piston was connected to the beam by a chain, not a rod, and thus couldn't exert a push. The pump end of the beam was heavier than the engine end, keeping the chain taut. The piston was sealed to the cylinder by a leather washer with a pool of water on top. In Newcomen's prototype engine the steam was condensed by pouring water into a jacket around the cylinder, and the valves for steam and water were worked by hand. In production models, water was squirted direct into the cylinder, and the valves were worked automatically by the movement of the piston. The engine gave about 3 kW. Newcomen was hampered by patents that Savery had taken out in 1698, and had to go into partnership with him. Despite the success of his engines he died poor. The engines survived him for a long time: one at Parkgate in Yorkshire was in use till 1934, despite its immense coal consumption.

John Smeaton (1724–92) was a scientific instrument maker who made his name by building the third Eddystone lighthouse, the first one that was not promptly swept away by the sea. He experimented to find the most efficient design of windmills and watermills before turning to steam engines. He worked in a scientific way, building working models and altering the design of every part till he arrived at the ideal combination. Later he built the Forth and Clyde Canal and Ramsgate harbour.

James Watt (1736–1819) realized that the chief cause of the inefficiency of the Newcomen engine was the waste of energy in alternately heating and cooling the large cylinder. He modified the design by adding a separate condenser. Instead of the steam being cooled in the cylinder, the cylinder was vented into a second, cold vessel into which some of the steam escaped and condensed, creating a vacuum which allowed the atmosphere to push more steam from the cylinder and pulled the piston down. Watt went into a successful partnership with Matthew Boulton. In all he built 496 engines of various sizes. Some remained in use into the twentieth century. Engines for mills rather than pumping needed to turn wheels. Watt couldn't use a crank to do this as the device had been patented. He designed a 'sun and planet gear' to do the same job, which usefully made the wheel turn at twice the rate of the piston. (You can demonstrate this with a set of epicyclic gears rescued from a derelict 3-speed bicycle hub.) This arrangement required a rigid piston rod rather than a chain, so for the first time movement was produced by the steam pushing the piston. Watt also invented the double-acting steam engine, in which steam was admitted alternately to each side of the piston; and the flyball governor to regulate the speed of the engine, in which a pair of metal weights hanging on levers was whirled around, so that their inertia raised them and they partly closed a valve to reduce the flow of steam.

Nedd Ludd may have been a mythical figure. The movement began in Nottinghamshire and spread to Lancashire, Yorkshire, and Cheshire between 1811 and 1816. Reprisals were severe: rioters were hanged or transported.

Richard Trevithick (1771–1833) invented the high pressure steam engine. A pumping engine he built in 1802 had a boiler made of cast iron 4 cm thick and ran at a pressure of $1\ \mathrm{MN/m^2}$, ten times that of the atmosphere. His design, known as the 'Cornish engine', was so much more compact and powerful than Watt's that it was soon being installed in mines and factories all over the country. Trevithick had a flair for publicity, but little business sense and no luck. He built two steam road carriages, both of which crashed, and in 1808 near Euston Square in London a circular railway for joyrides, with an engine called *Catch-me-who-can*. He died penniless.

An improvement in steam engine design, first used in 1780 but not exploited till some years later, was the compound engine. This has two to four cylinders of different sizes. High pressure steam from the boiler goes first to the smallest cylinder, emerging at a lower pressure but still able to produce useful movement, so it is piped to the next cylinder which is larger because of the lower pressure, and so on. Making greater use of the steam in this way increases the efficiency of the engine.

George Stephenson (1781–1848) was a mining engineer. In 1814 he built a locomotive, *Blücher*, for Killingworth colliery, and in 1825 *Locomotion* for the World's first passenger railway, the Stockton and Darlington.

In 1830 the directors of the new Liverpool and Manchester railway were uncertain whether to use horses or steam. They held a competition for locomotives at Rainhill, and the *Rocket*, built by George's son Robert (1803–59), won. This railway was the first to use steam power throughout. The Stephensons went on to build more locomotives and railways, and bridges including the Britannia Bridge over the Menai Strait.

Sadi Carnot (1796–1832) founded the science of thermodynamics. He realized that energy is never lost, simply transformed from one form to another, and that the efficiency of a steam engine depends on the temperature difference between the boiler and the condenser. At this time even the best steam engines were less than 10 per cent efficient. Later their efficiency was increased by superheating the steam above boiling-point in accordance with Carnot's principles.

Charles Parsons (1854–1931), despite being the son of the Earl of Rosse and having a degree in mathematics, apprenticed himself to an engineering firm where he built a novel high speed steam engine. He was later commissioned by another firm to build a high speed engine to drive a generator. His completely new idea, the axial flow turbine, resembled a row of windmills inside a cylindrical casing, with stationary blades between each set of moving blades to direct the flow of steam. His first turbine was built in 1884. In 1897 there was a grand naval review at Spithead to celebrate Queen Victoria's Diamond Jubilee. Parsons turned up unannounced in a turbine-powered boat, the *Turbinia*, and startled the Navy by going at $34\frac{1}{2}$ knots (64 km/h).

Papin had suggested an internal combustion engine powered by gunpowder, and the first patent for a gas engine was taken out in 1794 in Britain. Joseph Niepce, inventor of photography, built a practical engine but couldn't sell it. Étienne Lenoir (1822–1900) was the first to achieve any commercial success with his engine of 1859. It had electric ignition by a spark but the mixture was not compressed, reducing efficiency to less than that of a good steam engine.

Nikolaus Otto (1832–91) built an engine that also ran on gas but was much more efficient. The first petrol engine was probably built by the Austrian Siegfried Markus (1831–99) around 1864. He built several cars, antedating Benz by some years, but remained obscure; perhaps because he was a Jew in a violently anti-semitic country. Other early internal combustion engines ran on heavy oil – not the same as diesel fuel, and they were not diesel engines for they had an ignition system. Rudolf Diesel (1858–1913) patented his engine in 1892. It was designed according to scientific theory, which had caught up with technology. It is still the most efficient of all engines in large scale production. The fuel-air mixture is compressed so much (up to 25 times) that its temperature is raised to about 550 °C and it ignites of its own accord. The engine has to be very strongly built, and tends to be heavy for its power output. Diesel's original engine ran on powdered coal. Modern diesel fuel resembles kerosene.

Gottlieb Daimler (1834–1900) built a four stroke petrol engine in 1885 and installed it in a bicycle and a carriage the following year. Also in 1885, Karl Benz built a better engine and put it in a three wheeled carriage. The engine had electric ignition (Daimler's had a primitive system of hot tubes) but the cooling system left much to be desired. It used water but no radiator: the water simply boiled, and had to be replaced from time to time. The two men went into partnership and their firm, Daimler Benz AG, is still building cars (they are called Mercedes after the daughter of the French concessionaire, who didn't want to sell cars with a German name in France so soon after the Franco-Prussian war).

TECHNOLOGISTS, SCIENTISTS, AND HEAT ENGINES

PAGES
94 to **96**

For the principle of the steam engine, see the previous section.

Internal combustion

PAGES
94 to **95**

It is important that pupils should realize that what keeps the piston moving during strokes 1, 3, and 4 is not only the explosions in the other cylinders but also the kinetic energy of the crankshaft, which carries a heavy flywheel. Otherwise a single-cylinder engine would be impossible. The four-stroke cycle is not the only one, nor is the piston engine the only type of internal combustion engine. Many motorcycles use two-stroke engines, in which fuel and air are taken into the cylinder and ignited every time the piston rises. They have no valves, but ports (holes) in the cylinder wall uncovered by the moving piston. The engine's efficiency is increased by the more frequent firing but reduced by bad gas flow through the simple intake and exhaust system. The mixture is drawn in via the crankcase, which means that oil has to be mixed with the fuel to lubricate the engine. The result is a dirty exhaust. There are also two-stroke diesels with more advanced breathing arrangements. They are often used in trucks.

Spinning motion or to-and-fro?

PAGE
96

The 'sun and planet' drive is mentioned under James Watt, above. The first known machine to use a crank is a grindstone depicted in a French manuscript of the ninth century. The heavy stone acts as a flywheel. It was not realized till later that any crank-operated mechanism works better with a flywheel. An early use of a flywheel appears in a drawing of a lathe by Leonardo da Vinci (1452–1519).

Making spinning motion

PAGE
96

The gas turbine looks rather like Parson's steam turbine and works in the same way, but it is important to realize that the numerous rows of blades at the front end are an axial flow compressor, the exact opposite of a turbine. They draw air into the engine and compress it. It is mixed with fuel in the combustion chambers and the hot gas rushes through a smaller turbine at the rear. In a pure jet engine the turbine drives only the compressor. Most jet aircraft have bypass or fan jets, in which the turbine also drives a large front fan which blows air through a ring shaped duct around the engine, increasing fuel efficiency and reducing noise. In other gas turbines rotary rather than linear thrust is produced. Examples include the turboprop, with a propellor; the turboshaft, used in helicopters; and gas turbines used in warships and as standby electricity generators. The gas turbine is too thirsty and its hot exhaust too dangerous for it to be a success in road vehicles, though it has been tried in some experimental cars and trucks.

Notes on the activities

PAGES
170 to 177

The activities begin with a circus which puts on show the range of devices which have been developed for producing motion. We then look at a series of chemical reactions and ask which is the best for producing useful amounts of heat. The study of the eight reactions offers opportunities for the development both of scientific skills and of ideas to do with chemical substance and chemical reaction. The final section offers a challenge: to make a model of Savery's pump (mentioned in the picture story). A sequence of demonstrations establishes the key ideas to be applied in the design.

THIS IS NOT A CHAPTER ABOUT ENERGY!

In future years the children will be introduced to the concept of energy, which, in simple terms, can be defined as the *ability* to cause movement or to cause change in movement. In view of the highly abstract nature of the concept, and the good evidence that children find it difficult, we hope that its introduction will be delayed as long as possible. We would consider ourselves to have failed if the exciting things which happen in these activities could not be enjoyed, discussed, and explained, without introducing the concept of energy.

What is useful to technologists is to have a classification of those devices which can be used to produce or transfer movement. A classification such as the following. Devices which produce movement as a result of:

1 the emission of heat by certain unstable substances called radioactive materials;

2 chemical reactions including those in living cells;

3 the absorption of radiation such as visible light;

4 the flow of an electric current;

5 the release of a system under restraint, such as a catapult or clockspring;

6 the natural movement of air and water in the environment.

Armed with a list of such devices, a technologist can string them together in various sequences to produce the right sort of movement in the right place at the right time. For example, devices in categories 1, 3, and 4 are working in sequence to operate the systems of the Voyager spacecraft as they move outwards through the cold blackness of deep space.

PROBLEM 1:
HOW MANY WAYS CAN WE MAKE THINGS MOVE?
(THE MOVEMENT CIRCUS)

PAGES
170 to 172

As the reader pages make clear, this has been a genuine problem for crafts and technology for thousands of years. We want to introduce the children to the great variety of ways in which it has been solved. We want the children to make the devices work, to observe and later to investigate the conditions under which they work, to describe what they observe as comprehensively and as clearly as possible, and to recognize the usefulness of the devices.

You will notice that there is some overlap between the devices in this circus and those in the electrical devices circus in Chapter 5. This is almost inevitable because of the importance of electricity and electric motors, but if you would prefer to avoid it, you could replace the common items with some of those suggested in 'Additional activities' below.

In the notes which follow we will give a brief description of each of the exhibits mentioned in the activities, followed by some questions which you could ask the children in conversation (and answers you might hope for). Then we will suggest some things which the children might change (independent variables); and some which might change as a result and be measured (dependent variables).

A Hand pump, water turbine, and dynamo

PAGE
171

A 'stirrup pump' is operated by hand, producing a current of water which drives a turbine. This in turn drives a generator, the electricity from which can be used to light a bulb, run an electric motor, or move the needle on a meter.

How long could it go on for? (Until you got tired.)
So where does the movement of the generator start from? (Me . . . my muscles.)
What goes on in your muscles to make them work? (Reactions.)
What do you need to make the reactions go? (Food.)
Apart from your muscles, how many devices for making things move are involved here? (Two – unless a motor or meter is connected at the end.)

Independent variables: rate of operation of pump, length of connecting tubes.
Dependent variables: speed of generator (brightness of bulb, ammeter reading).

B Gravity lift

PAGE
171

A mass which can be let go to fall straight down is used to haul a loaded trolley up a slope. Alternatively, the trolley can be used to transport a series of bags from the top of the slope to the bottom, being returned to the top each time by the falling weight (a possible design exercise for the children).

What got the trolley moving? (The falling mass.)
How did the weights get on the hanger? (I put them on.)
So how did the movement really start? (From me . . . my muscles.)
What goes on in your muscles to make them work? . . . And so on as questions for exhibit A.

Independent variables: length and steepness of slope, load on trolley, load on hanger.
Dependent variables: speed of trolley, trips made per minute.

C Electric lift

PAGE 171

A power pack or, preferably, a rechargeable battery supplies electricity to an electric motor which can lift a load.

What made the movement happen – starting from the beginning? (The motor.)

Further back than that? (The electricity.)

What made the electricity flow? (The battery.)

How long could you keep lifting the load again and again? (Until the battery ran out of push.)

What happens inside the battery? (Reactions.)

Independent variables: load, height of lift, push (voltage) of battery – take care not to overload the motor though.

Dependent variable: time taken to lift load a given distance.

D Electric fan and windmill

PAGE 171

A battery or power pack supplies electricity to a small electric fan, the current of air from which turns a paper windmill.

What makes the windmill turn? (The wind from the fan.)

What is the wind made of? (Moving air.)

What started everything moving? (Electricity.)

... And so on as questions for exhibit C.

Independent variables: distance between windmill and fan, orientation of each with respect to the other, surroundings of fan (try a wind tunnel?), number of blades on windmill, speed of propellor (push [voltage] of power supply).

Dependent variable: speed of windmill.

E Steam engine and dynamo

PAGE 172

A model steam engine drives a generator, the electricity from which lights one or more bulbs or makes the needle of an ammeter move.

⚠ Check your LEA safety notes for references to the use of steam engines. Many model steam engines used to employ a liquid fuel such as methylated spirits. There have been many instances of children suffering very severe burns while attempting to refill such models. Either a residual flame or the hot metal has ignited the fuel, causing the whole bottle to burst into flames. Therefore LIQUID FUELS MUST NOT BE USED with model steam engines.

Solid fuels, either metaldehyde or a piece of candle, will usually work well and do not present the same hazard.

What makes the bulbs come on? (Electricity.)

Where does that come from? (The generator.)

The steam engine runs the generator – what makes the steam engine move? (Steam.)

How do you get the steam? (Fire heats the water.)

Where does the fire come from? (The fuel burns.)

Independent variables: the number of bulbs (in parallel), the speed of the engine (if adjustable).

Dependent variables: the brightness of the bulbs, the output current (ammeter needed to replace all bulbs).

F Clockwork spring and dynamo

PAGE
172

A clockwork spring which can be wound up then released is connected through its axle to a generator, the electricity from which lights one or more bulbs for a short time.

What made the bulb come on? (Electricity.)
Where from? (The generator.)
Where did the movement start? (In the spring.)
Ah, but how did the spring get wound up? (My muscles.)
... And so on as questions for exhibit A.

Independent variables: number of bulbs, number of turns on the spring.
Dependent variables: amount of light from bulb (qualitative judgment), current from generator.

G Electric pump

PAGE
172

Electricity, preferably from a battery, drives a motor which turns a turbine unit so that it works 'backwards' to act as a water pump which produces a flow of water.

What made the water move – go back to the first thing that happened? (Electricity.)
What made the electricity move? (The battery.)
... And so on as questions for exhibit C.

Independent variables: height of delivery tube of pump, and that of the water sump (reservoir), push (voltage) of battery – speed of pump.
Dependent variables: amount of light from bulb (qualitative judg-tube into measuring cylinder).

H Silicon solar cell

PAGE
172

Electricity generated by a silicon solar cell illuminated by a table lamp drives a small electric motor.

The children will probably have already seen this as part of the first circus of Chapter 5, and this is regrettable. However, the function of the cell is so important that it should be here as well. It would be ideal if you were able to put together an alternative apparatus, perhaps drawing on equipment from your local electronics hobby shop. The only criterion is that the cell must generate electricity and not simply control it.

What causes the movement here? (Electricity.)
But what gets the electricity going? (The solar cell.)
What makes the solar cell do that? (The light from the lamp.)
How do you know? (Switch off the lamp.)

Independent variables: ideally, the distance of the lamp, the colour of the light, the area of the solar cell illuminated. However, unless you are able to get hold of an extensive array of cells they will supply so little push, and the current will be so low, that these variables will barely show an effect on the dependent variable. Of course this will be the speed of the motor, or its ability to lift a (very small) weight.

PROBLEM 2:
HOW MUCH HEAT CAN YOU GET FROM CHEMICAL REACTIONS – AND HOW MUCH IS USEFUL?

PAGES
173 to 175

Here the children are set the task of exercising their scientific skills to follow the instructions, make the reactions go, carefully observe and equally carefully record the results. Apropos of the last, you might begin by helping them to make up a table of results:

Observations at the start, *e.g.* temperatures of reactants, appearance of reactants;
Observations during the reaction, *e.g.* changes in appearance;
Observations at the end, *e.g.* final temperatures reached.

The children are approaching the end of a two-year course which has aimed to develop their scientific skills, so they should by now be able to approach this in a thoroughly professional way.

When they have completed the investigations they have to formulate solutions to the problem itself and discuss them with you. This will include finding answers to the many questions in the text, and others such as: 'How do you know which produces the most heat?', and 'What does 'most useful' mean?'. All together, it is a demanding task and of sufficient value in itself to go no further.

The reactions fall into three groups:
1 reactions in solution: one neutralization and two displacement reactions;
2 three reactions with oxygen from the air;
3 two violent oxidation reactions *to be demonstrated.*
You may like to hold plenary discussions at the ends of the first two groups before going on to the next. The text provides discussion starter questions.

Reaction A

PAGE
173

If you followed our suggestion in the section on dyes as indicators in Chapter 4 of these notes, the children will already have met acids and alkalis. If you did not, you may like to do so now before getting them started on the reactions.
Explanation: when you dissolve an alkali in water to make a solution, the water breaks up the alkali into two separate kinds of stuff.

The same thing happens when an acid is mixed with water to dilute it. If you mix the solutions the four kinds of stuff join up to form two new substances.

One of these is water itself; the other is called a salt. With the chemicals in reaction A, the salt is the kind we use to flavour our food. As the substances form, heat is produced.

Moving around   **167**

Reaction B

PAGE 173

Explanation: when you dissolve copper sulphate in water, the water breaks it up into two kinds of stuff. One of these is copper in such tiny bits that you can't see them. You can call the other the 'sulphate' part. If you add zinc metal it joins up with the sulphate to make a substance called zinc sulphate, which the water can't break up again. At the same time, all the copper bits join up to form copper metal. As they form, the new substances give out heat.

Reaction C

PAGE 174

Explanation: sulphuric acid is actually a sulphate – you could call it hydrogen sulphate. When you mix it with water it breaks up into two separate kinds of stuff: hydrogen (ions) and a sulphate part. If you add magnesium, it will join up with the sulphate to form magnesium sulphate, which the water cannot break up again. The hydrogen bits join up to form hydrogen gas. As they form, the new substances give out heat.

Reaction D

PAGE 174

Explanation: if you heat magnesium metal in a flame it will combine with the oxygen in the nearby air to form a new substance called magnesium oxide. As it forms, it gives out heat, causing more magnesium to combine with more oxygen ... and so on until all the magnesium is used up.

Reaction E

PAGE 174

Explanation: Ethanol is an organic substance: it is made up of carbon, hydrogen, and oxygen. If you heat some of it, it reacts with the oxygen in the air. Some of the carbon will be released as soot and smoke; most will join up with oxygen to form gases such as carbon dioxide. The hydrogen will join with oxygen to form water (steam actually!). As the new substances form, heat is produced. Of course you know that the whole set of happenings is called burning.

Reaction F

PAGE 175

Explanation: a peanut is made up of organic substances. In particular, it contains much fat which is made up of carbon, hydrogen, and oxygen . . . . (And so on as for reaction E.)

Reaction G *(for the teacher to demonstrate)*

PAGE 175

Explanation: the detergent does not take part in the reaction – it is there to make bubbles of hydrogen gas which are easy to handle. If you heat hydrogen gas to a few hundred degrees C it will be attacked by the oxygen of the air and the two will join up to form water. Great amounts of heat will be given out and this will turn the water into superhot steam, expanding so fast that it sends a shock wave through the air. You will hear the shock wave as a pop.

PAGE 175

Reaction H *(for the teacher to demonstrate)*

Explanation: potassium manganate(VII) is made up of potassium, manganese, and lots of oxygen. Glycerol is an organic substance containing carbon, hydrogen, and oxygen. Put them together and the oxygen in the potassium manganate(VII) attacks the hydrogen in the glycerol. From then on the result is a sort of combination of reactions F and G.

PROBLEM 3: MAKING A MODEL OF SAVERY'S PUMP

PAGES
175 to 177

The problem is of a type often faced by technologists and scientists: by the former because they need a working model to try out improvements; and by the latter because they need one to investigate, make pattern statements about, and, ultimately, develop theories to explain.

Savery's pump
Thomas Savery (1650–1715), a Cornish inventor, developed a steam engine in which high pressure steam was forced down a tube to the water level in the mine where it opened a valve. Water rushed in, condensing the steam in the tube and leaving a partial vacuum. Atmospheric pressure acting on the surface of the water forced it in to fill the tube. It was drained off at a higher level.

Though the pump was an initial success, the technology of the day was not up to the problem of handling high pressure steam. Solder in the joints melted, rapid changes in temperature caused metal parts to fracture, boilers burst, injuries were caused, and time was lost. However, before the design was abandoned a major modification, of great help to designers of the next generation of pumps, had been introduced. This was to generate the steam in a vessel quite separate from that into which the cold water flowed.

Demonstrating the key ideas
The demonstrations, which can be taken in any order, and the discussions which follow are intended to develop four key ideas in the minds of the children. Your final discussion, after completing the demonstrations, should aim to make clear these ideas. They are:

1 The atmosphere presses suprisingly hard on things.
2 It can cause movement of a surface if you take away the air from the other side of the surface.
3 Specifically, it can be made to lift water up a tube by removing the air from above the surface of the water.
4 Air can be removed from a space by first filling it with steam then condensing the steam.

In a question at the end of demonstration E we have made a 'deliberate mistake', using the phrase 'suck up'. We hope that you will point out that the phrase, though commonplace, is muddling. It suggests that the partial vacuum in your mouth is pulling up the orange juice. That is nonsense of course: a vacuum is nothing so can do nothing. The orange juice is lifted by the atmospheric pressure on its surface in the beaker, acting against a reduced pressure in your mouth.

Designing the pump

At the centre of the model you will need a container which you can fill with steam under pressure and then cool. The steam will condense leaving a partial vacuum. The container will need two inlets and two outlets. One inlet is for the steam, the other to connect the partial vacuum to the water which is to be pumped up (perhaps via a receiving vessel).

This inlet must have a tap. One outlet is for condensed steam, and the other for a safety valve or safety tube, to release the steam pressure if there is a blockage.

⚠ It is very important that you check the children's designs before allowing a prototype to be constructed. Ideally you should have them double-checked by a colleague. Even after checking, you must run the prototype behind safety screens.

Ironically, the presence of poorly fitting seals acts as a further safety feature, as pressure differences cannot so readily build up inside the apparatus.

Additional activities

ADDITIONS TO THE CIRCUS

An appeal to the children to bring in their own powered toys, electric or clockwork, should produce some excellent subjects.

One of the children or one of your colleagues again (a model aircraft or power boat enthusiast) may be able to loan a miniature internal combustion engine for a really exciting demonstration.

A rich field of less exotic additions is that of the catapult variants. Model Roman siege engines, miniature crossbows, toy field guns, tennis ball 'machine guns', car catapults for use with low friction track, and the 'coin thrower' from Nuffield Secondary Science *Theme 6: Movement,* page 48, are examples.

ORGANIZE A RUBBER-BAND TANK DERBY

Worksheet 65 provides instructions for making these toys, which are still appealing despite their history of at least three generations! It would be fun to organize an inter-group competition with eliminations within the groups first.

WORKSHEET 66 'MAKE AN AEOLIPILE' AND
WORKSHEET 67 'MAKE A WATER PUMP'

These give instructions for making devices which could be included in the circus.

The children will need your help with the aeolipile, not least because the construction involves glass modelling and inserting glass tubing in bungs, both of which are potentially hazardous. Using a drop of glycerol as lubricant should reduce the latter hazard.

⚠ Any steam generating apparatus is potentially dangerous, not least because blockage in the outlet can cause pressure to build up to explosive dimensions. The aeolipile also produces jets of steam which can scald. For these reasons check all apparatus carefully and only observe the machine in action through safety screens.

The children can make the water pump at home, using (yet more!) squeezie containers.

POSTERS

The topic offers rich opportunities for poster and collage work. You could make a start with a collage of pictures which set out to show the usefulness or relevance of the devices in the circus. Others could have titles such as 'High-tech transport' and 'The history of transport'.

CHAPTER 12 # Pictures of the world

Introduction

This topic was chosen for several reasons. Photography involves a variety of science processes which are discussed in the reader section. The activities pages give further experience of technology. We can also see photography employed in a variety of science contexts to remind the children of what scientists do – the problems that interest scientists, and the methods scientists employ. The topic of photography therefore acts as a final overview for the whole course. We have deliberately chosen examples which, in many instances, echo ideas and images encountered earlier in the course.

Summary

Target

Read and discuss pages 97 'Pictures of the world'; 98 to 99 'The story of photography' (picture story); 100 to 101 'Observing, recording, and measuring – using pictures'; 101 'Freezing the action'; 102 'Blowing up observations'; 103 'Reaching out, down, and in'; 104 'Making invisible observations'; 105 'Measuring with pictures'; 106 to 107 'How do a horse's legs move?'; 107 'How far away are the stars?'; 108 'Why are round arches so strong?' and 'How can we improve our weather predictions?'

Images

Scientists developing photography, originally as an alternative to painting. Nowadays used to observe things and events which cannot be directly observed by the eye.

Skills

Designing experiments and investigations. Measuring. Making pattern statements.

Ideas

Basis of photography – light causing chemical changes. Techniques used to improve the process. Use of photography in a wide range of scientific contexts – in astronomy, to observe fast events, to observe very small objects, etc.

Activities

Making a camera obscura. Making light sensitive paper. Taking pictures with a camera obscura. Pinhole camera.

Worksheets

68 'Camera controls'
69 'Make a 35-mm negative'
70 'Make a print from your negatives'
71 'Develop a 126 cassette in daylight'

Reader pages

PAGES
97 to 108

The chapter starts with a description of photography being used to help scientists to carry out the familiar tasks of observing, recording,

172 Chapter 12

and measuring. The relevance of photography to the processes of science is then extended by seeing how pictures are used to make pattern statements and to help to solve problems.

Activities pages

PAGES
178 to 185

The activities focus on the technology of photography: the production of an image on a screen, the making of a permanent record of the image, and its reproduction on demand. The children begin by making a model camera obscura (we save the term 'pinhole camera' for a later, more elaborate device) and investigating its performance. A light sensitive chemical is prepared and studied; and sensitive paper is made.

The paper is tested by making a simple contact print. 'Factory-made' paper is used to take a picture using the camera obscura: the image is developed and fixed, then used to make a positive print. Finally, instructions are followed for making a pinhole camera from a standard 126 cassette. Three worksheets provide reference material for further work using good cameras and commercial equipment and materials.

PAGE
97

Background to the reader pages

THE STORY OF PHOTOGRAPHY (picture story)
1 The idea of a camera

PAGES
98 to 99

As Aristotle noticed, the holes in a sieve work as a kind of multiple pinhole camera. Normally you don't notice that the dots of light are images of the Sun, but when there is a partial eclipse each dot becomes crescent-shaped.

Abu Ali al-Hasan ibn al-Haytham (c.965 to 1038) was the first person to explain how a lens worked. He also refuted the common notion that when you looked at something, a ray went out of your eye and struck the object.

Giovanni Battista della Porta (1542–1597) was a sculptor. The camera obscura, or rather its successor the camera lucida, was to be much used by artists as a sketching aid. *Camera obscura* is Latin for a dark room. The original version was a room with a hole in one wall, throwing an image on to the other wall. The observers were inside the room. In the 17th century a concave mirror was put at an angle behind the lens to turn the picture right way up.

The pinhole camera used by the pupils in the activity should correctly be called a camera lucida – *lucida* means bright. The original version, used from the seventeenth century on, was a wooden box with a lens and a ground glass back to which a sheet of paper could be fixed. Vermeer (1632–75) used a camera lucida to make drawings for the backgrounds of some of his paintings.

Sir Isaac Newton (1642–1727) published his *Opticks* in 1704. It included an account of his well-known work on the spectrum.

2 The idea of a light-sensitive 'film'

By 1727 it had been known for some time that silver salts darkened. Johann Heinrich Schulze (1687–1744) was able to show that this was caused by light, not by air as had been supposed. After this discovery several people tried to make images with silver salts, but all attempts foundered on the problem of fixing the image.

In around 1790 Josiah Wedgwood (1730–1795) sent his son Thomas (1771–1805) to work with Sir Humphry Davy, but without success.

Joseph Nicéphore Niepce (pronounced Ni-APE-chay; 1765–1833) invented a practical internal combustion engine around 1801. No-one wanted it. Undeterred, he turned to the problem of what he called 'heliography'. Since silver salts had already been tried without success, in 1826 he used a different chemical, bitumen of Judea (which is white), dissolved in oil and spread on a pewter plate. The bitumen was hardened by light, not darkened. He washed off the soft parts of the bitumen with oil to reveal the dark pewter underneath. The first picture he took was of the view from his window.

Niepce went into business with a painter, Louis Daguerre (1789–1851), to improve the process. Daguerre had been working on silver iodide since 1831. Meanwhile the astronomer Sir John Herschel (1792–1871) had discovered that silver salts could be fixed with sodium thiosulphate (called 'hypo' because of the old name hyposulphite). Daguerre's process used silver iodide on a silver-coated copper plate. He treated the plate with mercury, which stuck to the blackened parts of the plate and gave bright silver-coloured highlights. The unblackened parts of the silver coating tarnished and turned black to make the dark parts of the picture. Thus it was a direct positive process, producing a 'right way round' image without a negative. It was impossible to make copies. The first daguerrotypes went on show in 1839. They were expensive. Exposure time was 15 minutes at first – tough on sitters, who had to have their heads clamped in place.

In the same year William Henry Fox Talbot (1800–1877) perfected his calotype process. The negative was made of translucent paper, which gave a grainy but rather attractive look to the positive print. In 1844 he published the first book of photographs.

The complete equipment for making daguerrotypes, on sale in 1847, weighed 50 kg. Cameras were heavy, but a lot of the weight came from the chemicals which had to be carried about. In all the early processes the plate had to be freshly coated and used while the chemicals were still wet, then processed at once.

George Eastman (1854–1932) invented the dry plate process, which he used first for glass, then for paper; but soon he took advantage of the new material, celluloid. It was celluloid film which was to make the invention of the cinema possible. The Kodak camera cost $25. It was a box about 15 cm each way, and very simple to use. The roll of film was long enough for a hundred pictures. When the film was finished you exchanged the whole camera for a new one with film already in it, and sent the old camera to the factory for processing.

OBSERVING, RECORDING, MEASURING – USING PICTURES

PAGES
100 to 106
Measuring, recording, and reporting are crucially important in meeting the criteria for acceptable scientific observations. Coming to the subject of Chapter 12 of Nuffield Science 11 to 13, you can see what an important tool has been put into the hands of scientists by the development of photography. Compare for instance the reported observations of witnesses to a bank hold-up with those made from the pictures taken by a hidden camera. And it is not only of great value in recording the phenomena within the range of our visual senses, it makes possible the observation and recording of many which are normally out of range.

Making a permanent record

PAGES
100 to 101
Microfilm was first used during the siege of Paris in the Franco-Prussian war of 1870–71, to carry out despatches and letters from and to the besieged city by balloon and carrier pigeon. Its first commercial use was in New York in 1928 to photograph cheques. During World War II, servicemen's letters were sometimes carried on 16-mm film. Today, microfilm is widely used for documents of all kinds, including newspaper archives. Most microfilming is done on rolls of 16 and 35-mm film. A typical reduction in size is to $\frac{1}{20}$ of the original. Microfiches – separate rectangles of microfilm – are used where there are large numbers of copies to be distributed, as to libraries or for parts lists for garages. Not being on a continuous strip, they can easily be updated by replacing only the necessary sheets. A typical microfiche is 15 × 10 cm, carrying 60 A4 pages at 20:1 reduction or 200 at 40:1. There are also ultrafiches, carrying 3000 at 150:1. The sheets are handled by a microfiche reader which projects a selected page on to a ground glass screen. Spies' microdots use an even greater reduction, with a whole page on a piece of film small enough to be disguised as a typewritten full stop.

Freezing the action

PAGE
101
Strobe photography is done with a xenon flash tube with an electronic control circuit to regulate the length and frequency of the flashes: more than 5000 flashes a second can be produced. Pictures can be taken with an ordinary camera with the shutter open, either using a single flash, automatically triggered at the right moment, for one picture or using multiple flashes to give a record of successive positions of the object in the same frame of film, as shown in the pupils' book with the photographs of the lacewing fly and the gymnast (pictures 10a and

10c). A succession of pictures which can be used as a movie film (for 'slow motion' presentation) calls for the use of a special high speed camera. This has a strip of film moving continuously, with a rotating mirror or prism moving each successive image along the film at the same speed as the film itself is moving.

Blowing up observations

PAGE
102
The first photomicrographs were taken in the 1840s. Pioneers included the French physicist Jean Foucault (1819–1868) and the American chemist John William Draper (1811–1882), who published a book of them in 1856. Exactly the opposite technique is used for engraving the components and circuits on microchips. The pattern to be engraved is drawn at a large size, then reduced on to a layer of photographic emulsion covering the silicon wafer. The emulsion is developed to remove the unexposed parts. Then the wafer is etched. The remaining exposed emulsion protects the parts of the wafer which it covers from the acid.

Reaching out, down, and in

PAGE
103
If possible, show the pupils some coloured astronomical photographs – pictures taken with ordinary visible light, not false colour or computer-enhanced ones. The beautiful colours are real, though you can't see them directly with your eyes. (The retinal cells which respond to colour do not function at low light levels.) They are brought out by long exposures, during which the telescope is tracked across the sky to keep the image sharp.

Pictures are sent back from unmanned space vehicles by radio, using a scanning technique similar to television but much slower. The brightness of each 'pixel' (picture element) or dot in the picture is encoded in digital form, which makes the information less likely to be corrupted in transmission. Inevitably there is some corruption, but this is removed when the image is enhanced by a computer. Colour pictures like the striking images of Jupiter, Saturn, and Uranus and their moons taken by Voyager II, or the Viking pictures of the surface of Mars, are made by taking three pictures successively through different colour filters, and transmitting each one separately.

Satellites can take extremely detailed pictures of things on the ground. The full power of military spy satellites is a secret, but they can certainly see not only individual people but also what they are doing. Pictures are sent back to earth either by radio, as above or, in the case of some Soviet satellites, by ejecting packages of film with a homing transmitter so that they can be found. Peaceful uses include geological surveys and monitoring vegetation and pollution. Often the pictures are taken at infra-red wavelengths: see below.

Devices for looking inside the body are collectively called endo-scopes. They include bronchoscopes for examining the lungs, gastro-scopes for the stomach, proctoscopes for the colon, and so on. Modern endoscopes are flexible thanks to glass optical fibres of such a high quality that they can carry a fine grained image. (Picture 18.) Some operations, such as the removal of polyps from the bowel, can now be done remotely with instruments on the tip of the endoscope. Older endoscopes were clumsy and bulky, with hinged joints, mirrors and prisms, and caused the patient much suffering.

Making invisible observations

PAGE
104

Electromagnetic radiation from X-rays through ultra-violet and visible light to infra-red can all be made to register on film. The film or camera may have to be modified. Ordinary film does not respond to infra-red. Its range of sensitivity extends from red some way into the ultra-violet. Old black and white film was insensitive to red light, causing red lipstick to come out black.

False colour photography is a useful research tool, showing things which cannot be seen in ordinary visible light. The medium (film or television) renders infra-red as visible colour. It is often used for satellite surveys of vegetation, since you can tell the health of plants by the amount of infra-red they absorb or reflect. False colour can also be imposed by computer on any black and white image, simply by transforming different levels of grey into selected colours.

On paintings, substances under the surface can reflect different amounts of infra-red light through the layers of paint, so that an infra-red photograph can make the initial sketch visible. Underpainting can be seen by X-raying the picture. (See picture 19 in the pupils' book.) Often both techniques are used on the same painting.

Ultra-violet light is useful for revealing later additions to cheques and other documents. A forger may match the original ink colour exactly as regards visible light, but it is most unlikely that the old and the new inks will have the same chemical composition. Ultra-violet light causes the ink to fluoresce – it absorbs ultra-violet and re-radiates in the visible part of the spectrum – and different inks fluoresce to a different extent. Ultra-violet fluorescence is also used to identify minerals and, with a fluorescent dye, to find cracks in castings. Picture 19b shows how the technique can be used to detect forged car number-plates.

X-rays were discovered in 1895 by Wilhelm Röntgen at the University of Würzburg. He was experimenting with a cathode ray tube and noticed that it made a sheet of paper covered with a fluorescent substance glow, even when a sheet of card or even metal foil was interposed between the tube and the screen. The medical value of X-rays was realized almost at once. Early in 1896 it was used in the USA to find a bullet in a man's leg.

Measuring with pictures

PAGE
105

The tracks of subatomic particles can be recorded directly on to film. (Picture 21.) In these special nuclear emulsions the emulsion layer is ten times as thick as in normal film. There are many other kinds of particle detector: cloud chambers, where the particles leave traces in a vapour; bubble chambers, where they leave a trail of bubbles in a liquid; spark chambers and scintillation counters. In all these the trace has to be photographed.

The thermal image of a boy and his dog is an example of false colour photography, mentioned above.

USING PICTURES TO MAKE PATTERN STATEMENTS AND TO SOLVE PROBLEMS

How do a horse's legs move?

PAGE 106
Eadweard Muybridge (1830–1904) was originally called Edward James Muggeridge. Born in England, he emigrated to the USA in 1852. At this time there was a vogue for everything Anglo-Saxon, and he changed his name to be in the fashion. Later he became a professional photographer. It took him two years to get a successful series of pictures of the horse (Stanford's favourite trotter, called Occident). (See picture 24.) During this time he was tried and acquitted of the murder of his wife's lover. The long exposure time of old film caused severe problems. He managed to reduce the exposure by using a white background. Muybridge's later photographs were published in 1887 in an important book, *Animal Locomotion*. He also invented a rotating device, the Zoopraxiscope, to display the pictures as a moving image. This was the best moving picture machine till Edison's Kinetoscope.

How far away are the stars?

PAGE 107
Henrietta Swan Leavitt (1868–1921) made a major step in discovering the size of the Universe, and her work pointed the way for that of other scientists such as Edwin Hubble (1889–1953), whose study of distant galaxies led in 1929 to the idea that the Universe is expanding, and that there might be distant objects receding so fast that there was no way of discovering them.

Why are round arches so strong?

PAGE 108
Polarized light is produced by passing light through a filter which stops all the light waves that are vibrating in a certain plane, and passes light waves that are vibrating at right angles to that plane. The filtering is explained by saying that long chains of atoms in the material act like the bars of a cage. Most filters are made out of 'Polaroid', a plastic sheet treated with iodine which forms the chains. But many other plastics polarize light to some extent and the way in which they do this is altered by stress, which distorts the long chain molecules of which they are composed. If light passes first through a vertical polarizer, then a horizontal polarizer, most of it is intercepted. If it passes through two vertical polarizers most of it gets through. Hence the different shades in the stress model.

How can we improve our weather predictions?

PAGE 108
Weather forecasting is described in the notes on Chapter 8. The way in which satellites send pictures to Earth is described above.

Notes on the activities

PAGES
178 to 185

The activities pages concentrate on the technology of photography, and offer several good opportunities for designing experiments and investigations, practising the skills of measurement, and making pattern statements. By now the children should be able to design and plan such work with little input from you.

TECHNOLOGY NOT SCIENCE?

Around 1780, the Swedish apothecary and great discoverer of new substances, Karl Wilhelm Scheele, discovered that light will liberate pure silver from certain silver salts and thus blacken them. In 1801 Johann Ritter in Germany discovered that the effect was most marked in an invisible region of the spectrum just beyond the violet. For many years, this 'invisible light' was called 'chemical rays'; today we call it ultra-violet radiation. Apart from this work, science had little part to play in the development of practical photography, which was carried out by craftsmen, inventors, and technologists. Having said that, the superb results of today's snapshot, commercial, and scientific photography owe much to commercial expenditure on scientific research over the last generation.

The inventors of photography had five problems to solve.

1 How to obtain a clear image of a distant scene on a flat screen. (Commercial artists were interested in the solution as a drawing aid).

2 How to record the image: how to make the light leave traces which would remain when the light was removed.

3 How to make the photographic record permanent and clearly visible.

4 How to prevent light further attacking the record.

5 How to make a copy of the record, preferably on paper.

By and large, these problems are reflected by the structure of our activities.

Forward planning

If you wish to follow our alternative suggestion for part C of problem 2 you will need to order your Kodak projection paper (P153) from your Kodak dealer before you begin. While the children are working on problem 1, you may like to prepare in advance the salted paper for problem 2 Part B. The same activities require a laboratory with good blackout and this may call for forward planning.

PROBLEM 1:
HOW CAN YOU MAKE A MODEL CAMERA OBSCURA?

Making the model

PAGES
178 to 179

Our use of the term 'camera obscura' is deliberate, but see the detailed note on the reader above. We prefer to reserve the more usual 'pinhole camera' for a later device (see problem 4) which can be used to 'take pictures'.

It seems important to us that every child should be able to make his or her own camera obscura and take it home to show it off. So we would prefer not to use the 'pinhole camera' kits available from apparatus suppliers. If you cannot afford plastic drainpipe (or equally wide cardboard mailing tubes) the children can bring empty salt drums (680 g size) or baked bean tins from home. You can either remove the bottom of a can with a rotary tin opener or punch a large hole through it with a nail. (Have one or two spares ready in case you write off a precious can!) Of course, the children will need to stick black paper (tightly) over the nail hole then make a pinhole through the paper. At least one person will need to be able to make several well-spread pinholes for step 9.

Lining the tube with black paper may seem elaborate, but the fact of doing it helps to establish the child's intuitive understanding of the device and the way it works. Making a shade for the screen also contributes to this. It is important that the black paper should fit snugly over the end of the tube. It is a good idea to start with a very small pinhole (don't waggle the pin about!) – you can always make it bigger later. A number 8 sewing needle makes a suitably-sized hole.

Apropos of the question in step 7, the brightness of the image will depend on the brightness of the subject you are viewing. A larger pinhole gives a brighter image too, but at the expense of sharpness. The original Nuffield Physics scheme suggested the use of 200-watt clear glass carbon filament bulbs as suitable objects. You may have some of these and they will give a good clear image. However, seeing this is no substitute for seeing a miniature, full colour (though upside down) image of the world outside.

Explaining the camera obscura
Despite the simplicity of the instrument, its operation is not easy to explain. You should let the children have a go at explaining it first. You will need a diagram for your explanation, and it will *not* be a good idea to use one from a textbook intended for fourth and fifth years. If you draw two rays, one from the bottom and one from the top of the object, crossing at the pinhole, you will give the impression that a fat beam of light from the whole object somehow squeezes itself through the pinhole then spreads out inside. Instead it is better to draw a very big object and a very big camera obscura with a pinhole as wide as a piece of chalk (or a broad OHP pen). Ask the children to imagine that they are looking out from the screen through the pinhole. From any part of the screen they can only see one tiny part of the object. Use a piece of chalk held flat or a broad pen to draw one thick line from the object through the pinhole to the screen. This represents a real, very narrow beam of light not a 'ray' (a construction line). From another part of the screen another part of the object can be seen. (Draw another thick beam from the object to the screen). Carry on until you have a complete fan (a cone actually) of beams.

An extension: using a lens

If you cut a T-shaped slot at the pinhole end of the tube (cross bar of the 'T' a centimetre or so from the edge) you can insert a magnifying glass (the sort with a straight handle). The upright of the 'T' will allow you to move the lens back and forth from the pinhole. If you start with a 'pepper' of pinholes around the original one, you will be able to produce the dramatic effect of making all of the separate images gather up into one.

PROBLEM 2:
HOW CAN YOU MAKE AND TEST LIGHT-SENSITIVE PAPER?

PAGES
180 to 181

You will need to work in a blacked out laboratory by the light of an orange safe-light for parts B and C of this.

The problem reflects the second, third, and fourth of the inventors' problems mentioned above. The long exposure time (probably about 10 minutes, though it might be a good idea to try up to 20 minutes) reflects a further problem. It took William Henry Fox-Talbot and others more than twenty years to get exposure times down to the point at which sitters for portraits no longer needed to have their heads clamped in position! It took a further half century to reach materials of the sensitivity we take for granted today.

Part A: Making a light-sensitive chemical

PAGE
180

The first step in producing a permanent photographic record is to produce a light-sensitive chemical. One such is silver bromide, which is unstable and breaks up under sunlight into dark grey silver and bromine which reacts with one of the other materials present in the film and processing tank.

If you want to see the effect, you obviously need to prepare fresh silver bromide. The 'photochemical reaction' is temperature-dependent, and an interesting extension would be to investigate this (using, say, ice cold, warm, and hot solutions). By now the children should be able to design the investigation themselves.

Part B: Making printing paper

PAGES
180 to 181

Ideally, you should do the whole of this part in orange safelight in a blacked-out laboratory. Apart from being intrinsically exciting, it makes an important point. It will help if you have prepared some salted paper in advance (see page 180). It is important to make sure that no-one accidentally switches on the normal lights or raises the blackout, and you should make a big show of putting the printing paper and silver nitrate in a dark box or under a black cloth before switching on the light.

Part C: Making a test print

PAGE
181

Back into the orange light for loading the printing frame! You will be surprised how easy it is to load the frame incorrectly with the layers in the wrong order or the wrong way up. We have already mentioned the long exposure time which may surprise some of the children. As good scientists they may like to try a range of exposure times around the ten minutes we suggest. You should make sure that everyone gets a print to stick into their books, even if this means repeating the best exposure.

William Henry Fox-Talbot used salt solution to fix his prints. You may like to let the children design an investigation to compare this simple fixer with a modern proprietory brand. You will need to standardize the fixing time (two minutes immersion with agitation would be suitable), and the washing time (five minutes under running water). You should add, as a control, a print which has not been fixed at all, and expose all the specimens to bright sunlight for the same length of time.

A further investigation design exercise would be to compare the home-made paper with a commercial product. One such is Kodak projection paper P153 which is designed for use in subdued daylight or tungsten light, but not fluorescent light.

PROBLEM 3:

PAGES
182 to 184

HOW CAN YOU TAKE PICTURES WITH A CAMERA OBSCURA?

Part A : Taking the picture

PAGES
182 to 183

Grade 1 (soft) bromide printing paper would be suitable for this. An alternative is to use positive film which has a better tonal range than bromide paper. The development time for film can also be varied to correct for under-exposure. However you will probably need to order it well in advance from your photographic dealer.

It will be a good idea to experiment with different exposure times ranging from half a minute to two minutes, and the children should be able to plan this in discussion with you. You will need to standardize the size of the pinhole as this effects the brightness of the image. Having everyone use a number 8 sewing needle will do this.

Of course the results will not compare with those from a proper camera, but they will be exciting nevertheless. Provided that is, that the instructions are followed exactly! It will be worth reading them through before making a start, and emphasizing the following points.
1 The paper or film must not be exposed to light (other than a darkroom safe-light). It needs to be fixed to the camera obscura in a blacked out laboratory, darkroom, or changing bag.
2 You must not make the pinhole in your new piece of black paper until you are ready to take the picture.
3 The shiny side of the sensitive paper must face into the tube.
4 The camera obscura must not be moved or shaken while you are taking the picture.
5 When the exposure is finished you must keep your finger over the pinhole until you get back into the dark.

6 You mustn't try to look at the image on the paper until it is immersed in the developer solution back in the dark.

PAGES
183 to 184

Part B : Developing and printing the picture
⚠ If the developer contains 'metol' (4-methylaminophenol – in 'MQ' developer) you should *protect your skin from it* (use barrier cream, rubber gloves, or photographic tweezers). The substance irritates some sensitive skins and can cause dermatitis. 'Amidol' developer is better.

The children will be greatly excited by the magical appearance of the image in the developer dish. It is worth taking some trouble to make sure that they can all experience it.

PAGE
184

Part C : Making a positive print
Using two sheets of printing paper, face to face, to copy (and reverse) the image from one to the other makes a powerful contribution to the children's understanding. You have the opportunity to design and carry out an experiment to get the exposure time just right. It will be a matter of seconds. To save paper, you can use a series of 2-cm 'test strips' laid under and across the middle of the 'negative', and each exposed for a different time.

PROBLEM 4:
HOW CAN YOU MAKE A BETTER PINHOLE CAMERA?

PAGE
184 to 185

The 126-cassette pinhole camera was designed by Peter Baker, the producer of the BBC Schools TV series 'Science Session'. It appeared in a programme transmitted in Autumn 1973, and the details were given in a pupils' magazine which accompanied the series. The camera was made and used with great success by many children working in groups of up to six per cassette. The only problems were those due to 'camera shake' during the opening and closing of the 'shutter'. Practice was and is needed to avoid this.

Originally, the intention was that the cassettes should be commercially developed and printed in the usual way and you may prefer to do this. However, we have developed a method of processing the film in a beaker in the laboratory. The details are on Worksheet 71. We have suggested the use of MQ developer and have given the appropriate warning to wear rubber gloves.

⚠ Solid sodium hydroxide pellets are very corrosive and must not be handled by the children. The 10-g quantities should have been weighed out in advance by you or one of the technical staff, and should be kept in small closed containers until needed. The children should tip them carefully onto a watch-glass, using a spatula if necessary to dislodge them, and then use the spatula to add the pellets one by one to the mix.

Additional activities

A GRAND POSTER-MAKING SESSION

It would be nice to wind up the two-year scheme with a grand poster- and collage-making session. The topic of photography is ideal for this. Some of the collages can reflect the reader pages: displaying collections of photographs which show observation, or measurement, or colour-shape patterns.

A final tip ... for impact, it is usually true that the less of the backing sheet that you can see the better. Stunning effects can be produced by butting the pictures right up to each other. If you do want the background to show (as you may if you want to get a lot of information from one picture at a time) use bordered prints and choose a dark or medium shade of cover paper.

MAKE A PHOTOPLAY

A photoplay consists of a series of photographs which tell a story. The end result is (say) twenty pictures stuck to a large (dark-coloured) backing sheet, each with a short handwritten or typed caption under it. Making it is most enjoyable, and it develops the children's practical and aesthetic understanding of the still picture medium. Also, subliminally, it develops their perception of the contribution of photographic technology to our culture. Divided into steps, the production goes as follows.

1 The class is divided into groups of up to twelve with one camera per group (loaned by one of them perhaps).

2 Each group makes up a story. This can be a documentary: some fourth-year pupils go into town for chips at lunchtime – wrappers and unwanted chips thrown down on steep steps in alleyway – old lady steps on them and falls ...; or a fictional story: junk shop – musty book about area near school – mentions arrest of Victorian burglar – swag not found – map on scrap of paper in pocket ....

3 Group allocates jobs: director(s), photographer(s), actors.

4 Group surveys the locations with an unloaded camera, carefully plans 20 shots (looking through viewfinder), decides whether they are close-ups, medium shots, or long shots.

5 A storyboard is made. This is a large sheet of paper with twenty 10-cm square boxes drawn on it and numbered. In each box a sketch is made of the picture to be taken. Rough captions are written underneath. The storyboard will constantly be referred to by the director on location. Everyone can make a mini-version.

6 The pictures are shot on location.

7 While the film is being developed and printed, the captions are finalized and written or typed on pieces of card.

8 The photoplays are pasted up and displayed for critical discussion by all the groups.

If the children enjoy the activity and there is time you can go on to the production of a tape-slide sequence.

THE PROFESSIONAL APPROACH

There may be sufficient interest amongst the children for you to introduce them to more advanced photographic techniques: the use of a single lens reflex camera (SLR); film developing using a tank; and printing using an enlarger. We have provided Worksheets 68, 69, and 70 as a resource for such work.

In the field you can experiment with photographs of the following.
1 Children standing still, running towards the camera, and running across the field of view shot with the camera held still and set at different speeds (with the exposure adjusted by aperture).
2 Children running across the field of view with the camera panned to follow them.
3 A line of children at distances of between half a metre and 6 metres with the aperture set at different stops (and the exposure adjusted by speed).
4 Ultra-close (macro) photography using spacing rings between the lens and camera body.

Apparatus lists

⚠️ *Eye protection should be provided where necessary.*

Chapter A1 'Life goes on'

Problem 1:
How can you study cells?
microscopes
microscope slides
onion
iodine solution
paint brushes (fine tipped)
scalpel
chopping or dissecting board
lolly sticks or spoons
coverslips
dropper pipettes
eosin stain
mounted needles
filter paper strips

Problem 2:
How do cells differ in their appearance? (microscope circus)
prepared slides of TS and LS of various parts of a variety of organisms (you may prefer to provide plants as well as animals)
microscopes

Chapter A2 'The body machine'

Problem 1:
How can you monitor your fitness?
tape measure
bathroom scales calibrated in newtons

large water manometer
bell jar
access to sink or large trough
length of hose pipe
OHP pen
metre rulers
stopwatch or stopclock
steps, box, or table

Chapter A3 'Keeping well'

Problem 1:
How can you grow microbes?

Part A:
What do yeasts need to grow?
beaker, 250-ml
boiling-tube fitted with a fermentation lock and bung
thermometer, – 10 °C to 110 °C
spatula
dried yeast
sugar
olive oil
boiled water
hot water
ice
limewater (bench molarity but FRESH!)

Part B:
How can you demonstrate Pasteur's great investigation?
boiling-tubes fitted with fermentation locks and bungs, 2
glass beaker, 250-ml
nutrient broth, 50 ml
test-tube holder
test-tube rack
Bunsen burner
heat-resistant mat
tripod
gauze

Problem 2:
How can you catch a microbe?
Petri dishes containing nutrient agar, 2
sellotape
chinagraph pencil
Bunsen burner
heat-resistant mat
tripod
gauze
access to a scrubbing brush and soap
acces to an oven at 37 °C

Problem 3:
How can microbes give
themselves away?
labelled samples of:
long life milk bought yesterday, opened
and kept in a fridge
long life milk bought yesterday,
unopened and kept in a fridge
long life milk bought yesterday, opened
and not kept in a fridge
long life milk bought today, opened and
not kept in a fridge
(This investigation could alternatively be
done using fresh milk)

Each group will then need:
McCartney bottle
beaker, 100-ml
glass rod
water bath at 37 °C
graduated pipette, 10-ml or syringe,
10-ml
sterile distilled water
Resazurin tablets

Chapter A4
'A colourful world'

Problem 1:
How can you make natural
dyes?
pestle and mortar or blender
scalpel
scissors

chopping board
fresh grass, flower petals, beetroot
silver sand
glass beakers, 250-ml, 2
Bunsen burner
heat-resistant mat
tripod
gauze
filter funnel
filter paper
clamp stand
strips of cotton linen, 10-cm × 2-cm
glass stirring rod
tongs
large piece of sugar paper
glue

Problem 2:
Do all fabrics dye the same?

Part A:
Trying different fabrics,
Part B: Testing fastness
squares of 3 different fabrics, 2-cm × 2-
cm (3 of each, i.e. 9 pieces in all)
plant dye
glass beaker, 250-ml
Bunsen burner
heat-resistant mat
tripod
gauze
glass stirring rod
tongs
scissors
access to water
detergent

Problem 3:
How can you make dyes stick?

Part A:
Using a mordant
glass beakers, 250-ml, 2
washing-up bowls or plastic buckets
containing warm water, 2
soap powder
scissors
tongs

plant dye
Bunsen burner
heat-resistant mat
tripod
gauze
glass stirring rod
access to water
woollen squares, 5-cm × 5-cm, 5
tin(II) chloride, 0.25 g
cream of tartar, I g

Part B:
Making more mordants
iron(II) sulphate, 0.5 g
cream of tartar, I g
glass beaker, 250-ml
alum, 2 g
cream of tartar, 0.5 g
glass beaker, 250-ml

Problem 4:
How can you make dye patterns?

Part A: Fabric printing
cotton or linen
plant dye
potato

Part B: Tie dyeing
buckets, 2
string
marbles
scissors
tongs
rubber gloves
cotton or linen
commercial dye mix

Part C: Batik
knife
newspaper
candle
tongs
rubber gloves
white cotton or linen
bucket of dye solution

electric iron
sugar paper

Chapter 5
'An electrical world'

Problem 1:
What can electricity do?

Investigation A:
Electric heating
ammeter, 0 to 10 A
power pack, 6-V d.c.
connecting leads, nichrome, 26 s.w.g., 25 cm, 2
pencil
terminal strip or 2 barrel connectors

Investigation B:
Electric lighting
variable resistor
ammeter, 0 to I A
pea bulb and holder, 6-V
connecting leads
power pack, 6-V d.c.

Investigation C:
Electromagnet
plastic insulated wire, 50 cm
large nail
paper-clips or tacks
power pack
connecting leads

Investigation D: Relay
power pack
relay
connecting leads

Investigation E:
Electric motor
small electric motor
loads, 0.1-N
string
G-clamps
power pack

dipole throw switch
connecting leads
stopclock

Investigation F: Electroplating

power pack
nickel ammonium sulphate solution
glass beaker
connecting leads
copper foil

Problem 2:
How can you get electric
current going?

Investigation A: Using heat

copper wire, 26 s.w.g., 20 cm
Eureka wire, 22 to 26 s.w.g. (about
0.4 mm diameter), 20 cm
centre zero galvanometer
Bunsen burner
heat-resistant mat

Investigation B: Using light

torch
solar cell
low voltage mini electric motor
connecting leads
selection of coloured filters

Investigation C:
Using magnetism

plastic insulated wire, 50 cm
boiling-tube or broom handle
bar magnet
centre zero galvanometer
connecting leads

Investigation D: Using a motor

motor/dynamo
dipole throw switch
G-clamps
flywheel
power pack
connecting leads
pea bulbs and holders, two 2-V

Investigation E:
Using a chemical reaction

strip of copper
strip of magnesium ribbon
connecting leads
beaker
pea bulb and holder, 2-V
dilute sulphuric acid, 250 ml
stopclock
tissue
sandpaper

Investigation F:
Using a reversible chemical
reaction

lead plates for model lead/acid
accumulator, 2
dilute sulphuric acid
stopclock
power pack
beaker or glass jar
connecting leads
pea bulb and holder, 2-V

Chapter A6
'The restless Earth'

Problem 1:
What are rocks like?

Part A

samples of:
basalt
conglomerate
clay
gabbro
granite
limestone
marble
obsidian
rhyolite
slate
shale
schist
sandstone
hand lens
steel nail

Part B
microscope
microslides of rock slices

Problem 2:
What are soils like?
Part A: Sedimentation test
tall glass container such as gas jar, coffee jar, or measuring cylinder
stirring rod

Part B:
How do sand, silt, and clay differ?
microscope
microslide

Part C: How acid is our soil?
test-tube
test-tube rack
spatula
barium sulphate
Universal Indicator solution
pH/colour chart for Universal Indicator solution

Problem 3:
How do we get metals from their ores?
malachite
carbon powder
tin lid or nickel crucible
Bunsen burner
heat-resistant mat
tripod
gauze
tongs
beaker, 100-ml
shallow dish

Problem 4:
How are rocks formed?
Part A: Making sandstone (sedimentary rock)
Petri dishes, 3
plastic beaker, 100-ml

stirring rod
spatula
sand
salt solution (saturated)
sugar solution (saturated)
plaster of Paris
hand lens

Part B: Making crystals (igneous rock)
test-tubes, 3
spatula
test-tube holder
Bunsen burner
heat-resistant mat
lead iodide

Chapter A7
'Water, water, everywhere'

Problem 1:
How can you measure the dirtiness of water?
Part B: Measuring turbidity
acrylic tube, 1 m long
bung to fit above
sticky cm tape stuck to side
permanent marker pen
sample of dirty water

Problem 2:
How can you make muddy water clear?
Part A: Investigating straining
tea strainer
cotton wool
cloth
newspaper

Part B: Filtration
filter paper
filter funnel

Part C:
A model sewage plant filter
sand
gravel
yoghurt pot with small holes in bottom
plastic beaker, 100-ml

Problem 3:
How can you separate copper sulphate and water?
Part A:
Filtering copper sulphate
test-tube
copper sulphate crystals
spatula
filter paper
filter funnel
beaker

Part B: Evaporating
watchglass

Part C:
Evaporating copper sulphate solution
test-tube
0.1M copper sulphate solution, 10 ml
evaporating basin
Bunsen burner
heat-resistant mat
tripod
gauze

Part D:
Condensing the water vapour
boiling-tube
1-hole bung to fit above
glass tube to fit above for distillation
Bunsen burner
heat-resistant mat
large damp cloth
beaker, 100-ml
clamp
boss
retort stand
Leibig condenser

Problem 4:
How can you tell that it is water?
Part B:
Tracking down the water
test-tubes, 5
thermometers, $-10\,^\circ C$ to $110\,^\circ C$
cobalt chloride paper
Universal Indicator solution
pH/colour charts for above
filter paper strips, 15 cm × 2 cm
Bunsen burner
heat-resistant mat
tripod
gauze
glass beaker, 100-ml
access to a fridge or ice

samples, labelled with just a letter, of:
pure water

and, for example:
0.1M acetic acid
0.1M calcium hydroxide solution
glycerol
0.1M sodium chloride solution

Chapter A8 '... into thin air'

Problem 2:
How can you forecast the weather?
(See apparatus for Worksheets 53 to 59 inclusive.)
maximum – minimum thermometer
or $-10\,^\circ C$ to $110\,^\circ C$ thermometer

Chapter A9 'Fire!'

Problem 1:
What happens to the masses of things when they are heated?
crucible and lid
tongs
Bunsen burner
tripod

gauze
pipe-clay triangle
heat-resistant mat
top pan balance

samples of . . .
cobalt chloride
copper metal foil, 5 cm × 5 cm
copper sulphate
ice
magnesium ribbon
nichrome wire
potassium permanganate
silver sand
solder
steel wool
wood chips
zinc oxide

⚠ For teacher's use only
iodine
sulphur
lead oxide

Problem 2:
Why does copper gain in mass when you heat it – and how can you test the explanation?

Part A:
Try keeping the air out!

Experiment 1
copper foil, 5 cm × 5 cm
tongs
Bunsen burner
tripod
gauze
heat-resistant mat
hammer

Experiment 2
copper foil
clamp
retort stand
boss
Bunsen burner
heat-resistant mat
test-tube

Experiment 3
copper foil
clamp
retort stand
boss
Bunsen burner
heat-resistant mat
test-tube
vacuum pump

Chapter A10 'Rocket!'

Problem 1:
How can you make a model rocket?
plastic washing-up liquid bottles, 2
football inflater valve
broom handle
bicycle pump connectors, 5
hammer
foot pump
scissors
ruler
felt-tip pens
access to water

Problem 2:
Are there patterns in the water rocket flight?

Part A
rocket from previous experiment
clinometer (protractor with plumb bob)

Part B
rocket from previous experiment
measuring cylinder

Problem 3:
Can you design another model rocket?
string
balloon
straws
scissors
sticky tape

elastic band
trolley
Plasticine
drawing pins or panel pins
matches
cotton thread

Problem 4:
Can the recoil pattern be extended?
large apparatus trolley
sandbags, 10

Chapter A11 'Moving around'

Problem 1:
How many ways can we make things move? (The movement circus)
hand pump
water turbine
dynamo

trolley
fixed pulley
masses on hanger, 100-g, 10
string, 2 m

electric motor with pulley attached
string, 1 m
lab pack
leads
masses on hanger, 10-g, 10

electric fan (small motor with propeller attached will do)
lab pack
leads
toy plastic windmill on a stick

steam engine
drive belt
dynamo
G-clamps, 2
leads
pea bulb and holder, 2-V

clockwork spring
dynamo
G-clamps, 2

leads
pea bulb and holder, 2-V

electric pump
(electric motor and turbine module)

silicon solar cell
lamp, 100-W
small motor, 1-V d.c.
leads

Problem 2:
How much heat can you get from chemical reactions – and how much is useful?

Reaction A
test-tubes, 2
bottle dilute hydrochloric acid, 250-ml
bottle dilute sodium hydroxide, 250-ml
stirring thermometer, – 10 °C to 110 °C
stopclock

Reaction B
test-tube
spatula
bottle 0.1M copper sulphate solution, 250-ml
zinc powder
stopclock

Reaction C
test-tube
stirring thermometer, – 10 °C to 110 °C
dilute sulphuric acid
pieces of magnesium ribbon, 2 each 2 cm long

Reaction D
Bunsen burner
heat-resistant mat
tongs
piece of blue glass
piece of magnesium ribbon, 3 cm long

Reaction E

measuring syringe, 5-ml
ethanol (methylated not absolute)
crucible
boiling-tube
tongs
wooden spill
heat-resistant mat

Reaction F

peanut
optical pin
Bunsen burner
heat-resistant mat
tongs
boiling-tube
measuring syringe, 5-ml

Reaction G

shallow dish
strong detergent solution
glass tubing jet
hydrogen supply
rubber tubing
Bunsen burner
heat-resistant mat

Reaction H

large tin lid
potassium manganate(VII) crystals
glycerol in dropping bottle
spatula

Problem 3:
Making a model of Savery's pump

Demonstration A

vacuum pump
balloon
large glass flask
1-hole bung to fit above
thick-walled rubber tubing to connect to
vacuum pump
safety screen

Demonstration B

thick-walled rubber tubing
Magdeburg hemispheres
vacuum pump

Demonstration C

collapsing can with cork bung
Bunsen burner
heat-resistant mat
tripod
gauze
tongs
kettle

Demonstration D

plastic glass
stiff card
access to water
large sink!

Demonstration E

long paper straws
glass of orange juice

Make the model

The apparatus for making a model of
Savery's pump depends on what pupils
decide (with guidance, particularly on
safety, from the teacher)

Chapter A12
'Pictures of the world'

Problem 1:
How can you make a model camera obscura?

tube, 15-cm × 8-cm
black sugar paper
greaseproof (tracing) paper
elastic bands
sticky tape
pin
large sheet of newspaper

Problem 2:
How can you make and test light-sensitive paper?

Part A:
Making a light-sensitive chemical
test-tube
0.01M silver nitrate solution
0.1M sodium bromide solution

Part B: Making printing paper
silver nitrate crystals
salt
safe-light
developing dish (any shallow tray)
drawing paper
top pan balance
brown glass bottle with stopper

Part C: Making a test print
sheet of the printing paper from part B
sheet of glass or perspex same size as paper
piece of wood, plyboard, or hardboard of similar size
elastic bands
strong salt solution, 250 ml
shape such as a leaf, or a special design
stopclock

Problem 3:
How can you take pictures with a camera obscura?

Part A: Taking the picture
camera obscura made earlier
black paper
commercial printing paper
boss
retort stand
clamp
darkroom or black changing bag
pin
stopclock

Part B:
Developing and printing the picture
commercial universal developer
commercial fixer
or sodium thiosulphate solution (250 g per litre)
shallow trays, 3
access to water
safe-light
stopclock
access to a darkroom

Part C: Making a positive print
commercial printing paper
'negative' from part B
sheet of glass
lamp, 100-W
commercial universal developer
commercial fixer
or sodium thiosulphate solution (250 g per litre)
shallow trays, 3
access to water
safe-light
stopclock
access to a darkroom

Problem 4:
How can you make a better pinhole camera?
black card, 1 mm thick
elastic bands
aluminium foil
black sticky tape
fine sewing needle
126 film cassette
wooden lolly stick
pencils
rulers
scissors
craft knife or Stanley knife.

Worksheets

Worksheet 33:
'Make a microbe poster'
acetate OHP sheet
OHP
A4 coloured card
scissors
glue
small white cards

Worksheet 34:
'How to use a microscope'
microscope
microslide

Worksheet 35:
'Monitor the energy value of your food'
coloured beads, e.g. blue, 15
coloured beads, e.g. red, 15
small boxes, 2

Worksheet 37:
'Make a body machine poster'
acetate OHP sheet
OHP
A4 coloured card
scissors
glue

Worksheet 38:
'Health do's and don'ts'
selection of booklets on diet, safety, etc.
from Health Education Council, etc.

Worksheet 40:
'Test your own dyes'
own made dyes
plus pupils' apparatus

Worksheet 44:
'Puzzle circuits'
battery or power pack
connecting leads
pea bulbs and holders, 2
switches, 3

Worksheet 47:
'Make an "Age of the Earth" strip chart'
tally roll
felt-tip pens
scissors
tape measure
ruler

Worksheet 48:
'Make your own fossils'
plastic beaker
card
scissors
paper-clips
Plasticine
plaster of Paris
leaf or shell

Worksheet 49:
'A floating test for liquids'
Plasticine
drinking straw
waterproof marker pen

samples of . . .
cooking oil
methylated spirit
paraffin
sugar solution
salt solution
turpentine
white vinegar
unlabelled liquids (one must be pure water), 3
salt
sea water

Worksheet 50:
'Make a golf-ball submarine'
tall glass beaker or measuring cylinder
plastic golf ball
paper-clips
Sellotape
salt
spatula or teaspoon
stirring rod

Worksheet 51:
'What makes steel rust'
round-bottomed flasks, 4
wire wool
glass beakers, 4
one-hole bungs to fit above, 4
straight glass tubing to fit above, 4

100 ml of . . .
methylated spirit
water coloured with ink

access to molten wax

Worksheet 52:
'Do you live in a hard or soft water area?'
packet of soap flakes, e.g. Lux
test-tube
bung to fit above
samples of hard and soft water

Worksheet 56:
'Making weather instruments A'
A4 card
scissors
stiff wire, 30 cm
cork
cork borer
plastic washing-up liquid bottle
old pen top or birthday candle holder
steel knitting needle
glue
plastic protractor, 15 cm diameter
table tennis ball
spirit level
length of wooden rod, 40 cm
screw
plastic cement
monofilament fishing line
needle
steel knitting needle

Worksheet 57:
'Making weather instruments B'
milk bottle
balloon
drinking straw
rubber glue
elastic band
filter funnel
measuring cylinder, 100-ml

Worksheet 58:
'Making weather instruments C'
softwood batten, 20 cm
nails, about 7 cm long
empty cotton-reel
small mass, e.g. 50-g
drinking straw
human hair, at least 30 cm long
dilute sodium hydroxide solution, 50 ml
glue stick
tweezers or forceps
stirring rod
hammer

Worksheet 60:
'Investigating the effect of heat on potassium manganate(VII)'
hard-glass test-tubes, 3
delivery tube and 1-hole bung to fit above
bungs to fit above, 2
potassium manganate(VII)
trough
Bunsen burner
heat-resistant mat

Worksheet 61:
'Investigating the effect of heat on potassium manganate(VII)'
potassium manganate(VII) in labelled containers, containing 100 mg, 200 mg, etc. up to 500 mg
gas syringe
Rocksil wool
top pan balance
hard glass test-tube fitted with bung and tube to attach to gas syringe

Worksheet 62:
'Make a fizzy rocket'
plastic washing-up liquid bottle
cork or rubber bung
balsa wood cut and shaped like a boat
(size to attach to washing-up liquid
bottle)
rubber bands, 2
sodium hydrogen carbonate
dilute hydrochloric acid
spatula
access to a large sink or bath
sharp pointed scissors

Worksheet 63:
'Make a rocket poster'
acetate for an OHP
OHP
pencils
felt-tip pens
scissors
glue
white card
coloured card (dark blue preferably)

Worksheet 65:
'Make a rubber band "tank"'
wooden cotton-reel with groove cut at
one end
candle
rubber band
matchstick
metal rod or nail
ruler or tape measure

Worksheet 66:
'Make an aeolipile'
tin with tight-fitting press-on lid and two
holes cut in the sides to take two tight-
fitting 1-hole bungs
glass tubing to fit bungs, 30 cm
nylon fishing line
fishing swivel
file for cutting glass
Bunsen burner
heat-resistant mat
heat-resistant gloves

Worksheet 67:
'Make a water pump'
washing-up liquid bottles, 2
marbles, 2
plastic cup
plastic tubing, 30 cm
cork borer of slightly smaller size than
tubing

Worksheet 69:
'Make a 35-mm negative'
commercial developing tank
35-mm film
lightproof changing bag
commercial universal developer
commercial fixer
stopclock
measuring cylinder, 250-ml
length of string, 10-m
bulldog clip
magnifying glass

Worksheet 70:
'Make a print from your negatives'
commercial enlarger
access to a dark room
safe-light
commercial printing paper
scissors
commercial universal developer
commercial fixer
stopclock
measuring cylinder, 250-ml
shallow trays, 3
access to a sink

Worksheet 71:
'Develop a 126 cassette in daylight'
126 film cartridge
ice lolly stick
large beaker to take cassette
measuring cylinder, 500-ml
warm distilled water, 500 ml
anhydrous sodium sulphite, 50 g
hydroquinone, 12 g
metol, 6 g
sodium hydroxide, 10 g
sodium thiosulphate, 90 g
flask, 2000-ml
rubber gloves

Index